The One and Only

A Celebration of One Hit Wonders
from Chesney Hawkes to 'The Chicken Song'

Tom Bromley

PENGUIN BOOKS

PENGUIN BOOKS

Published by the Penguin Group
Penguin Books Ltd, 80 Strand, London WC2R 0RL, England
Penguin Group (USA) Inc., 375 Hudson Street, New York, New York 10014, USA
Penguin Books Australia Ltd, 250 Camberwell Road, Camberwell, Victoria 3124, Australia
Penguin Books Canada Ltd, 10 Alcorn Avenue, Toronto, Ontario, Canada M4V 3B2
Penguin Books India (P) Ltd, 11 Community Centre, Panchsheel Park, New Delhi – 110 017, India
Penguin Group (NZ), cnr Airborne and Rosedale Roads, Albany, Auckland 1310, New Zealand
Penguin Books (South Africa) (Pty) Ltd, 24 Sturdee Avenue, Rosebank 2196, South Africa

Penguin Books Ltd, Registered Offices: 80 Strand, London WC2R 0RL, England

www.penguin.com

First published 2004
1

All images appear courtesy of Redferns Music Picture Library,
except back-cover photo of Stefan Dennis © Jenny Acheson/Retna

The moral right of the author has been asserted

Set in ITC American Typewriter and TheSans
Designed by Richard Marston
Illustrations by David Mackintosh
Printed in England by Clays Ltd, St Ives plc

'One is the Loneliest Number . . .'
Harry Nilsson, 'One'

For my one and only

Contents

Foreword

You may be under the impression that to get to the charts is a gargantuan struggle of talent versus commerce. Indeed, it can be. Every band I have ever seen, must have at some time wanted to have a hit single. It validates your work. It says that you were liked enough by people all over the UK to have your name read out by Mark Goodier on a Sunday evening on Radio One. You put your heart, soul and a great deal of effort into into writing, recording your song, making a video and then promoting your masterwork. The record company ploughs thousands of pounds (money they'll get back off the band) into radio and TV pluggers, press adverts, and those ambiguous 'marketing teams' who go out to the regions to 'pre-position' your single (i.e., buy stacks of copies that end up in a sack at a dump). Anyway, the efforts of thousands of people are channelled into taking you into the top forty – and what happens? Nothing. And the reason that nothing happens is because that week the British people decided they'd rather buy a song about a duck or a puppet frog or someone's ding-a-ling or a kung fu fighter. The powerful vagaries of the UK record-buying public make fools of we pundits, elevate the mediocre and laugh in the delicately chiselled faces of the arbiters of taste.

In a previous life, I used to work for an excellent Liverpool band called the La's. They had an achingly lovely song called 'There She Goes', which by rights should have been at the very least a top-ten hit. But it wasn't, and to this day I can't tell you why. However, faux Italian cabaret turn Joe Dolce Music Theatre has been to number 1 with 'Shaddap You Face'. There's a band in Harlow called The Sweeney who have a number called 'Why', which is simply one of the most uplifting and beautiful pop songs I have ever heard in my life. Despite being championed by John Peel and Steve Lamacq, it failed to come close to denting the top forty. Meanwhile, an outfit called Babylon Zoo who had simply *awful* record used in a jeans advert, shot to the top of the charts without so much as a by your leave. Do you see a pattern forming? That's right! Chart hits have *nothing* to do with talent. For every mustard-keen indie kid nipping down the road to pick up the latest one by the Ordinary Boys there are a dozen nans and granddads buying that one by those lovely Fast Food Rockers for little Britney's birthday. The charts are not a measure of artistic achievement or a place of justice. They are merely, a big shiny abacus, and at the end of the week the one with the most beans wins.

Tom Bromley has taken a good hard look at the phenomena of the one hit wonder and I for one am grateful. For good or ill, such aberrations of good taste are part of our national psyche and as such should be analysed and even embraced, and the reason is this: would you rather have a dozen consecutive insanely random one hit wonders, or a dozen consecutive Westlife number ones? See ... they're not so bad ...

Phill Jupitus
April 2004

Introduction

It was late on a Sunday night when the phone call came – late enough that I had been asleep for an hour and a half. Crashing down the stairs, my thoughts were full of calamity, of someone ringing with Bad News. Instead, on the other end of the phone was Adrian. Adrian, I racked my brains. The only Adrian I knew was my girlfriend's brother, and this wasn't him. Adrian Bennett, the caller continued: I was no wiser. Adrian Bennett, he finally revealed, from the Tweets.

'Of course,' I said. 'How are you?'

'I've been umming and aahing about doing this interview for your book,' Adrian explained. 'And I've decided I want to do it.'

'Well that's great,' I said. 'Let me get my diary and we can fix up a . . .'

'No,' said Adrian firmly. 'I want to do it now.'

'Who is it?' my girlfriend shouted from upstairs. 'Is everything all right?'

'It's fine,' I shouted back. 'It's Adrian from the Tweets. He wants to talk about "The Birdie Song" . . .'

Welcome, dear reader, to the strange and curious world of one hit wonders, that twilight world occupied by musicians of all kinds who boast, in their repertoire, one solitary hit. I've done research for books before, but this was different. For my last novel, *Half a World Away*, I found myself visiting Nick Drake's grave. This time, by contrast, I had a drink in the pub with a no-longer-underage member of St Winifred's School Choir, I have exchanged email pleasantries with Joe Dolce, chatted on the phone to Noel Edmonds about Mr Blobby and quizzed the lead singer of the Vapors about what 'Turning Japanese' was really about. Like a real-life Marti Debergi, I wanted to catch the sights and the sounds of what being a one hit wonder was all about (the smells I could make do without). But like Marti, I got more. Much more.

Joe and Adrian and Noel were some of the friendlier one hit wonders I encountered. Because

Planet One Hit Wonder is not a place that every inhabitant is happy to call home. In estate agent parlance, some prefer to call it Celebrity Borders or Greater Stardom. I could not tell you the countless times that a shirty PR person said 'no thanks' or 'I don't think we'd want to be associated with that' or launched into a lengthy diatribe about how they'd worked with their star for almost seventeen years and never once had they considered them to be a one hit wonder. There were others, too, who didn't reply – or who did, but really didn't want to talk. It was a long time ago. They'd moved on. It might bring back bad memories. The latter I could certainly vouch for – for some of the ones I did speak to it was like picking an old scab. On more than one occasion I wondered if I'd tuned in to Simon Bates's *Our Tune* by mistake.

As a nation, we have not been kind to our one hit wonders. We have allowed them a brief glimpse of fame – not even fifteen minutes, more like three and a half – and then ridiculed them back into obscurity. If you'd like some idea of what it might be like to live such an existence, try going into a second-hand record shop and buying a copy of, say, 'The One And Only' by Chesney Hawkes. I can't remember the last time I was so openly laughed at in public, both by the guy at the till and the man behind me in the queue.

'I'm researching a book on one hit wonders,' I tried to explain.

'Sure you are,' the shop assistant smirked as he took my fifty-pence piece.

Alternatively, take a look at one hit wonders in literature. In Nick Hornby's second novel, *About a Boy*, the lead character, Will Freeman, lives off the royalties of his father's solitary hit, a toe-curling Christmas classic called 'Santa's Super Sleigh'. The song may remove the need for Will to get a job, but it does his head in every December as it blares out over the supermarket Tannoys. In Lisa Jewell's *One Hit Wonder* the story revolves around the sister of an eighties Madonna-lite star. The kudos at school of having a sister on *Top of the Pops* quickly degenerates into piss-taking as the hits stop coming. Meanwhile, back in the real world, we have Tony Hawks's comedy travelogue *One Hit Wonderland*: so ashamed is the author of his mono musical status that he travels the world in order to rid himself of his tag. He thinks he has shifted it: I disagree, and you'll find my reasons later in the book. But, in the meantime, I suppose now is as good a time as any to discuss just what exactly constitutes a one hit wonder.

A Discussion of Just What Exactly Constitutes a One Hit Wonder

This might seem a fairly banal point, but by God, the drunken arguments I have had over this definition. The purist argument, and this is endorsed by the *Guinness Book of British Hit Singles*, is one solitary top-seventy-five hit. If you want to be super-pure about proceedings, then that hit has to reach number 1 as well. Now, although I applaud the sentiment, it would result in this being a rather short book: specifically, it would contain, at the time of writing, a maximum of forty songs. It would also, and this is probably the more important point, rule out a succession of songs and artists that in the public consciousness are members of that most exclusive club, Club One Hit Wonder.

As soon as we start moving away from this definition, the question becomes one of where we draw the line. In the old days (I'm showing my age here – either way – by defining that as the eighties) it was the top forty that was sacrosanct. That, after all, was what Bruno Brookes or Mark Goodier would count down between five and seven on a Sunday night. But if you recorded the top forty like I did on a C90 cassette, then you'd press record and play at about half past five and only actually get the top thirty. Would that be a better definition?

At the other end of the musical scale, all this talk between top thirties and top forties is now largely redundant: in today's chart, only really a top-ten hit is seen as a success: anything else is a failure. Maybe that would be a better marker. In the end I decided to flick back through the chart histories to see what happened to Chesney Hawkes, singer of 'The One And Only', and perhaps the paragon of one hit wonderdom. The follow-up single, 'I'm A Man Not A Boy', only got as high as number 27. If I wanted the likes of Chesney in this book, a top-twenty hit would seem to be a fair compromise. It also fitted with the selection procedure of the compilation album *The Best One Hit Wonders in the World ... Ever!*, a record that apart from people like me researching books on one hit wonders, I can't quite see who'd buy, but that's another story.

Even this criterion, though, is not quite perfect. Let us take another classic one hitter, Babylon Zoo, whose less than seminal second single 'Animal Army' got to number 17. Should they be excluded from this book? After more soul searching, I decided to bring into play a second criterion: that strange and rather wobbly lump called the public consciousness. Some artists just *are*, in the nation's perception, one hit wonders. There's something about the song that marks them out as such. It's almost like a scent – less CK One, more UK One – an odour that however much the artist tries to wash off, never quite goes away. How far I am a good judge of the public consciousness is, I'll readily admit, open to question. For the handful of artists included here who have broken my rule and had a second top-twenty hit, I think I've judged right but I'm ready to be proved wrong. So here's the deal – if between the book's hardback publication and the time the paperback goes into production (let's say 1 May 2005) I receive 100 letters (c/o Penguin Books, 80 Strand, London WC2R ORL) supporting Babylon Zoo or whoever's non-inclusion, then I will hold my hands up, admit I'm wrong, and remove the offending song from my list.

The Songs in this Book

The 130-odd songs included in this book have been chosen and divided thematically in order, I hope, to give some sense as to how and why the phenomenon occurs. The final chapter boasts what I consider to be the greatest one hit wonders of all time. It is a selection that clearly suffers from being based on my own personal taste. You have been warned.

The book, as the subtitle suggests, is a celebration of the one hit wonder phenomenon – it is intended to be about the songs, about the people, where they came from and what happened next. Although there may be the occasional cheap joke, this is not intended to be some sort of 'put-the-boot-in' narrative. It seems a little too easy, a little too lazy simply to write, 'Ooh, do you remember Mr Blobby? He was a bit crap, wasn't he?' It is more interesting, I think, to try and understand how and why Mr Blobby occurred in the first place.

Some of the songs in the book you'll remember like old friends. Others you'll groan at the memory. You may well be depressed to discover just how many songs you have stored away in your mind, brain cells that could really be used for something more worthwhile. For example, if I say the words 'I Eat Cannibals' by Toto Coelo, the chances are I have triggered off the said song playing in your internal jukebox, again and again for the rest of the day. Sorry about that. The only way to get rid of it is to trump it with something else like, say, 'The Birdie Song'. Is that going round now instead? I'll stop.

There are great songs here, too. If I say the words Turning and Japanese, hopefully you'll now have a decent song to hum along to. Nestled among these songs are many of pop's finest nuggets and gems, either great songs in their own right or masters of a particular genre. And though these bands may not have enjoyed the sort of career that deserves a full-length biography, they are still more than worthy of their paragraph for posterity. This, as much as anything else, is their book.

Are One Hit Wonders a Dying Breed?

What struck me in writing this book is how increasingly anomalous the whole concept of one hit wonders is becoming and whether it is something that will soon be assigned to pop-culture history. Although there is the occasional modern example – Gary Jules and his 'Mad World' (though the jury's out, of course) – they are fewer and further apart.

One of the reasons for this, of course, is the decline of singles and the singles chart. When I was growing up, I used to sit and listen religiously to the top forty, my own form of Sunday worship, writing down the charts and storing them up as though they were the equivalent of the Dead Sea Scrolls. Now, admittedly, I may simply be a little bit sad, but I know I am not alone: I remember a particularly disturbing evening at university where not one but two incredibly bright people confessed to doing exactly the same thing. One of them even went so far as to use different-coloured pens depending on whether the song went up, down or was a non-mover.

Do eleven-year-old boys still huddle around the radio with the same hushed reverence and sense of excitement? Sadly, I think not. They've got a myriad of more exciting things to do with their lives, be it Game Boys or PlayStations or surfing for pictures of Britney Spears on the Internet. And on one level, who can blame them? The charts are not so interesting now. In the old days, the trajectory of a single would be as follows: a new entry in the twenties or thirties, a steady climb up towards the top ten before hitting its eventual peak. Indeed, after the number 1 position and the highest new-entry slot, the most coveted accolade in the chart was that of the highest climber.

These days, nothing ever climbs. And rather than a new entry in the top ten or even at number 1 being a moment of wonder and chart history, now it is an everyday occurrence, and all the duller for it. Blame, of course, has to lie squarely at the doors of the major record companies: they simply got too good, and too slick, at marketing. Pricing policies in the 1990s also didn't help: with singles sold at half-price in the week of release, the incentive was there for fans to rush out and buy the song immediately, thus guaranteeing a high chart entry. The next week, as the price went up again, the single would crash down the chart at a rate of knots. This, coupled with radio stations playing songs on heavy rotation five or six weeks before release, often means people have tired of songs before they have even been released.

Singles sales are in decline. In January 2004 the top forty achieved its lowest ever combined weekly sales figure – 400,000 all in. It is undoubtedly a vicious circle: the less interesting the chart is, the fewer records are sold; the fewer records are sold, the less interesting the chart is. And though it is true that figures have been hit by downloading on the Internet, it is noticeable that album sales have not been so – in fact, in 2003 album sales in the UK rose. We are still buying and listening to music, we are just not buying singles. And if we are not buying singles, we are not buying one hit wonders either.

Some Reasons behind One Hit Wonders

So why are some songs and bands destined for one hit wonder status? There is, of course, a myriad of reasons, but having spent many months locked in a darkened room with these songs, some reasons seem more prevalent than others.

The first reason that one hit wonders seem to occur is seasonality, of which two cases in particular are important: Christmas and summer. I'm not completely sure why – alcohol, I suspect, may have something to do with it. The Christmas chart sometimes appears to have a set of rules all its own. And though a funny dance routine may seem a laugh when you're off your face on Bacardi Breezers in Torremolinos, once you're back home in Basingstoke the charm appears to fade. Similarly, songs that celebrate Christmas normally come with a label that reads 'Best before 25 December'.

The second factor is that most favoured of musical chestnuts – the gimmick. This can come in many forms, and the chapters included here reflect this. There are chapters on puppets, child stars and instrumental songs. All of these categories, which may initially seem cute and of novelty value, lack the sustainability of a longer musical career. We like our pop stars to be in the news, on the front pages of the tabloids and making outrageous statements about Jordan (the model, not the country). Pop stars who are mute, six years old or made of fur simply don't make good copy; they don't end up in the sort of dodgy situations that help the musical wheels turn round.

Next are songs whose success is not entirely musically related – these could be songs that rose to prominence through their use in a film or TV show, from adverts or, God forbid, sung by celebrities. However good the song might be, it is their exposure in another medium that has pushed them into the public consciousness. Once the Hollywood circus has moved on, the public have bought their pair of Levi's, the band are left trying to replicate their success without the initial reason for it.

Dance music, more than other genres, is ripe for single-hit acts. The constant desire for immediacy, the search for something new leads to a huge turnover of records. At the same time, advances in technology have made it cheaper and easier to produce records, allowing smaller and unknown acts to become successful. The way the song becomes successful is different, too – unlike rock or chart pop, the star is not important: the beat is all that matters. Anonymity is possible here much more than elsewhere. Indeed, one could argue that one hit wonders are not dying – they have adapted into records by the likes of DJ Nobody vs MC Who He?

Emotion matters too. When I was writing this book, one thing that struck me is how much buying music, especially singles, is linked to a particular event or moment we are keen to remember. As long as there are people falling for each other, there will be people buying what Paul McCartney once referred to as 'silly love songs'. And like it or not, there is little choice about the popular ballad of the time. No matter how syrupy the song, it is still 'their song' and will always hold a place of affection in their heart.

Where the star comes from also makes a difference. If English isn't the singer's first language and your home market is Italy, Germany or Luxembourg, the barriers to a long career in the UK are that much higher. In music, as elsewhere, the British can be incredibly parochial, and while songs sung in English have little problem being successful on the Continent, it rarely happens the other way round.

Some songs just stick out. There are those that attain notoriety through rudeness – great at getting initial attention or exposure, but you can only really get away with shocking the public once. Then there are songs that are simply funny peculiar – choruses about eating cannibals or telling people to 'shaddap'. Again, we'll put up with weirdness once, but don't expect to make a career out of it. These are songs, it has to be said, with an inherently short shelf-life. What once seemed quirky and different doesn't take long to flip over into annoying and irritating. Comedy songs are another example. It doesn't matter how good the joke is: by the time you've heard it for the nth time, you're not laughing any more.

Moving away from the music to the industry itself, various sets of circumstances seem to crop up with a certain regularity. There are a number of bands who have had success too quickly, too early in their career, and were simply unable to handle the success and the accompanying pressure. Sometimes the band's hectic rise to prominence meant they lacked any sort of base to fall back on. If you've been touring the toilets for years before you have a hit, then you've got plenty of fans to fall back on by single number 2. If you've been together a couple of weeks and suddenly find yourself on *Top of the Pops*, you're in a far more precarious position. Some bands are good enough that they can overcome this potential curse – Radiohead, for example, were almost derailed by the early success of 'Creep' and took a while, particularly in the US, to shake off the label of being the 'Creep' band. Others, as we will see, were less successful.

In the seventies and eighties the staggering of singles releases around the world also made a difference. It doesn't happen so much now – with the Internet and Amazon and videos and MTV, simultaneous releases are both that much easier and also necessary. Twenty years ago, however, personal appearances and pressing the flesh were all the more important: if a new band had a hit single, they could find themselves following its success around the world from country to country. This happened to, among others, Joe Dolce, the Vapors and Men at Work. The problem is that when you finished plugging a particular song (and it could take a year or more), by the time you returned to base and released the next single, no one remembered who you were. Men at Work, who had a number 1 in the UK with 'Down Under' eighteen months after it did the same in Australia, ended up releasing their second album three months after the first. In anyone's book, that is a lot of men to stomach at once.

The decline of Radio One and the fragmentary nature of the modern radio audience (as well as the same thing happening in TV) also make a difference. Whatever your thoughts on the musical tastes of say, Dave Lee Travis or Peter Powell, in the 1970s and 1980s their huge audience figures and less rigid playlists allowed them more power and more free rein than their modern counterparts. Noel Edmonds, for example, a fan of both helicopters and *M*A*S*H*, could play 'Suicide Is Painless' and push it to number 1. Simon Mayo could get old songs like 'Kinky Boots' or 'Always Look On The Bright Side Of Life' into the higher echelons of the charts. Now, though, with listeners haemorrhaging left, right and centre, that power is substantially diminished – and tighter playlists allow the DJs less choice to play such records. Some of the audience figures and associated power have drifted to Radio Two – witness Terry Wogan and Eva Cassidy, for example. And though Radio Two can sometimes push a single into the charts, the artists they support are more album-orientated (as are their listeners) and their influence is stronger there.

What Do One Hit Wonders Say about Us?

Looking back over the songs in this book, what does this strange compilation of music say about us, the nation, or more specifically, the record-buying public? We are quite often accused, or rather we quite often boast, of being an ironic nation, far more aware of postmodern nods and winks than our American and Continental cousins. We 'get' kitsch, we revel in 'car-crash' TV, we love things that are so-bad-they're-good. Certainly, this helps explain (and gives a convenient intellectual veneer to) the myriad of nostalgia programmes on TV – I Love this, Top Ten that – not to mention grown men and women dressing up in school uniform and pogoing the night away to A Flock of Seagulls. It may even have been one of the reasons you have bought this book. But did we buy the songs included here the first time around for any of these reasons? Unfortunately, I think all this being cool and detached is a little retrospective.

Instead, what I think the success of these one hit wonders suggests is something precisely the opposite: we are more sentimental, soppier and sillier as a nation than we sometimes like to let on. Some of us still feel the twinge of an old romantic moment when 'Save Your Love' is heard. For others, 'Macarena' pinpoints all the sights and sounds of a particular holiday. We may not like to admit it, but 600,000 people bought 'Mr Blobby' because they liked Mr Blobby. They found him funny. Noel Edmonds describes how the *House Party* office was swamped with letters and pictures of Mr Blobby as soon as he'd been on TV. We may not always share the same musical tastes as the nation, but the fact that people are buying these records, I think, is healthy if misplaced: it shows we have a heart. Being cool and ironic and detached is not the only way to look at things.

This leads on to an associated factor, which is this: one hit wonders say something about why we buy records. They show how much music is a fabric of our world, a soundtrack to our lives, and how songs can capture a memory or an emotion in a way that little else can. It has to be said that quite often, the records that achieve this are not necessarily the ones we are most proud of owning. To give you two examples from my own life, neither one hit wonders, but hopefully you get the point: on summer holidays as a child, my family would make the long drive from York to the south coast, soundtracked by a relentless playing of *Abbey Road* by the Beatles. Even now, there are bits of that album I can't listen to without feeling carsick. Or take my first proper girlfriend – our two and a half months for ever encapsulated (should I be admitting this?) by Climie Fisher's 'Love Changes Everything'. Maybe this is one of the reasons we are so mean to our one hit wonders: we are embarrassed by having bought them in the first place.

One hit wonders, too, say something about what pop music should be all about: in fact, in many respects they are pop music in its purest form, distilled down to its very essence: their ephemeral nature. Pop at its best should be fun and fleeting, a quick fix, a little buzz, and then on to the next one, thank you very much. They may not stand up to close scrutiny, but that was never their intention in the first place. Not every band wants to be Radiohead, and there should be more than enough room for both.

These songs also reinforce our insatiable desire for something new, our consistent cultural need for instant gratification, the phenomenal turnover of music and stars and stories that our TV and radio and newspapers and magazines and gossip columns and websites feed upon. Maybe they show how short our attention spans are, that we can't focus on things for more than three minutes. The best bands and the musicians that have long careers tend to know this, and continually reinvent themselves, coming up with different sounds and styles – think, for example, how Blur and the Beatles and U2 fluctuate over the years. Only fans of Status Quo like things the same – but when they tried something different ('In The Army Now') they had one of their biggest hits for years.

Finally, one hit wonders tap into that part of the national psyche we never seem able to resist – the underdog. We like to champion the little guy, revel in the sensation of getting one over on the powers that be. And nowhere is this more apparent than in an unknown singer keeping a long-established star off the top spot. Think Joe Dolce and 'Vienna' by Ultravox. Mr Blobby and Take That. Or more recently, Gary Jules spoiling the perfect end to the year of the Darkness. Will we ever buy another record by Gary Jules in our entire lives? Probably not, but that doesn't spoil the moment of delight when we learned he'd pipped the favourites to number 1.

This, then, is Chesney's book. Renato's and Noel's and Berlin's and Nena's and Strawberry Switchblade's and Men at Work's. They may only have had one hit, but it is one hit more than I've ever had, and I suspect you too. These artists are worthy of their paragraph in the annals of rock history, and our musical story, frankly, would have been duller for their absence. So put your feet up and get ready to remember, be prepared to cringe occasionally but mainly to smile, as we return to a place, as Martha and the Muffins once put it, far away in time . . .

Tom Bromley
Salisbury, March 2004

A Guide to the Symbols and Recommendations

Along with each song discussed, there are various symbols and recommendations to help you on your way.

Symbols

I have included a symbol for each of the chapter types, because many songs (inevitably) fall into more than one category. The full list is as follows:

 Summer A song that was a holiday hit

 Christmas A hit at Christmas

 Puppet The artist is a cartoon character, a puppet or a grown man dressed up in a silly costume

 Day job A one hit wonder who is an actor, a soap star, a footballer, a DJ – anything, in fact, apart from a singer

 Instrumental A song without words or with gibberish

 Comedy A song that is humorous, intentionally, at least

 Child An artist who is not old enough to know better

 TV/film A song whose success is related to a TV show or film

 Smooch A love song

 Dance Artist filed under dance of whatever description

 Saucy Songs that are just a little bit rude

 Euro Artists from across the European Continent

Bizarre Artists or songs that are just a little odd

 80s/90s Big pop hits that defined the decades

 Awful Just terrible one hit wonders

 Great Just fantastic one hit wonders

 Dead One hit wonders who, sniff, are sadly no longer with us

 Panto Artists who have trodden the boards at Christmas time

 Reformed Artists who split up and then got back together again

 Student Artists who ended up doing the student union circuit

 Cover Songs that are cover versions

 Borrow Songs that contain samples of other songs, bits of classical music, lines from a poem and so forth

 Radio Songs that received a helping hand from a DJ

 New version Songs that have been recorded. And then rerecorded

 Still going Artists who have ploughed a hit-free furrow ever since

 Germany I'm not saying that Germany is a retirement home for one hit wonders, but like Ringo Starr's All Star Band, quite a few of them seem to end up here

 Anorak I mentioned in the introduction that occasionally the artist in question has had a second top-twenty hit. I don't think it takes away from their status. You might disagree. If you're feeling argumentative, these are the ones to get picky about

 Recognisability In a *Name That Tune* sort of way, this refers to how quickly you recognise the hit in question and thus your reaction time in either changing radio station or turning up the volume

 Durability Some songs have a longer shelf-life than others. This icon shows you could play this song indefinitely and not get bored …

 Offability …whereas here, as soon as you recognise the song, it's off

Stickability This icon warns that once you've been exposed to the song your brain is going to give it heavy rotation, whether you like it or not

 Philibilty Named in honour of Phil Collins and his classic eighties ballad 'Against All Odds'. Because against the odds is what these one hit wonders battled against to get into the charts

 Chedibility The flip side of credibility, this icon tells you how chedible – or cheesy – a song or artist is. Resplendent in its pungency

Recommendations

Having read what I've written, some of you may want to listen to the records to refresh your memory. So for each song I have made three suggestions – please note that the years of release and record labels may relate to reissues rather than to the original release.

Listen Here Where you can hear the song in question. I've tried, where possible, to choose compilations first (one song may be enough for you), greatest hits albums second, albums third, and if all else fails, the single details.

Listen On So you've heard the song. If you want to check out something else by the same artist, here's where to go.

Listen Further If you fancy delving deeper into something or someone similar, here's where to start.

1 Costa Del Awful
– Summer Hits

Peter Powell, erstwhile Radio One DJ of the 1980s, used to have a summer jingle that he would dust down once a year with great excitement. 'Sum-mer radio,' the jingle went, 'on the Pete-Peter Powell show, hear the music flow on the Peter Powell show . . .' He'd then gush about how fantastic it was that summer had arrived, before spinning the latest song by Howard Jones.

Summer hits have changed over the years in the same way that where we take our holidays has. Last of the old guard, perhaps, were 'Seaside Shuffle' by Terry Dactyl and the Dinosaurs (number 2, 1972), a squeezebox-driven ditty about promenades and the like, and Fiddler's Dram (we'll come back to them later) with their day trip to Bangor. Instead, hits from Sylvia ('Y Viva España') and Typically Tropical ('Barbados') matched our increasing desire to travel abroad.

Of course, returning home slightly burned, we always bring back something that seemed a good idea at the time. It could be a local food or drink that just doesn't taste the same back in Britain, a fledgling relationship that should have been snuffed out in Spain or, worst of all, that funny dance routine that everyone was doing in the disco. 'The Birdie Song', 'Macarena', the Lambada, 'Agadoo', Whigfield's 'Saturday Night' . . . we've done many dances over the years. Quite fun when you're on holiday. Less so back home.

Black Lace and Whigfield are, sadly, just too successful for this book. But don't worry, there are plenty more where they came from . . .

Y Viva España Sylvia
No. 4 1974

Franco goes to Hollywood

If any one hit wonder is the mother of all summer records, then surely it must be Sylvia: a decade before 'Agadoo', seventeen years before Whigfield, at a time when Las Ketchup were not even a twinkle in their flamenco father's eyes. An unofficial national anthem, 'Y Viva España' is a celebration of all those wonderful things Iberian. And what a lot there are: influenza, omelettes with potatoes in, the Armada, Michael Portillo, bullfighting, Franco, the Inquisition, ETA, throwing donkeys out of windows, the Costa del Crime, Julio Iglesias. 'Y Viva España' indeed, Sylvia!

Sylvia Vrethammar might not sound like a particularly Spanish name, and that's because it's not. Sylvia is, of all things for a song celebrating Spain, Swedish. Born in Uddevalla on the Swedish west coast (slightly chillier, I believe, than the Californian variety), Sylvia grew up in Stockholm. By the end of the sixties she was co-hosting the nation's biggest TV show, the not-un-Swedish-stereotype-sounding *Hylands Hörna*. Then a trip to Rio for Brazil's International Song Festival opened her eyes, or rather her ears, to the delights of samba. Returning to Scandinavia with the Brazilian group Trio Pandeiros de Ouro in her luggage, Sylvia was dubbed the 'Samba Queen'.

Next stop on Sylvia's Latin love-in was Spain. 'Y Viva España' opens with a paean (or is it a paella?) to silent movie star Rudolph Valentino, as a precursor to talking all things love. Sylvia makes the pertinent point, and one that clearly struck a chord with much of the British Isles, that it is hard to be a smouldering lover when it is pissing down with rain (I'm paraphrasing slightly here). Therefore a quick plane ride to 'sunny Spain' is the answer.

Even with General Franco still in charge, Sylvia's sunny Spain is clearly a forerunner for Club 18–30: there are just pulling opportunities aplenty for everyone. For the gentlemen, there are 'señoritas by the score'. And as well as the locals, there are the female tourists, who go from 'pasty' to 'tasty' in no time at all. For the laydeez, there is always a matador, but the 'finest bet', according to Sylvia, are the flamenco dancers. She describes kissing one 'behind the castanet', which I presume must be some sort of Swedish euphemism. Particularly because it excited the dancer so much he, ahem, 'rattled his maracas'.

> Sylvia is, of all things for a song celebrating Spain, Swedish.

Never big in Britain again, Sylvia, in case you're worried she is eating into the Swedish social security system, remained popular on the Continent, especially in Germany. She has toured with Bert Kaempfert and recorded an album with Georgie Fame. In 1980 she became a United Nations Peace Ambassador. In the 1990s she developed a taste for big band and is still playing, performing and rattling those castanets.

Listen Here *Schooldisco.com – The Revision Guide* (Columbia, 2003). Sylvia's finest four minutes is halfway down CD 2, between 'Copacabana' by Barry Manilow and 'In The Summertime' by Mungo Jerry.

Listen On Sylvia's 1992 available-in-Germany album *Ricardo* (Papagayo, 1992), which features the no doubt deeply poignant 'Na-Na-Na Nee-Nee-Nee No-No-No'.

Listen Further For another take on all things Iberian, try Miles Davis's quite wonderful *Sketches of Spain* (Sony Jazz, 1997).

Barbados Typically Tropical
No. 1 1975

Cruise control

This is the story of a man who went on holiday with his dad, came back, wrote a song about it in two hours and ended up at number 1. It really *was* that simple.

Jeff Calvert was a trainee engineer at London's Morgan recording studios. Max West was a member of a not exactly progressing progressive rock band called Quasar. Late at night, they would sneak into the studio to mess around and record tracks. 'They tended to be gimmicky, sometimes comic or sci-fi-ish, though we weren't always trying to be novelties', Jeff explains.* And then came the Caribbean cruise: 'I was into the whole atmosphere, so when I got back, we thought we'd do something for a giggle. At the end of

* *Q* magazine, February 1995.
** *Q* magazine, February 1995.

the day, it was a bit of a wind-up, with the put-on accent. We never intended to release it.'**

'Barbados' tells the story of a London bus driver, who has had enough of 'London town' and its rain, a man who has seen more than enough of Brixton 'in de night'. Thus he boards, ahem, Coconut Airways Flight 372 to Bridgetown, flown by one Captain Tobias Wilcox (Jeff's voice sped up, fact fans). The bus driver is looking forward to heading 'backa' to the palm trees, the 'sunny Caribbean sea' (can a sea technically be sunny? Discuss), and his 'girlfriend' Mary Jane, which is either an innocent coincidence or a knowing nod to the wacky baccy.

Two hours in the writing, Jeff and Max's masterpiece captures two of the Caribbean's great strengths, seafood and music. Or, to be slightly more specific, cod and reggae. A singles deal with a small record label followed, followed by a rerecorded version accompanied by the likes of Vic Flick and Chris Spedding. And Spedding up the charts was exactly what the song did, hitting number 1 in July 1975, selling just short of half a million copies and enjoying the perhaps slightly dubious accolade of being the only song for which Pan's People, the *Top of the Pops* dance troupe, did a striptease.

> Barbados captures two of the Caribbean's great strengths, seafood and music. Or more specifically, cod and reggae.

So where did Typically Tropical go from there? Like a vinyl Freddie Laker, they overstretched themselves with new routes. They tried 'Rocket Now', in which the Coconut Airways captain Tobias Wilcox went to the moon. That didn't work. They tried switching from the Caribbean to the Yorkshire coast on 'Bridlington'. That didn't work either. What was more successful was returning to the *Top of the Pops* dance troupe, now Hot Gossip rather than Pan's People, and boasting one Sarah Brightman, later to be cast under the spell of Andrew Lloyd Webber. Max and Jeff penned her debut hit, 'I Lost My Heart To A Starship Trooper', which reached number 6 in 1979. Even more bizarrely, Max and Jeff then used all their reggae prowess to produce, of all things, Judas Priest's second album, *Sad Wings of Destiny*.

For twenty-five years destiny's sad wings was where Max and Jeff stayed. Until they got a call from the Vengaboys, a sort of Hi-NRG Dutch Abba, with ghastly party anthems, such as 'We Like To Party!' and 'Boom, Boom, Boom, Boom!!', the latter what many people would like to have done to Kim, Robin, Roy and Denice given a sufficient supply of dynamite. Anyway, the Vengaboys were still in party mode, but rather than head for Barbados they were more in the mood for some Balearic beats. 'We're Going To Ibiza!' kept the same tune as 'Barbados' but switched the island in question. The result brought the Typically Tropical sound to a whole new generation, hitting number 1 in September 1999 and filling two very happy people's coffers one more time. With enough left over, presumably, for another Caribbean cruise.

Listen Here 'Barbados' can be found on the Ronseal-titled three-CD compilation, *One Hit Wonders* (K Tel, 2003).

Listen On Sarah Brightman's disco stomp, 'I Lost My Heart To A Starship Trooper' (Ariola, 1978). Not a palm tree in sight.

Listen Further *The Party Album* by the Vengaboys (Positiva, 1999), which includes the Barbados-relocating 'We're Going To Ibiza'.

The Birdie Song
The Tweets
No. 2 1981

They could have been the Wombles

A little bit of this. A little bit of that. And shake your bum. Not, as some might suggest, the entire career plan of Kylie Minogue, but in fact the unofficial words to one of the most derided songs of all time: so much so, that in a survey on dotmusic.co.uk a couple of years ago, 'The Birdie Song' beat 'Barbie Girl' and 'Teletubbies Say Eh-Oh!' to the title of worst song of all time.

'The Birdie Song' is the kind of universal hit that crosses generations, reaches everyone from toddlers to grandparents. Actually, and this is my own theory, it is the sort of song that only reaches toddlers and grandparents, in other words, those who are yet to develop any sort of music appreciation, and those who can't hear any more. Its key, I think, lies in its dance, which is simple enough for a birdbrain to follow. Step one, perform 'the beak', as if you are Rod Hull with a pair of Emus. Step two, 'the wings', as if you are Ian Wright feeling like Chicken Tonight. Step three, 'the wriggle': sort of Elvis with piles, 'That's got a good beat' crossed with a pneumatic drill. Joy. No eighties wedding/school disco/Kraftwerk concert was complete without one.

The origins of 'The Birdie Song' are, perhaps unsurprisingly, Continental. It was written in the 1950s by a Swiss accordion player called Werner Thomas, who tended a flock of ducks and geese (hence the avian theme). And for three decades, on the Continent the 'Vogel Tanz' stayed, a staple of German beer festivals and the like. Until 1981, when a canny pair of Dutchmen called the Electronicas decided to 'commit' the song to vinyl, and make their fortune.

Ah yes. The Electronicas. You probably don't remember them, or their 'Original Bird Dance', which stalled at number 22. Because in Britain at least, they were beaten to the peck by a bunch of session musicians and a record company boss with an eye for a quick buck. Before the Electronicas knew what was happening, the Tweets' version of the 'Bird Dance' was flying up the charts, stealing their thunder and place in pop history. The plan was so simple it was brilliant: the musicians even dressed up in giant bird costumes (the origins of the Flaming Lips stage show, anyone?) and no one could recognise them. Eight million copies sold worldwide later, the perpetrators of this musical bank heist – this swoop? – are still at large.

I managed to track one Tweet member down, keyboardist Adrian Bennett, now living in Portugal. What did he think when he first heard the song? 'I thought it was a load of shit,' he remembers fondly. The thing to remember is that Adrian, like the rest of the Tweets, was a decent musician, with a sterling career of session work behind him: 'The Birdie Song' was originally just another job, one with that fateful choice between session fee and royalty cut. But unlike the other session work, this time things took off. The

costumes arrived, and a decade and a half before the Spice Girls, so did the names: Tubby Tweet, Tweety Tweet, Tricky Tweet and Troy Tweet.

Birded up, the band hit the promotional road. Adrian recalls a photo-opportunity in Trafalgar Square, a slight problem for him as he has a phobia about birds. 'Are you the Tweets?' asked one snap-happy Japanese tourist. 'We ain't fucking Bucks Fizz,' was the reply. The costumes were, in a word, 'hot'. And though they kept the band's anonymity in the public eye, they didn't backstage. In the green room after *Top of the Pops*, the heads came off to cries of 'oh, it's *you*' from their fellow musicians.

Adrian feels the Tweets were a missed opportunity: 'It could have been brilliant, we could have been like the Wombles.' The characters were there, the songs (a bird-themed set of 'Rocking Robin', 'The Funky Chicken' and the like) – 'The Birdie Song' their springboard to stardom. But the money and the promotion just weren't there: while other chart acts were swanning around in limousines, the Tweets were still making do with a clapped-out old Transit van. On the way to one gig, at a children's hospital in Nottingham, the van broke down and they never made it. 'Tweets Snub Autistic Children' was the next day's headline. A second single, 'Let's All Sing Like The Birdies Sing', only reached number 44 and the Tweets split up. Adrian opened up his own studio, before migrating south to Spain and Portugal and the music industry there.

'The Birdie Song' has one other, surprising, claim to fame. In 1981, after five years on the job, it became the

> A little bit of this. A little bit of that. And shake your bum.

last performance of the *Top of the Pops* dance troupe of Lulu, Gill, Pauline, Patti, Rosie and Sue, better known as Legs and Co. What a way to go. And what a way to destroy some much-loved teenage memories. Sigh.

Listen Here The somewhat cheddary compilation *The Ultimate Cheese Party* (WSM, 2003). As well as the Tweets, there's everything from Jive Bunny to the Cheeky Girls.

Listen On The follow-up single, 'Let's All Sing Like The Birdies Sing' (PRT, 1981),

Listen Further Electronicas' rival version, the stalled-at-number-22 'Original Bird Dance' (Polydor, 1981).

The Chicken Song
Spitting Image
No. 1 1986

Black comedy lace

Ah. Casseroling your grandmother. Using spears to disembowel yourself. Splashing a coat of green Dulux on your left knee. Setting up your very own string quartet. Getting a spade, digging a hole and putting all your clothes in it. Placing a deckchair up your nostrils (tip: it's best to fold it up first). Becoming fluent in Arapaho. Parting an Eskimo from his head. Fowling the air. Having a Renault 4 for supper (serving suggestion: salami in your ears). Pretending your name is Moon, Richards, Penelope or Chegwin.

If ever a song defined a good night out in mid-eighties Britain, then 'The Chicken Song' was it.

Spitting Image's target with this obscenely successful song was those (these?) irritating summer singles, and more specifically, Black Lace – the band rather than the erotic fiction* – 'two wet gits' according to the lyrics, with 'girly curly hair', who, like the *Blue Peter* tortoise and Peter Powell's Summer Radio jingle, would emerge annually from hibernation as soon as the weather started to perk up. For those of you with bad-music-proof memories, Black Lace's criminal records were the top-ten smashes 'Superman', 'Agadoo' and 'Do The Conga' – a triumvirate of silly dances that no Lanzarote discotheque was complete without. Actually, to be fair to Black Lace (and believe me, I never thought I'd write these words), by the time 'The Chicken Song' came out, the charts had been pretty much free of their charms for eighteen months: singles 'El Vino Collapso' and 'I Speaka Da Lingo' had both bombed, while the scraping-the-barrel number 'Hokey Cokey' had not so much peaked as flatlined at number 31. No matter. Britain's best satirical show since *That Was The Week That Was* had the poor buggers in their sights. And that, said Alice, was that.

> Out of all the songs Spitting Image did, 'The Chicken Song' is perhaps the least humorous.

* Though there is a highly regarded erotic classic, *The Lady with the Pineapples*, in which a 'superman' sounds his horn, pushes his lady friend's pineapples and then, once her tree is sufficiently shaken, gives her what can only be described as a jolly good congaing.

Spitting Image, unlike Black Lace, was stock full of talent: Steve Coogan, Ian Hislop, John Sessions, Rory Bremner, Harry Enfield, Alistair MacGowan, Richard Curtis and John O'Farrell were among the many performers and writers who contributed to the show. 'The Chicken Song' itself was composed by stalwart Philip Pope (who also wrote the theme tune to *Only Fools and Horses*), while the lyrics were the responsibility of Rob Grant and Doug Naylor, who achieved fame as the writers of *Red Dwarf*. Lead vocals, meanwhile, were supplied by Michael Fenton Stevens – who, along with a young Angus Deayton, was a member of parody group the Hee Bee Gee Bees* – and Kate Robbins, later part of Radio 4's *Dead Ringers*.

The funny thing is that out of all the songs Spitting Image did, 'The Chicken Song' is perhaps the least humorous. The B-side, 'I've Never Met a Nice South African', was far better. Likewise the bonus tracks on the 12-inch, the Phil Collins pastiche 'Hello You Must Be Going' and the We Are the World parody 'We're Scared Of Bob'. Then there was their take on Prince ('Black Moustache') and perhaps their finest musical five minutes, the ZZ Top classic 'We've Got Beards'.** Nevertheless, it was 'The Chicken Song' that tickled the nation's funny bone, out-Black Lacing Black Lace. And if anyone ever said how irritating the song was, they could just smile, count their royalties, and say, yes, that's exactly the point.

* Best known for their Gibbs jibe, 'Meaningless Songs In Very High Voices'.
** The joke, of course, was that though 'the Top' were fronted by the hirsute axe attack of Billy Gibbons and Dusty Hill, drumming duties were carried out by the ironically beardless Frank Beard.

Listen Here The Spitting Image album, *Spit in Your Ear* (Virgin, 1995). The album that's like the TV show, except without the pictures.

Listen On ZZ Top pastiche 'We've Got Beards', on the same album.

Listen Further Black Lace's *Greatest Ever Party Album* (Metro, 2000). All the songs 'The Chicken Song' was taking the Michael out of.

Itsy Bitsy Teeny Weeny Yellow Polka Dot Bikini
Bombalurina
No. 1 1990

Oh yeah? Oh *no*.

In 1961 Billy Wilder released his Cold War satire, *One, Two, Three*, starring James Cagney. Cagney is a Coca-Cola executive, marketing the 'Real Thing' behind the Iron Curtain, who gets caught up with a volatile communist, Otto Piffl. I know this sounds tangential, but please, bear with me. Arrested by the East German police, Piffl is subjected to the most vicious form of torture to break him. Thumb screws? The rack? The comfy chair? No, something far, far more sinister. Piffl's resistance, his very spirit is broken by repeated listening to 'Itsy Bitsy Teeny Weeny Yellow Polka Dot Bikini'.

For the rest of us, the torture turned up in 1990,

thanks to a most unholy trinity of musical suspects. The clue to the identity of the first suspect is in the group's name: Bombalurina is the name of a cat from the musical *Cats*, and yes, the guiding hand of the lovely Andrew Lloyd Webber is at work here. 'Itsy Bitsy' is supposedly one of his favourite songs, originally a hit for Brian 'the Voice of Summer' Hyland back in 1961. The next link in the chain is record producer Nigel Wright: I could go on, but let us just say 'keyboard player' and 'Shakatak' and leave it at that. All that was missing was a children's TV presenter with stupid glasses and a sponge mallet . . .

The missing link between Roland Rat and Chris Evans, Timmy Mallett had the sort of energy in the early hours of the morning normally associated with small, hyperactive children. That was fine: his tartrazine TV show *Wacaday* could entertain all the overexcited small children while the rest of us had a lie-in. But then came 'Itsy Bitsy', and Timmy started appearing at other points in the day. Two words: those shirts. Princess Di didn't help matters by wearing an itsy bitsy bikini, and the song shot to number 1. On the Monday morning after the charts were announced Chris Evans turned up at Timmy's house at 7 a.m. with a bottle of champagne. I could put that into context, but actually, it's funnier if I leave it vague like that.

There was a follow-up single, 'Seven Little Girls Sitting In The Backseat', but thankfully, it didn't repeat 'Itsy Bitsy''s success. Andrew Lloyd Webber continued doing his lovely musicals and made friends with Ben Elton. Dawn, one of Timmy's backing singers, ended up marrying Gary Barlow. And Timmy can be found

> The missing link between Roland Rat and Chris Evans.

doing the student union rounds, no doubt with a drunken disco remix of 'Itsy Bitsy' and a hilarious version of Mallett's Mallet, complete with a bit of swearing thrown in for good measure.

Listen Here *Huggin' an' a Kissin'* (1990). A whole album of Timmy Mallett, available from his website in three different versions: standard, non-stop party mix and karaoke.

Listen On Timmy's version of 'My Boomerang Won't Come Back' on the same album.

Listen Further 'Tetris' by Doctor Spin (Carpet, 1992). Andrew Lloyd Webber in cunning disguise once more, reaching number 6 in 1992.

Macarena Los Del Rio
No. 2 1996

Hey!

Blame Diana Patricia Cubillan. She's a five-foot-three flamenco dancer from Caracas in Venezuela. And if she hadn't performed one night in front of Rafael Ruiz and Antonio Romero, an ageing Spanish musical duo, none of this would ever have happened.

Antonio was not the first bloke ever to shout encouragement to a woman dancing in a club, but he is the only one to make a mint from it. So inspired was he by Diana's strutting, the words to their international hit came tumbling out. 'Give your body joy!' he exclaimed. 'Because your body is for giving happiness and good things.' Yes, I think it probably sounds better in the original Spanish too. The rest of the lyrics followed soon after. To summarise: the Macarena in question is something of a saucy minx whose boyfriend Vittorino has gone off to join the army, and while he's away, basically it's party time. Vittorino's two friends were 'soooooo fine' she felt unable to resist. And if you 'move' and 'jam' with her and your 'jam' is good, then you'll get the invite back home too.

'Macarena' then followed the traditional summer holiday hit route. It was big first on the Continent, this time a number 1 in Spain in 1993. Then, yes, they did it in the German beerhalls and it became a 'cruise staple'. And then, yes, some bright-spark tourist saw the 'irritating hit' dollar signs in front of their eyes. A remix by the Bayside Boys, the addition of English lyrics and a giggling Macarena, and global domination was theirs. In 1996 everyone did the Macarena: Nationalist Party rallies in Malta; Hillary Clinton and Al Gore at the Democratic Party convention; 50,000 people at the Yankee Stadium in New York, breaking the world line-dancing record. The Americans in particular seemed to go mad for this song.

As for the dance, its origins are unclear, but suspicion lies with Mia Frye, the French choreographer of the video, who now makes a living doing a Simon Cowell impression on the French version of *Popstars*. Quite how that gives her the right to criticise, but anyway. As for Los Del Rio, well, they were always sanguine about their success. Interviewed at the time about their one hit wonder status, Rafael Ruiz said, 'Go ask Frank Sinatra if he has come up with another "New York, New York".' I'll leave that one with you.

Here, should you want to relive that drunken night in Saints and Sinners, is how to 'do' the Macarena: 1. Put your right arm out in front of you with your palm down. 2. Do the same with your left. 3. Put your right arm out again, this time palm up. 4. That's right, now with your left. 5. Grab your left elbow. This is best done with your right hand. 6. Grab your right elbow. 7. Grab the back of your neck, first with your right hand and then, 8. You're ahead of me here, aren't you? 9. Right hand, front-left pocket. 10. Left hand, front-right pocket. 11. Right hand, right-rear pocket. 12. Left hand, left-rear pocket. No, I don't know what to do if you haven't got pockets either. Just improvise for now. 13. Shake your booty to the left. 14. And then to the right. 15. Go on, once more for luck, to the left again. 16. Clap, turn to the right and shout 'Hey! Macarena!'

If you are sat reading this on the toilet and have just 'done' the Macarena, then you are a deeply sad individual.

> Macarena is something of a saucy minx whose boyfriend has gone off to join the army.

Listen Here Los Del Rio's album *Macarena Non Stop* (RCA, 1999). Eight tracks, six different versions of you-know-what.

Listen On Summer goes Santa with the follow-up single, 'Macarena Christmas' (Ariola, 1996).

Listen Further *The Best Latin Party Album in the World . . . Ever!* (Virgin, 1999). That's Latin Party as in samba rather than toga.

Mambo No. 5 (A Little Bit of . . .) Lou Bega
No. 1 1999

In 1984 Prince sang about partying like it was 1999. But in 1999, everyone was partying like it was 1948

In the beginning, believe it or not, there was English country dancing. Then, in the seventeenth century, there was the French *contredanse* and the Spanish *contradanza*. By the time it hit Cuba a century later *contradanza* became *danza*, the national dance. This mutated into *danzon*, played by brass-bands or *tipicas* and later by smaller groups called *charangas*: a hotch-potch of violin, cello, piano, guiro, clarinet, flute, bass and drums. The most successful of these was that of Antonio Arcano. In 1938 his cellist, Orestes Lopez, composed a *danzon* with a single-word title, which Arcano would shout out when it was time for the band to solo. Its name? 'Mambo'.

Slowly, mambo began to spread, largely thanks to one man, Perez Prado, the 'Prez', the Mambo King, who took the music from Cuba to Mexico and finally to America. In Mexico City in December 1949 he cut a 78, two tracks that would be his launch pad for taking America by storm: 'Que Rico El Mambo' and 'Mambo No. 5'. By the early 1950s everyone was going mambo crazy.

So far, so history lesson. Now enter Lou Bega, real name David Lubega (do you see what he did there?), a Munich-born singer with a Sicilian mother and Ugandan father. In 1993 he went to Miami, working in various studios to earn some money, and it was during this stay that he came across Perez Prado and the mambo. If you came across Perez and his mambo, you might be struck too. It's one of those records, like Coolio's 'Gangster's Paradise' and Stevie Wonder's 'Pastime Paradise', where once you hear the original, you realise that's where the hook, where all the good bits are. Anyway, Prado's version was instrumental, which was where Lou came in. 'That was my chance,' he explained in an interview. 'I decided to use lyrics, make it accessible to the '90s somehow, and bring it back.'

And what lyrics. Not so much a little bit ooh, a little bit aah, as a little bit nudge, a little bit wink. Monica, Erica, Rita, Tina, Sandra, Mary, Jessica. Did these ladies once enjoy a little bit of Lou? Who knows. Maybe they were wowed by his outfit: the pinstripe suit, the polka-dot handkerchief, the spats and Borsalino hat. 'Mambo No. 5' did four better than number 5 and ruled the roost across the world. The follow-up, 'I Got A Girl', did all the fives, mambo number 55, and that, for Lou, was that, in this country at least. The words 'big', 'in' and 'Germany' are once again appropriate.

And if Lou isn't still big here, his, or rather Perez Prado's, mambo lives on. The following year 'Mambo No. 5' hit the top spot again, this time sung by Bob the Builder and this time about building rather than the laydeez. For Monica, think timber. No jokes about wood please. And at the same time Channel 4, having taken over coverage of cricket from the BBC, needed a

> Did these ladies once enjoy a little bit of Lou?

new theme to replace the Booker T. & the MG's classic 'Soul Limbo'. Who better to encapsulate the great game than a Cuban-inspired German singer?

Listen Here Lou's modestly titled album, *King of Mambo* (Camden, 2003).

Listen On Hear the King of Mambo do basic maths on the I-can-count classic '1+1=2'.

Listen Further Another album called *King of Mambo* (RCA, 1994), this time by the original master, Perez 'Prez' Prado.

The Ketchup Song
Las Ketchup
No. 1 2002

(Rap classic + silly name) × dance routine = international hit

This isn't the first time that rock and roll and condiments have gone together. There's the Beatles' 'Mean Mr Mustard'. Vinegar Joe. The questionable influence of Simon Mayo (see 'Kinky Boots'). Brown Sauce. Salt 'n' Pepa. And then in 2002 there came the daddy of all sauces. Actually, the daddy of all sauces is probably Daddy's Tomato Sauce, but you know what I mean.

The reason behind all the tomato stuff is depressingly straightforward. Las Ketchup consists of three not unattractive Spanish sisters, Lola (the brunette one), Lucia (the brunette one) and Pilar (the brunette

one), whose father is a big-in-Seville flamenco guitarist called Tomate. And just in case you missed the point, their hit song 'Asereje' was renamed 'The Ketchup Song' for the international market, complete with record sleeves covered in tomatoes.

The inspiration for 'The Ketchup Song' comes from, of all places, late-seventies American rap. The Sugarhill Gang, in fact, whose crossover anthem 'Rapper's Delight' provided the inspiration for songwriter Manuel Ruiz (if you listen to the chorus carefully, you can hear it). The lyrics, which I'm sorry to say have nothing whatsoever to do with ketchup, tell the tale of Diego, described on the record company website as 'a young fashion-conscious gypsy with Rastafarian leanings'. No, I don't know what that means either. Anyway, it's Friday night, Diego is at the disco checking out the talent, and he's making up his own lyrics because he doesn't understand the words to the song. Which is ironic, because that's what everyone else ended up doing as well.

But for the song to go exponential, what any summer anthem needs is its own dance routine. And Las Ketchup didn't disappoint. Before you knew what was happening, the words 'new' and 'Macarena' were everywhere. You start by crossing your hands across your torso, left hand over right, right over left, six times. Then you get your thumb out, hitch a ride to the right and the left. Next up, it's hand in the air, making circles above your head, before we come to the Las Ketchup classic move: one hand on the back of the head, the other on your forehead and move your knees

> The words 'new' and 'Macarena' were everywhere.

together and out times four. And then just wiggle your butt.

As summer dances go, I'm not convinced 'The Ketchup Song' is the best. The hitching a ride stuff, surely, is taken straight from the routine to Black Lace's 'Superman'. It's a surprise the girls don't 'ski' and 'spray' as well. The butt wiggling at the end, too, feels like a choreographer running out of ideas. But the move that really gets me is the knees knocking together bit. It's the sort of move that attractive young Spanish girls called Pilar can just about get away with, but leaves everyone else looking like an idiot.

Not that their record company thought they were a one hit wonder or anything, but the Las Ketchup album features no fewer than four versions of the song. Among the remaining tracks there's a number called 'Krapuleo'. Which kind of says it all.

Listen Here Choose your favourite version on the Las Ketchup album, *Las Ketchup* (Columbia, 2002).

Listen On Album track 'Me Persigue Un Chulo', enticingly described by Amazon as 'a rumba version of Madness's "Baggy Trousers"'.

Listen Further 'Rapper's Delight' by the Sugarhill Gang (Sugarhill, 1979). In an ideal world, Las Ketchup would turn a generation of teenage girls into hip-hop fans . . .

Big in Britain

One Hit Wonders in the USA

Take That
'Back For Good' (No. 7)

Everything But The Girl
'Missing' (No. 2)

Madness
'Our House' (No. 7)

Spandau Ballet
'True' (No. 4)

Dexy's Midnight Runners
'Come On Eileen' (No. 1)

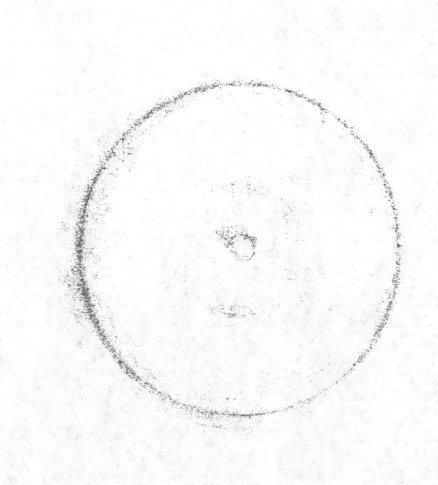

2 Complete Turkeys
– Christmas Hits

What is it about the Christmas chart that makes it open season for strange and bizarre records? It's the time of year when practically anything goes: you could almost sell your grandmother for charity, say 'Hey, come on! It's Christmas!' and people will forgive you. Maybe it's the combined mix of office parties (drunken silly dancing), Christmas itself (for a couple of weeks, sentimentality is the new cool) and a media struggling for stories in a quiet news period.

The 'race' for the Christmas number 1 is not so much Le Mans as an episode of *Wacky Races*. Here are some of the victors over the years: 'Lily The Pink' by the Scaffold, 'Two Little Boys' by Rolf Harris, 'Ernie (The Fastest Milkman In The West)' by Benny Hill, Little Jimmy Osmond's 'Long Haired Lover From Liverpool', 'Mull Of Kintyre', 'There's No One Quite Like Grandma', 'Save Your Love'...If you think things were better back then, in this case you'd be right. In the mid-1960s the Beatles successfully kept the loons at bay.

But for all the odd songs, there is a second strand of Christmas song that is all the more surprising. From Greg Lake to Gary Jules, there is a tradition and an appetite for more sombre, moodier, darker music. As much as we go for the jolly holly stuff, we like a bit of the portentous stuff too. Maybe Christmas means something to us after all. If you ever feel like writing a Christmas song and want to end up earning royalties year after year on one of those Christmas compilations, here's my advice: give the stuff about Santa the sack and send for the clanging chimes of doom ...

I Believe In Father Christmas Greg Lake

No. 2 1975

ELF?

I'm not sure it is possible to be more 'prog' than Greg Lake without having been born a hobbit. This is a singer who started off in King Crimson, getting the nod over both Bryan Ferry and Elton John for the part. Then he put the Lake into Emerson, Lake and Palmer: ELP to their fans, 'ELP to everybody else. Cue overblown and overlong songs, tricky time signatures, adaptations of classical music and experimentations with early synthesizers. In 1974 the band released *Welcome Back My Friends to the Show that Never Ends...*, a title that wasn't far off given that it was a triple LP.

With the band taking a break, Greg entered the dangerous waters of releasing a Christmas single, and before he knew it, posterity had him marked down not as the bloke from ELP but as the one on *The Best Christmas Album in the World... Ever!* when everyone goes 'Greg who?' 'I Believe In Father Christmas' has everything you could ask for from a Christmas song: sleigh bells, choirs, the London Philharmonic Orchestra, a bit nicked from Prokofiev, the kitchen sink and a lyric with a message.

Greg is not, I think it would be fair to say, the most cheerful of elves. In the first verse he describes how he was promised snow at Christmas but all he got

instead was rain. And as the sound of a choir comes wafting across the speakers, Greg describes hearing the sound of a choir, with eyes full of, what can only be described as a somewhat painful combination, of tinsel and fire. Greg's feelings of let-down continue in verse two. Where's the dream of Christmas he was promised? What about that silent night? Greg mentions some fairy story about some baby or other in the Middle East, before he gets to the crux of his disappointment. He 'believed' (note the past tense) in Father Christmas, until he woke up with a yawn and realised that, bugger me, it was his dad after all (I'm paraphrasing slightly).

Actually, Greg isn't dealing with issues from his childhood at all but is making a point about how commercial Christmas has become: the Christmas you get, he suggests, is the Christmas that you deserve. Putting aside quite what I've done to get *The Great Escape* on the telly *again*, he's got a point about all the commercialism. If it's not kids screaming for the latest toy that was sold out months ago, then it's Tango sponsoring the Christmas lights down Regent Street so they're all bloody orange. And if it's not Tango, it's clapped-out old proggers releasing cash-in festive singles, that get played year after year, racking up the royalties.

> Everything you could ask for from a Christmas song: sleigh bells, choirs, the London Philharmonic, Prokofiev, the kitchen sink . .

Listen Here *The Best Christmas Album in the World... Ever!* (Virgin, 2000). Nestled between Band Aid and 'A Spaceman Came Travelling'.

Listen On *Tarkus* by Emerson Lake and Palmer (Victory, 1971). Greg's day job: be warned, prog virgins – the title track is twenty minutes long.

Listen Further *Alexander Nevsky/Lieutenant Kijé* by Prokofiev (The Originals, 1995). The London Symphony Orchestra do the 'sleigh ride' bit that gives the song that Christmassy feel.

Stop The Cavalry
Jona Lewie
No. 3 1980

Dum-a num-a num num . . .

Christmas. Peace on earth. It's a tradition that stretches back 2,000 years or so, give or take the Soviet Union invading Afghanistan on 25 December 1979. One thinks, for example, of the famous football match during the First World War, when the English and Germans left their trenches to kick a ball about in the snow. One thinks, too, of the music that champions this link: John Lennon's festive anthem, 'Happy Xmas (War is Over)'; Simon and Garfunkel's 'Silent Night', interspersed with a news report about the Vietnam War; David Bowie pa-ruppa pum pumming it with Bing Crosby.

Jona Lewie's 'Stop The Cavalry' is a Christmas classic that fits firmly into this tradition, right from its introduction of trumpet fanfare and 'Little Drummer Boy' drum roll. With its 'umpa-umpa' backbeat, brass-band interludes and Jona's Ian Dury-esque vocals, it is one of those songs that simply sounds like nothing else. It is a song that remains fresh through being played once a year, dusted down and welcomed like an old friend – the warm glow of recognition quickly followed by one of the 'oh, what *was* his name?'-type conversations.

'Stop The Cavalry' was partly inspired by the Charge of the Light Brigade and, slightly more obliquely, Peter Berger's *Invitation to Sociology: A Humanist Perspective*, which had impressed Jona back in his college days. But whatever the philosophical underpinning, the song's message is wider and more straightforward: Jona sings from the perspective of the universal soldier through the centuries, who has had it with war, from those congratulated by 'Mister Churchill', back to clip-clopping cavalry days, and forward (this being the early 1980s) to nuclear fallout zones. With the brass-band and sleigh bells behind, Jona then adds perhaps the ultimate Christmas sentiment: he wishes he could be home for Christmas. It doesn't matter whether you're fighting a war, stuck in a strange hotel with your in-laws or have drawn the short straw on the 24-hour garage rota: we can all relate to that. This is only my suggestion, but part of the song's success may lie in the tragic events of 8 December that year. Just as perhaps Stiltskin's 'Inside' chimed with the death of Kurt Cobain, so Jona Lewie's sentiment and sombreness connected with the mood following the death of John Lennon.

> A song that remains fresh through being played once a year, dusted down and welcomed like an old friend.

Jona's real name is John. His surname is actually Lewis, but clearly he didn't like the idea of being mistaken for a department store. When he wasn't reading up on the latest sociological theories, Jona spent his late-sixties student days jamming with Dave Brock – who would go on to form the riff-heavy Hawkwind. Jona's blues piano playing led to him joining Brett Marvin and the Thunderbirds and a coveted support slot for Eric Clapton's Derek and the Dominos. Under the pseudonym Terry Dactyl and the Dinosaurs, the band had a hit record with 'Seaside Shuffle', before Jona left the band and rock and roll and became a sociology lecturer. But in the late 1970s he got the music bug again, and got a solo deal with, of all people, fledgling punk label Stiff Records. A restless mix of everything from music hall to early electronica, Jona's eclectic music struggled to find an audience, until the Hairy Cornflake himself, Dave Lee Travis, heard his single 'You'll Always Find Me In The Kitchen At Parties' and Jona got some airplay. And then he called in the cavalry.

Listen Here Also on *The Best Christmas Album in the World … Ever!* (Virgin, 2000). An appropriate record label for a Yuletide album, if ever there was one.

Listen On *The Best of Jona Lewie* (Metro, 2002). All his best bits on one handy record.

Listen Further 'Happy Xmas (War Is Over)' by John Lennon (Apple, 1972). Another classic piece of peacenik music. Unlike the dreadful cover by the Pop Idols, which tends to bring out violence in the common man.

Nellie The Elephant
The Toy Dolls
No. 4 1984

Ooooooooooooooooohhh . . .

Rock and roll and nursery rhymes began their strange relationship back with the Beatles. In 1966 John Lennon did his wind-Paul-up trick for 'Paperback Writer' by singing 'Frère Jacques' as his backing vocals. In 1972 it was Paul's turn, questioning his vegetarian credentials with his top-ten single 'Mary Had A Little Lamb'. In 1993 Green Jelly huffed and puffed their way through 'Three Little Pigs', and in 2001 Travis closed their *Invisible Band* album with their Humpty-Dumpty-inspired 'Humpty Dumpty Love Song'. But this Mother Goose of all nursery-rhyme hits reached number 4 in the week of Christmas 1984 and came courtesy of a punk band from Sunderland.

> The Toy Dolls version, it has to be said, trumpety-trumps the original.

Formed in late 1979, the Toy Dolls were originally a four-piece, but after original singer Pete Zulu left (along with the origins of the band name), and Billy Idol-a-like replacement Hud followed suit, guitarist Olga (not his real name) stepped up to take over microphone duties. There followed enough changes in both bassist and drummer to make the Blue Aeroplanes look like a stable line-up. Among those passing through were Mr Scott (his girlfriend Val demanded he be paid at least a tenner a gig), Trevor the Frog (he didn't like being called a frog), Flip, Teddy and Happy Bob.

Meanwhile, the band were beginning to get a following for their punk rock music meets Half Man Half Biscuit humour: songs included 'Deirdre's A Slag' (about *Coronation Street* character Deirdre Barlow), 'Yul Brynner Was A Skinhead' and 'When You're Jimmy Savile'. A deal with EMI and debut album *Dig That Groove Baby* came and went, and then in 1984 success finally hit. With Bonny Baz on bass and Dicky on drums, Olga rerecorded one of the band's earlier songs.

Originally sung by Mandy Miller in the 1950s, 'Nellie The Elephant' is one of those classic *Children's Favourites* songs, up there with 'Tubby The Tuba' and 'Sparky's Magic Piano'. It is the story of the 'intelligent elephant' who waved farewell to the circus and, with what can only be described as a trumpety trump, headed back to the jungle. The Toy Dolls version, it has to be said, trumpety-trumps the original, all anticipation with its 'oooohs' and jumping up and down with its punky crash through the chorus. Not so much Sid Vicious as Sid Family Friendly, it is what the words 'student' and 'disco' were invented for.

The Toy Dolls took success in their stride. Subsequent single 'James Bond Lives Down Our Street' was a bit of a Dr No-no, and the band went back to the serious business of getting through drummers and bassists. Their small but loyal following has kept them in gigs around the world ever since, with a new album and world tour (and line-up?) pencilled in for 2004.

Listen Here *The Best of the Toy Dolls* (Music Club, 2001). Can you guess which track is track one?

Listen On According to the Toy Dolls website, their new album will be released by the time you read this. Possible songs include the lovingly titled 'I Gave My Heart To A Slag Called Sharon From Whitley Bay'.

Listen Further *Hello Children Everywhere* – Various Artists (EMI Gold, 2002). The original version of 'Nellie' by Mandy Miller, along with 'Runaway Train', 'When I See An Elephant Fly' and many, many more.

Do They Know It's Christmas?
Band Aid II
No. 1 1989

'Clanging chimes' indeed

1984 was arguably the high-water mark of eighties pop: there was Frankie and their three number 1s; Duran Duran swanning about on yachts, as opposed to nearly drowning on them; Wham! switching from shuttlecocks down their pants to designer stubble. But something else happened that year too: Bob Geldof saw Michael Buerk's report on the famine in Ethiopia and felt compelled to do something. He rang up Midge Ure, and together they wrote a song. 'Do

They Know It's Christmas?' may not be the greatest song ever written, but there's no doubting its heart or its urgency: witness their acoustic performance at the inaugural Comic Relief. There's also no denying its impact. Bob rang up the rock glitterati, told them to fucking get down to the studio, *now*, and together they had the biggest-selling single of all time. Millions of pounds and international awareness were raised.

And then, unfortunately, in 1989, someone decided to do it all over again.

You don't often get Band Aid II's version of 'Do They Know It's Christmas?' on those Christmas compilation CDs. 1989, you see, wasn't such a vintage year for pop. Three words sum it up best: Stock. Aitken. Waterman. They produced this Christmas 'cracker' with their classic Hit Factory sound, and while the original version featured the good, the bad and the Phil Collins, second time round it has to be said that they couldn't get the staff.

Observe.

Verse one, all the don't be frightened stuff, letting in light and banishing the nasty shade. The Band Aid version starts with Paul Young's finest four lines; Band Aid II combines Kylie (when she was shit) with, well, Chris Rea. And while the Band Aid baton is passed to Boy George, arms thrown around the world, spreading his smiles of joy, Mark Two gets its grins from Jimmy Somerville, Big Fun and Matt Goss. Yes, I'd forgotten Big Fun existed too. I blame the boogie.

On to verse two. Bob sets his stall out with George Michael. The Stock, Aitken and Waterman version responds with Cliff Richard. Simon Le Bon singing about worlds outside of windows? Step forward Marti 'You can hear the smile' Pellow. Bob goes for broke, bringing on Sting for the dread and fear and only

water flowing section, swiftly joined by Bono for a rollicking closing couplet, 'Well tonight'. 'Insteaaad'. 'Woooah'. How do you compete with that? The Hit Factory offers up Kylie and Jason, plus a little bit more Bros.

You can almost hear the cries from outside Addis Ababa. 'It's all right! Really, we're not that hungry after all.' But the treats on Band Aid II just keep on coming. Cliff does a bit with Bananarama. Lisa Stansfield chimes in with Sonia. There's an entire 'Feed the world' chorus from the Pasadenas. And then finally the 'ensemble' kick in: all of the above plus Cathy Dennis! Technotronic! D Mob! Kevin Godley! Wet Wet Wet! Glen Goldsmith! No, I've no idea who Glen Goldsmith is. Apparently he got to number 12 with a song called 'Dreaming'. No, I can't remember it either.

In 2002 Bob Geldof was approached by the BBC and ITV about the possibility of the contestants of *Fame Academy* and *Popstars: the Rivals* getting together to form a sort of Band Aid III. This time, thankfully, he saw sense.

Listen Here You'll have to track down the single (PWL/Polydor, 1989); the original Band Aid is the preferred choice of the Christmas compilations.

Listen On The original Band Aid version, which can be found on the Band Aid II B-side.

Listen Further *The Hit Factory: Pete Waterman's Greatest Hits* – Various Artists (Universal, 2000). Contains many of the suspects, sorry, singers.

Kinky Boots
Patrick Macnee and Honor Blackman
No. 5 1990

Do you want mayo with that?

The Avengers is one of those classic television series that men of a certain age get all misty-eyed and nostalgic about. A mixture of action, adventure, Englishness and just a hint of the bizarre, it starred Patrick Macnee as super-spy John Steed, armed and ready to tackle any adversary with his bowler hat and umbrella. And before Diana Rigg arrived as his infamous accomplice Emma Peel, it was Honor Blackman who put the kick into Steed's sidekick as Cathy Gale. Rather than reaching for a gun in her handbag, the producers decided to send Honor on a crash course in martial arts. But with flowery dresses not going hand in hand with hand-to-hand combat, a new wardrobe was needed, which led to some bright spark suggesting something a little saucy. Kitted out in skintight leather, all sorts of naughty things were implied by Honor's character, which had the nation been more sexually aware they might not have got away with. And finishing off the costume, of course, was a pair of kinky boots.

But forgetting all the frisson and tension and crinkle, Honor and Patrick agreed to capitalise on the show's success by recording this throwaway single. 'Kinky Boots', it has to be so said, couldn't be less kinky

if it tried. It's a three-way tie for the most irritating part of the record. Is it the fluffy little sixties pop-lite bubbling along in the background? Is it the backing singers doing their best train impression by going 'boop boop' every ten seconds or so? Or is it the way that every third line is repeated, is repeated, as if (boop boop!) the record has got stuck.

Back on the vocal track, meanwhile, Patrick and Honor manfully and womanfully struggle through the words in a talking, singing, stick-to-the-day-job sort of a way. Kinky boots, apparently, are the new sensation that's sweeping the nation. Everyone's wearing them, from 'maiden aunties' to (the second 'best' rhyme in the song, this) 'Mayfair debutantes'. But what surprises as much as the sexlessness is the cynicism of the lyrics: the kinky boots wearers are like 'sheep', doing what the advertising men tell them to do. And when the sixties equivalent of Trinny and Susannah say 'wear 'em', off everyone obeys like women (are you ready for a rhyme classic?) 'in a harem'.

Released in 1964, the British public showed that actually they could ignore what the ad men told them to do and gave the record the boot. Not that the flop damaged anybody's career. Honor moved from one iconic character to another, appearing as Pussy Galore in the Bond film *Goldfinger*, James Bond famously getting his innuendo away with her in a stable. Patrick, meanwhile, continued saving Blighty with a little help from Diana Rigg, and *The Avengers* went from strength to strength. He even enjoyed a crowning rock and roll moment, appearing as record boss Sir

> 'Kinky Boots', it has to be so said, couldn't be less kinky if it tried.

Denis Eaton-Hogg in the, if you will, rockumentary *This is Spinal Tap*. As for 'Kinky Boots', it turned up in Kenny Everett's 'Bottom Thirty' as one of the worst records of all time.

    . . . and then came Simon Mayo. The year was 1990, and Simon, as he was commonly known, held the coveted crown of breakfast show DJ on Radio One. With the words 'Smashy' and 'Nicey' just around the corner, Simon woke the nation up in time to listen to what is widely regarded as the classic Radio One line-up of all time: Simon 'Our Tune' Bates, Gary 'Willy on the Plonker' Davies and Steve 'In the Afternoon' Wright. With 75 squillion people tuning in each morning, Simon had as much power as Margaret Thatcher and Debbie McGee put together. Fortunately, he only ever saw fit to put it to the fairly benign use of shoehorning a single up the Christmas chart. In 1989 it was the turn of fifties Scottish crooner Andy Stewart, who saw his 'Donald, Where's Yer Troosers?' catapult to number 4. And then, in 1990, 'Kinky Boots' was the office party favourite. Such is the fickleness of both pop and fashion: a record that was forgotten and abused can suddenly become a smash hit twenty-five years on, all thanks to the joys of 'kitsch' and 'irony'.

Listen Here *Chegger's Choice* – Various Artists (Global TV, 1999). Keith Chegwin fronts a double album of '40 Clucking Awful Trax'.

Look On *The Avengers: The Definitive Dossier 1963/1964* (DVD, 2003). The Patrick and Honor era in all their kinky-boots glory.

Listen Further *20 Scottish Favourites* – Andy Stewart (EMI Gold, 2001). Contains 'Donald, Where's

Yer Troosers?', which Simon Mayo shoved up the charts a year earlier.

Mr Hankey The Christmas Poo
Mr Hankey
No. 4 1999

Howdy-ho!

There are hundreds upon hundreds of artists listed in the *Guinness Book of British Hit Singles* but only one that is described as 'US, male Christmas excrement vocalist'. That honour goes to Mr Hankey, the talking turd from everyone's favourite offensive cartoon series, *South Park*. Not that he was the only piece of crap in the top ten that Christmas: this was also the year of Cliff's 'Millennium Prayer', yodelling hamsters (see the Cuban Boys) and Westlife's dreary cover of 'I Have A Dream'.

    The origins of Mr Hankey can be traced back to the father of *South Park* creator Trey Parker. Struggling to get his three-year-old son to flush the toilet, he told him that if he didn't pull the chain, the said turd would come to life, leap out of the toilet and kill him.* It may sound cruel, but not only did it work, it was the only toilet-training tactic to spawn a hit single.

* The power a parent has over their young child cannot be over-estimated. I myself was told by my father at a similar age that Rolf Harris had been deported from Australia because nobody liked him. It was many years before I discovered it was a lie.

In the *South Park* episode 'Mr Hankey the Christmas Poo', it is Kyle who doesn't flush. But his Mr Hankey is a rather more benign form of excrement: rather than attacking non-flushers, he comes out of the toilet to give presents to everyone who has a lot of fibre in their diet. Unfortunately for Kyle, he is the only one who believes in Mr Hankey, and whereas he sees a happy little turd, complete with Santa hat and high-pitched 'Howdy-ho!' greeting, everyone else just sees him talking to a lump of shit. He is committed to a mental institution, until Chef reveals that he too believes in Mr Hankey. Soon everyone believes in Mr Hankey, Kyle is released, and they sing this happy Christmas song. The end.

The point of Mr Hankey, in that usual *South Park* double-whammy way, is to offer some vague moral message (here, the meaning of Christmas) and gross you out at the same time (here, the suggested popping of Mr Hankey in your mouth). In that other *South Park* double-whammy way, it is both puerile and clever-clever – how many other hits can you name with the word 'vicariously' in the chorus? But the thing is, despite the fact that he is made of shit and leaves a trail wherever he bounces, normally sane people like Mr Hankey. People like my girlfriend, for example, who creases up in laughter when we watch that episode. Or those who have bought that popular piece of merchandise, the Mr Hankey soft toy.

Ultimately, though, as shocking as *South Park* would like to think they are with Mr Hankey, their singing poo is more part of a tradition than a first in musical history: the Rolling Stones' finest album, *Exile on Main Street.*, features the blues blast of 'Turd On The Run'; the Prodigy's *Fat of the Land*, meanwhile, focuses on the more musical sort of stool with 'Funky

Shit'; and Elvis, of course, the King himself, died on the throne.

Listen Here *Mr Hankey's Christmas Classics* (Columbia, 2002). Is there a name for a collection of turds?

Listen On Mr Hankey and Kenny's 'The Most Offensive Song Ever'. They're a little bit rude about the birth of Christ.

Listen Further *Classics in the Key of G* – Kenny G (Arista, 1999). There's crap. And there's really crap.

Cognoscenti Vs Intelligentsia
The Cuban Boys
No. 4 1999

FW: FW: FW: Re: FW: You've got to see this!!! It is SO funnnyy!!!
This is a story that starts with a hamster. His name is Hampton the Hampster (*sic*), and he is the pride and joy of a Canadian art student called Deirdre LaCarte. In August 1998 Deirdre started a website, www.hamsterdance.com, dedicated to her furry friend. To a speeded-up sample of Roger Miller's 'Whistle Stop', taken from the soundtrack to Walt Disney's *Robin Hood*, an animated Hampton and rodent friends grooved away. For seven months nothing happened. The website languished in Internet

obscurity. The counter stood at a paltry 800 hits. Hampton, to quote the Generation X song, was dancing with himself. Though not in the way that Billy Idol was singing about. That would have been rude.

And then that mystical modern media phenomenon, the 'tipping point', was reached. For whatever reason, the website took off: in the next four days the hits on the site jumped from 800 to 60,000. By June 1999 the number totalled 17,000,000. In every office around the world someone was forwarding the site details to everyone they knew. Like Claire Swires and Mahir and his 'I Kiss You!!!' catchphrase, Hampton was fast becoming an Internet icon, attracting squeals of delight and groans of despair in equal measure.

Like the Tweets and 'The Birdie Song' almost two decades earlier, it was only a matter of time before someone saw the potential of a cash-in single. That honour fell to the Cuban Boys, a band who weren't actually Cuban – they're from Preston and Eastbourne – and aren't even all boys – there's Jenny as well as Skreen, BL and Ricardo. The band met, appropriately, on the Internet and were soon sending each other tracks and material by email. Sent the site like the rest of the world, the band had the bright idea of looping the Hampsterdance tune, sticking on a disco beat and adding a few voice samples. And then, as they always did, they stuck it on a CD and sent it to John Peel in the vain hope that he might play it.

Except this time, on 7 April 1999, John Peel *did* play it. In prophetic fashion, he suggested it had the potential to become the most irritating hit of the year. That didn't stop the normally well-adjusted Peel fans emailing by the bucketload for the song to be played again. It became the most requested song the show had had since the Sex Pistols' 'God Save The

Queen'. Having spent years in the indie wilderness, the Cuban Boys suddenly found themselves being courted by all the major record labels as well as, er, Jonathan King, who drove the band round London in his Rolls Royce. They signed to EMI.

'Cognoscenti Vs Intelligentsia' was a title the band chose as a joke to see if they could get away with it. They could. EMI, disappointed not to have the word 'hamster' in the title, suggested the band dress up as hamsters and appear on the Capital Radio roadshow. They wouldn't. After much haggling, the band agreed to a picture of a hamster on the single sleeve. But even then, the single's novelty Christmas status was not assured. Originally slated for release in September, it was put back over wrangles about samples. Rescheduled for November, the single was about to be pushed back to January when a pincer movement of Jo Whiley and Dr Fox finally convinced the record company to go for the Christmas number 1. It didn't quite make it – peaking at number 4 – but the band shifted 200,000 copies and got the number 1 they really wanted: in John Peel's Festive Fifty.

> A pincer movement of Jo Whiley and Dr Fox convinced the record company to go for the Christmas number one.

Back in Hampsterland, the Cuban Boys' brilliant wheeze was swiftly imitated – Hampton the Hampster's Hampsterdance Song cleaned up internationally. Albums, cuddly toys, cartoon series, all were in abundance in a concerted attempt to cash in on the Hampton phenomenon. It is not known whether Hampton himself has ever seen any of this money.

Listen Here *Dance Box* – Various Artists (EMI International, 2002). There's Fragma and Kevin and Perry thrown in for good measure.

Listen On *Eastwood* – the Cuban Boys (EMI, 2001). The album includes a cover of the Offspring's 'Self Esteem'.

Listen Further *Hampster Dance Party* – Hampton the Hampster (BMG, 2002). 'Hampton' gets in on the act. Includes the heartbreaking 'Even Hampsters Fall In Love'.

Mad World Michael Andrews featuring Gary Jules
No. 1 2003

Very, very

The race for Christmas number 1 in 2003 was meant to be over before it began. The second season of *Pop Idol* was in full flow, Simon Cowell was being rude to all and sundry, and the single recorded by all twelve finalists was in the bag. With the call-trading-standards name of the Idols, the desperate dozen groped their way through 'Happy Xmas (War is Over)'. It may not have been the best cover version ever recorded, but it had number 1 written all over it. Avid Merrion, Basil Brush, Noddy, Cliff Richard, they didn't stand a chance. The only serious contenders were the Darkness, topping off a top year with a Yuletide single, 'Christmas Time (Don't Let The Bells End)'. And then there was Gary.

Just occasionally, the charts don't go the way the corporations want and something wonderful can work its way into the public consciousness. That is exactly what happened with Gary Jules and his cover of Tears for Fears' 1983 single 'Mad World'. The song was originally featured on the soundtrack to *Donnie Darko*, a rather fabulous if slightly incomprehensible film about a teenage boy, giant rabbits, plane crashes and time travelling. The film was out a year earlier to rave reviews without exactly setting the world alight. So much so, that the film's rather good soundtrack didn't get a release, which meant that this song wasn't initially available.

I keep on talking about Gary and certainly he's got a great voice in a Michael Stipe sort of way, but the real genius of the piece is probably Michael Andrews: Gary's childhood friend, the man responsible for the *Donnie Darko* soundtrack, the person who saw that Tears for Fears' angsty, early-eighties pop song could be pared down into something rather beautiful. With the faintest of piano chords and Gary's haunting vocals, Tears for Fears suddenly became acclaimed as songwriters of great poignancy and depth. Who'd have thought it?

Why 'Mad World' pipped the Darkness to the post, despite a huge promotional push for the latter, is that it fitted the Christmas vibe that little bit better. There may

> Tears for Fears suddenly became acclaimed as songwriters of great poignancy and depth.

be no Yuletide references, the nearest nod being the mobile in the video that looks a little like baubles, but like Greg Lake and Jona Lewie years earlier, there is a satisfying weight to the song: not heavy, but just having enough gravitas to remind us that Christmas is not just a commercial exercise. The position of 'Mad World' on future Christmas compilations for years to come is assured. And the Pop Idols? Who cares?

Listen Here *Trading Snakeoil for Wolftickets* (Sanctuary, 2004). Nice enough, but at the time of writing, no second single has been forthcoming.

Listen On *Tears Roll Down* – Tears for Fears (Mercury, 1992). All the best bits of the boys from Bath.

Watch Further *Donnie Darko* (DVD, 2003). If anyone can explain exactly what happens, please do get in touch.

Five further sporting one hit wonders

'Chalk Dust (The Umpire Strikes Back)'
The Brat

'Slam Jam'
WWF Superstars

'N-n-nineteen Not Out'
Commentators

'Sven Sven Sven'
Bell and Spurling

'Nice One Cyril'
Cockerel Chorus

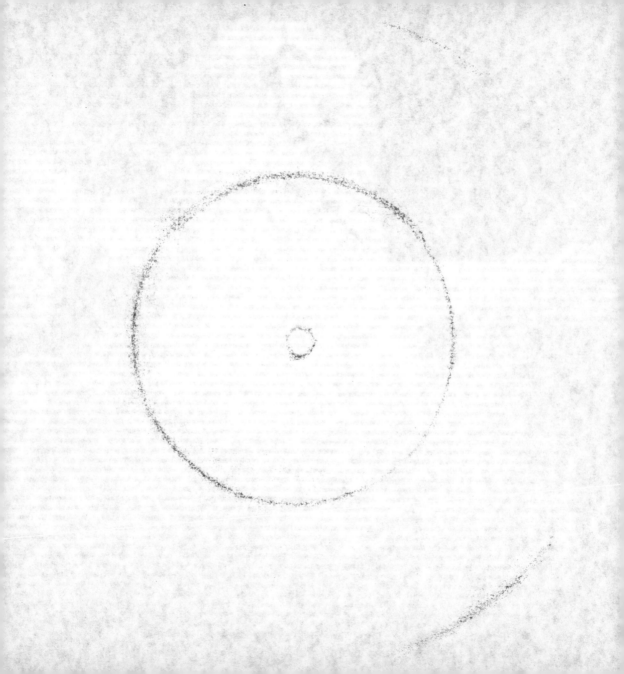

3 I Hate That Duck
– Puppet and Cartoon Hits

If you ever thought that pop stars were little more than puppets of the record industry, this chapter is the 'living' proof. An oddball – furball? – collection of puppets, Muppets, cartoon characters and people in silly costumes, these are, in Ed Stewart parlance, children's favourites, and in everyone else's parlance, a tad annoying.

Here's the thing about children and musical taste: they don't have any. Here's another thing about children: they don't get irony. Here's a third thing about children: they like things repeated again and again. Put the three together and you have a recipe to irritate the rest of the nation. Fortunately, though, here's a fourth thing about children: they get bored very quickly. And so these creations never hang around for long.

The rest of us are not totally free from blame either. Be it Flat Eric or ITV Digital's Monkey or Phillip Schofield's Gordon the Gopher, we maintain a soft spot for small, cute, furry things, the more cheap and cheerfully put together the better. It hasn't happened yet, but the day someone makes a glove puppet out of a sock and it gets into the chart can only be months away . . .

Sugar, Sugar
The Archies
No. 1 1969

The sweet smell of success

I'm not saying that Britain was a depressing place to live at the end of the sixties, but in the final weeks of the decade two songs hogged the number 1 spot that made you wonder if the Beatles and the Stones and Bob Dylan and everything else ever actually happened. Seeing in the seventies was Rolf Harris and his just awful 'Two Little Boys'. If Rolf thought he could see us crying, chances are he was probably right. In despair. And for eight weeks previously – that's two whole late-sixties months – the biggest-selling single wasn't by a band at all, but a bunch of cartoon characters: the Archies.

The Archies was a children's cartoon show put together by Don Kirshner, the man responsible for the Monkees. By the late 1960s his original cute foursome were getting a bit bored with saying things like 'Hey! Hey!' and were featuring in strange psychedelic films like *Head* instead. There were going to be no such problems with a load of cartoon characters. Originally a comic book written by Bob Montana in the 1940s, *The Archies* followed the adventures of a group of school kids at Riverdale High. There was lead character Archie Andrews, Jughead Jones, his perpetual sidekick, the rich and slightly full of herself Veronica Lake, down-to-earth Betty Cooper and shaggy hound

Hotdog. Together with Reggie Mantle on drums, they had a band that soon followed the Monkees into the charts proper.

After a couple of minor hit singles in the States, 'Sugar Sugar' was a smash hit everywhere. Depending on who you listen to, it shifted between five and ten million copies worldwide, including 900,000 in the UK. Not so much light as lite, the song's music is about as saccharine as its lyrics, with a hefty lump of sugar puns in there for good measure – and some future song titles for both New Edition ('Candy Girl') and, er, Def Leppard ('Pour Some Sugar On Me'). What can I say? Bubblegum, banal and inoffensive, it was cute to the point of making your teeth hurt.

What happened to the Archies was that the singer providing the lead vocals, a man called Ron Dante, got incredibly worried about being typecast and refused to take part in either a live Archies Revue show or further recordings. In fact his own band, the Cuff Links, enjoyed a couple of top-ten hits of their own at the same time. When his solo career stalled, he did return to sing some more Archies songs, but by then the 'band' (if not the TV show) were on the slide. Ron went on to produce Barry Manilow, while the cartoon shows drew to a close in 1977.

> The song's music is about as saccharine as its lyrics, with a hefty lump of sugar puns in there for good measure.

Listen Here *Absolutely the Best of the Archies* (Varese, 2001). Sixteen classic cartoon cuts.

Listen On   *The Very Best of the Archies* (Cleopatra, 1999). Fewer tracks than the *Absolutely* collection but has a couple of nineties remixes of 'Sugar, Sugar' thrown in.

Listen Further   *The Definitive Monkees* – the Monkees (Warner, 2001). Don Kirshner's original – and best – TV band.

Halfway Down The Stairs The Muppets
No. 7 1977

It isn't at the bottom. Yet, neither, indeed, is it at the top

In the silver jubilee summer of 1977, all the chart talk was centred on the Sex Pistols and whether their 'God Save The Queen' single was being artificially kept off the top spot by a mixture of a conservative record industry and Rod Stewart's 'I Don't Want To Talk About It'. Meanwhile, further down the top ten, slipped in this almost unnoticed one hit wonder, by a small green frog who made a virtual living out of being ignored.

In the Muppet Hall of Fame, Robin is not quite at the bottom, yet nor is he at the top – not like, say, Fozzy Bear or Miss Piggy or his uncle, Kermit the Frog. Indeed, in the first two series of *The Muppet Show* Kermit went out of his way to prove that the show wasn't nepotistic: Robin appears just twice – once, failing to get anyone's attention and only stopped from leaving by guest star Bernadette Peters; the other, singing this song.

'Halfway Down The Stairs' was originally written by A. A. Milne in his 1924 book of children's verse, *When We Were Very Young*. It's a poem about sitting halfway down the stairs. Well, obviously, but beyond that, it's quietly ambiguous: one might argue that it's about being normal, about having a place not at the top or bottom of life's pile, but perfectly happy in the middle. Or one could argue it is about having a place to think – a stair of one's own? – and the importance of contemplation. The Muppet version (Robin's voice supplied by Jerry Nelson) is sweet without being saccharine, and unlike that later ball of greenness, Orville, Robin's shyness is 'dry' rather than 'wet' and so maintains our affection.

A quick word about frogs and popular music. 'Halfway Down The Stairs' isn't at the bottom of amphibious music: that honour surely goes to Paul McCartney and his Frog Chorus, with their can-frogs-actually-do-this single, 'We All Stand Together'. But neither is it at the top: for my money that goes to the Doors and their rather fantastic 'Peace Frog'. Instead, Robin's musical nest is on a lily pad somewhere in the middle, next lily perhaps, to the band with the worst name ever in the history of music: Toad the Wet Sprockett. No, I can't imagine why they didn't make it big in the UK either.

Backed by a cover of another one hit wonder on the B-side (the Muppet version of 'Mah Na Mah Na'),

> Unlike that later ball of greenness, Orville, Robin's shyness is 'dry' rather than 'wet'.

Robin reached number 7 as the British public clapped and cheered the Queen/stuck safety pins through their noses (delete as appropriate). But the fact that Robin was the only Muppet to achieve chart success did not go to his head: there was no 'I don't do stairs' behaviour from him. Instead, *The Muppet Show* remained very much his uncle's domain, though Robin did get a starring role in the Muppet film *The Frog Prince*.

Listen Here   *The Muppet Show* (Arista, 1977). The album won a Grammy for 'Best Recording for Children'.

Listen On   *Kermit Unpigged* (BMG, 1994). Kermit and Robin team up on 'Can't Get Along Without You'.

Look Further   *The Frog Prince* (VHS). Robin's full-length film role, currently available only on video.

Orville's Song Keith Harris and Orville

No. 4 1982

I hate that duck

Why is it that some children's television programmes are looked back on fondly and others with a grimace and a groan? If I said *Button Moon*, you'd go, 'aah'. Mr Spoon! The spaceship made out of a baked beans can and a funnel! If I say *Bagpuss*, you'd go Professer

Yaffle! The marvellous mechanical mouse organ! The episode with the chocolate-biscuit-making factory! If I said *The Clangers*, you'd start making whistling noises, go all goosepimply as you thought about soup dragons. But if I mentioned Keith Harris and Orville …

Now, I don't know what it's like where you come from, but apart from the time that mallard ate the stale crust I threw into the pond, I have never, *ever*, seen a duck that was green. And certainly not one that wears nappies. Not that it stopped Keith Harris from becoming the most famous man since Peter Davison in *All Creatures Great and Small* for having his hand up a creature's arse. It was the culmination of a career that had started early in childhood: Keith used to earn his pocket money by pretending to be a ventriloquist's dummy on his dad's knee. Armed (literally) with Orville and permanently sniffing monkey Cuddles, Keith starred in BBC1's cleverly titled *The Keith Harris Show* for most of the eighties. He even got a call from the royals, entertaining Prince William at his third birthday party.

But his entry in the rock and roll hall of shame was achieved with this 1982 single. It was written by Bobby Crush, who was sharing a summer-season billing with Keith at the Scarborough Opera House. Even Bobby admitted, 'it was a bit stomach churning to be honest but it was the best four days' work I ever did'.* The gist of 'Orville's Song' can be summed up thus: Orville wishes he was able to fly. Keith says he can. Orville says he can't. Keith says he can again.

> To be fair to Orville, he does have a point: he can't fly.

* *Q* magazine, February 1995.

Orville says, no, he really can't. And that's about it. I think it grates not because Orville is so wet, though that doesn't help, but more that he is so defeatist about the situation. As a nation, we British don't like whingers: heroic failures yes, moping ducks no. Though to be fair to Orville, and I never thought I'd say that, he does have a point: he can't fly. And maybe Keith should give it to him straight, sit him down and tell the duck the truth. Or maybe he can't because the truth is more sinister. Orville *can* fly, it's just that he is being held down by Keith Harris clinging on tightly to what remains of his career.

In 2002 Louis Theroux did one of his *When Louis Met . . .* shows with Keith and Orville. And though Louis did his best to do his normal stitch-up routine, on this occasion he failed. Sure, Keith had a car with the number plate ORV 1L. Sure, he wasn't on the telly any more. But rather than being bitter and twisted or a prima donna or anything like that, Keith came across as what he was: the last of a generation of good, old-fashioned northern entertainers, whose end-of-the-pier show had been washed away by 24-hour cartoon channels and PlayStations and the like. But you know what? He was still doing ok. There is a roaring trade in panto. And Orville may be in incontinence pants rather than nappies these days, but there are plenty of student unions to perform at, with Keith's children's-telly-plus-a-bit-of-swearing show, the aptly named *Duck Off*.

Listen Here *Chegger's Choice* – Various Artists (Global TV, 1999). It's the opening song on CD 2.

Listen On 'Come To My Party' – Keith Harris and Orville with Dippy (BBC, 1983). Basically, we didn't.

Listen Further *The Best of Bobby Crush* (Spectrum, 2001). 'Orville's Song' strangely not included.

Rat Rapping Roland Rat Superstar
No. 14 1983

The yeaaaaaaaaah of the rat

In early-eighties Britain getting up was very simple. Half the country didn't, because Margaret Thatcher had put them out of work, and the rest tuned in to Mike Read on Radio One. Then in 1983 came what can only be defined as a cultural watershed for the nation: breakfast television was invented. While the BBC show saw Frank Bough cracking the whip and Selina Scott getting the nation up in a different way, the TV-am sofa sagged under the heavyweight presentership of Anna Ford, Angela Rippon, David Frost and the like. So enter up-and-coming programme maker Greg Dyke. Enter children's programmes whiz Anne 'Teletubbies' Wood. And enter the rat that saved the sinking ship.

Roland Rat was a rodent puppet with not so much the gift of the gab as the gift of the gob: brash, loudmouthed and full of it, he was a sort of furry,

> A sort of furry, flea-ridden Fonz, or at least he thought he was.

flea-ridden Fonz, or at least he thought he was, who alternated between his two hilarious catchphrases: 'Yeaaaaaaaaaaah' and 'Ratfans!' The Comedy Dave to his Chris Moyles was Kevin the Gerbil, a sycophantic blob of orange, apparently from Leeds. Also part of the show were Errol the Hamster, whose sole job was to 'run VT', Little Reggie, Roland's annoying little brother, and Glenis the Guinea Pig, Roland's bit of (quite literally) fluff. Let's leave aside the question of whether rats can mate with guinea pigs for another time.

Like Jesus Christ before him and Har Mar afterwards, Roland Rat awarded himself the dubious second surname of 'Superstar'. I say dubious because his only entry into the top twenty was this 1983 single. 'Rat Rapping' revolves around one particularly hilarious pun (you may want to grab hold of something before I tell you what it is): Roland and Kevin 'scratch', but not records like real rap acts: they scratch because they've got fleas. Roland 'raps' a bit too, one part John Barnes to two parts Victoria Aitken, all about his superstar status. There's a penthouse suite, a swimming pool and lots of 'pretty young guinea pigs' knocking around. Really, let's not dwell on the rat–guinea pig thing.

Roland Rat may have saved breakfast television, but nobody came to save his record career. Subsequent singles 'Love Me Tender' and 'No. 1 Rat Fan' flopped, along with Kevin the Gerbil's cover of 'Summer Holiday'. Even a second album recorded with Stock, Aitken and Waterman (strangely true) failed to do the business. Roland steadfastly refused to change his name to Roland Rat Has-Been, and stuck to the small screen. He moved to the BBC for his own children's TV series and later to Los Angeles for the Channel 5 show

LA Rat. Not that his career was on the skids or anything, but he even appeared in panto with Gary Wilmot.

Still, let's not be too cruel on Roland. Without his early morning rescue act, breakfast television might never have taken off. Just think of all those things we have Roland to be thankful for: Timmy Mallett; Anne Diamond and Nick Owen; Mike Morris's moustache; Paula Yates's bed; Ulrika-ka the weathergirl; Kelly Brook, the worst presenter on television . . . until, of course, Kate Lawlor joined *RI:SE*.

Suddenly, Chris Moyles doing the Radio One breakfast show doesn't seem so bad . . .

Listen Here 'Rat Rapping' (Rodent, 1983). The single has the lovingly crafted catalogue number, RAT 1.

Listen On 'Summer Holiday' – Kevin the Gerbil (Magnet, 1984). Roland's right-hand rodent does Cliff to minimal chart success.

Look Further *Rat on the Road* – twentieth-anniversary DVD of some of Roland's best bits.

Mr Blobby
Mr Blobby
No. 1 1993

Blobby! Blobby blobby, er, blobby!!

Here's the thing about Mr Blobby. You hate him. Your instinctive reaction is to think, 'Oh God, *I* remember him, how *awful*, wasn't he just like *the worst*?' And you wouldn't be alone in that: a 2002 poll conducted by HMV saw his eponymous single voted the worst Christmas number 1 of all time. But here's the other thing. You were a little bit tickled by the memory too. You saw the word 'Blobby!' at the top of this entry and you smiled as you imagined him saying it. You may even, without any prompting from me, have said the word 'Blobby!' out loud in a Mr Blobby style. And you wouldn't be alone in trying to keep that guilty smirk off your face either. I think I need to get out more.

'I watch *Noel's House Party*,' Alan Partridge said in the last of his radio shows, 'and I think thank *God* for the BBC.' In the early 1990s the home of Saturday-night entertainment was Crinkley Bottom, where each week Noel Edmonds would invite the viewing public into his 'house' for a series of wacky games and sketches. It was cosy and almost offensively inoffensive TV – perhaps necessarily so after the tragic end of *The Late Late Breakfast Show* – but it was also, it has to be said, extremely good for what it was and hugely popular. There was a slot called NTV in which Noel hid a camera in some unsuspecting viewer's sitting room.

There was another called Wait Till I Get You Home in which cute little kids were prodded to say rude things about their parents in return for prizes. But the biggest pull in the show was Noel's Gotchas in which celebrities were strung along to do silly things, before ta-da! Noel would appear and show them how they had been cunningly fooled.

I say all this, because it is in this context that Mr Blobby was created: as a parody of a children's television character. It's worth repeating that word. Parody. Like the inbred love child of Bungle and Zippy, Mr Blobby, with his glazed eyes, rictus grin, yellow spots and Christopher Biggins bow tie, would crash around in a lovable way, hugging people and breaking things and shouting 'Blobby!' Originally created by Michael Leggo, the show's producer, on the back of a napkin, the character came about for budgetary reasons: a cheap way of getting many celebrities 'gotchaed' in a short space of time. Mr Blobby and Blobbyland were created: Will Carling, Valerie Singleton, Wayne Sleep and Gary Davies were among those invited on to the fake children's TV programme. At the last moment, Noel would slip into the costume and 'gotcha' the sleb. 'Appallingly constructed' is how he remembers the costume: it was 'near as dammit airtight' which made breathing difficult; Noel's eyes were at Blobby's mouth level, which made it difficult to see; and an internal mechanism to make the head spring off was somewhat temperamental – it dug into the back of Noel's neck, and where he thought he'd been sweating, in fact he'd been bleeding.

But like some sort of light entertainment

> The inbred love child of Bungle and Zippy.

Frankenstein, Noel and the *House Party* team had created a monster he was ultimately unable to control. Mr Blobby was huge. Children, who don't get irony or the concept of parody, thought Mr Blobby was for real. The BBC was inundated with letters and drawings and models of their new favourite character. They loved his mixture of enthusiasm and destruction. Mr Blobby quickly graduated from the 'gotcha' slot to the show proper. Then came his own TV show, regular slots on *Live and Kicking*, a Blobbyland theme park, an appearance on *Larry King Live* ('don't go for the toupee or glasses,' a PA foolishly warned beforehand) and, of course, this number 1 single. 'Mr Blobby' (the song) built on Mr Blobby (the blob)'s signature tune, the 'Farty Song', so called because of its use of sampled blown raspberries. Its writers, Paul Shaw and David Rodgers, remain proud of their achievement: 'There are certain novelty songs I might not have been proud of, naming no names, but I think Mr Blobby was pretty musical'.* The song shifted by the bucketload – 650,000 copies in total – and not even the then unstoppable Take That could keep him from the top.

It is worth pointing out that for all the talk of Britain being a sophisticated culture, so much more ironic and knowing than our European and American cousins, Mr Blobby suggests otherwise. Like Loadsamoney before him and Ali G afterwards, Mr Blobby started as parody and, before he knew it, was sucked into the culture as the real thing. It is therefore, I think, a bit harsh to complain that Mr Blobby was awful because, in essence, that was exactly what he was meant to be. Sometimes, it seems, we are not quite as clever as we would like to think.

* *Q* magazine, February 1995.

Listen Here *Mr Blobby – The Album* (Destiny, 1994). Also contains 'Old MacBlobby Had A Farm' and 'Blobbylocks And The Three Bears'.

Listen On 'Christmas in Blobbyland' (Destiny, 1995). Flop second single proves we prefer our Christmases white to pink with yellow spots.

Look Further *Noel's Gotchas* (BBC Video, 1993). A collection of the pranks from where it all began . . .

Teletubbies Say Eh-Oh!
Teletubbies
No. 1 1997

Not again, not again
In 1997 the BBC launched a new children's television show that delighted and infuriated in equal measure. The Teletubbies, with their bright primary colours, nonsensical language, strange names, endless repetition and surreal setting, were the perfect entertainment for those with short attention spans and high boredom thresholds. And as well as the clubbers coming down after a full night's funking, it went down a treat with the nation's children too.

Created by Anne Wood, whose previous credits included Roland Rat, the Teletubbies consist of Tinky Winky (vocals), Dipsy (guitar), Laa Laa (bass) and Po (drums), four brightly coloured blobs with a television in their stomachs. One can only assume their parents had one too many TV dinners. The Teletubbies live in

Teletubbyland, in some sort of Pre-Millennium Dome, which gets about as many visitors, where they live on a not especially healthy – some would say student – diet of toast, with an occasional helping of whatever-there-is-left-in-the-fridge, in their case, custard. Also like the studentworld life, *Teletubbies* is meant to have an educational element, but all Tinky Winky and co. appear to do is arse about and watch telly. I don't know where Teletubbyland is, but the reception on their TV screens is dreadful: much to their chagrin, no doubt, they can't even pick up *Countdown* or *This Morning*.

What I think really irritates people about the Teletubbies, which is most people over the age of two, is that the show makes no effort whatsoever to accommodate them. There is no knowingness or clever references or *Toy Story* winks or *Magic Roundabout* rumours. There was some fatuous story that did the rounds about how Tinky Winky was gay because he had a triangle on his head and had a handbag, but really, it wasn't exactly of *Captain Pugwash* proportions. Children eighteen months old don't get clever references. They like doing things more than once, which is why, much to the frustration of any adult watching, the 'tubbies have a tendency to say things like 'Again, again!' and then a whole chunk of the show is repeated once more.

All this inanity and repetition, of course, made them perfect candidates to make a pop record. 'Teletubbies Say Eh-Oh!' sits in that rich seam of pop songs that answers the Who's 1978 hit 'Who Are You': the Monkees hey-heying about being the Monkees, Adam Ant Ant-rapping about being an, um, ant; Prince's 'My Name Is Prince' (which was ironic, because he wasn't for much longer); and Eminem's 'My Name Is' (clearly learning from Prince's mistake by not actually putting his name in the title). In the Teletubbies' song each Teletubby is prompted to introduce themself, then they all shout 'Teletubbies' followed by 'Eh-oh!', which is Teletubby-speak for 'Hello'. This is then repeated 'again, again!' until the tape is ejected from the car stereo and thrown out of the window by parents desperate to hold on to their sanity.

'Teletubbies Say Eh-Oh!' was written by Andrew McCrorie-Shand, who in the 1970s had enjoyed a middling musical career as a keyboardist for prog rock bands such as Druid and Curved Air (alongside subsequent Police stalwart Stewart Copeland). His switch from progressive to regressive was clearly lucrative as the single shifted 1.2 million copies and was nominated for an Ivor Novello award. Without wanting to diss the record, one reason for the large volume of sales may have been the Teletubbies' position as the 1997 must-have Christmas toy that no one could get hold of. With no Tinky Winky doll to keep little Johnny quiet, for many people the single may have been the next best thing. The Teletubbies spent two weeks at number 1 before having the Christmas number 1 snaffled from under their noses by the Spice Girls.

The Teletubbies made one further, if bizarre, entry into the world of rock and roll. In 2001 they helped answer the question of whatever happened to Steve Strange, when the former lead singer of eighties duo Visage was caught stealing a Teletubby from a Woolworths in South Wales. Suggestions that the

> The Teletubbies helped answer the question of whatever happened to Steve Strange.

arresting police said, 'Eh oh, eh oh, eh oh', have been completely made up by me in order to finish this section with a joke.

Listen Here   *Teletubbies – The Album* (BBC, 1998). Contains four separate dances – the Puddle Dance, the Twisty Dance, the Running Away Dance and the Up and Down Dance. Not that the idea is to exhaust the children and send them to bed or anything.

Listen On   *Bedtime and Playtime Stories* (Rhino, 2000). Includes the floor-filler 'Big Wind And Come Back Everything'.

Listen Further   *Fade to Grey* – Visage (Polydor, 1993). With all the greatest songs on one disc, it's something of a steal.

Chocolate Salty Balls
Chef
No. 1 1998

Ingredients:
1 foul-mouthed cartoon series
1 soul legend (mature)
1 helpful DJ
And a large helping of sauce

This is a delicious chart-topping recipe that can be enjoyed by all the family, or at least the ones who aren't easily offended. It is particularly popular at Christmas time, when it serves as a useful alternative to more Spice-laden offerings.

First, find yourself a screwball cartoon comedy series. I'm using *South Park*, which I'd recommend, particularly the early couple of series if you can get hold of them. Don't worry if the animation appears a little basic: that's part of the charm and adds to its flavour. You should find a certain coarseness to the texture: indeed the coarser the better – 'You bastard!' 'Screw you guys!' 'Bitch bitch bitch . . .' and so on – just enough to take the edge off the programme's underlying sweetness. For this recipe we're going to need to put aside the show's more popular elements – the Kyle, the Stan, the succulent Cartman and the Kenny (which must always be killed to enjoy fully) – in order to focus on one of its minor but equally delicious parts.

Next, add to the cartoon series a character called Jerome McElroy, more commonly known as Chef. Ostensibly there to cook school dinners in the South Park school, what this character really adds to the programme is worldly advice for the children on all matters birds and bees, and hot loving for any female characters who want it. Although this part could theoretically be played by any particular soul legend, in reality only an Isaac Hayes will do. There's something about his sixties time with Stax, his *Hot Buttered Soul* and *Black Moses* albums that appeals. And this is all topped off with his soundtrack to *Shaft*, a song whose stunning introduction, the tickling of the hi-hat, the

> Popular at Christmas time, when it serves as a useful alternative to more Spice-laden offerings.

wobbling of the wah-wah, can be replicated at home to much satisfaction.

Now, bring said Chef to the fore in what is known as the 'Chef's Salty Chocolate Balls' episode. Here a film festival, not dissimilar to Sundance, comes to South Park and threatens to completely take over the town. Chef sets up a stall to make some money, but his assorted cookies – 'Fudge 'Ems', 'Go Fudge Yourself' and so forth – aren't selling well. So he switches to another recipe, his 'Chocolate Salty Balls', for which he sings this accompanying song (serving suggestion: suck them). Meanwhile, the film festival is threatening the town's sewer system, and the livelihood of one Mr Hankey (see 'Mr Hankey The Christmas Poo'). Close to death, Mr Hankey is re-energised by sucking on one of Chef's Chocolate Salty Balls and then drives the film festival out of town.

Now add a DJ into the melting pot. For best results, try the Cartman of Radio One, Chris Moyles. Get him to play the song again and again on his afternoon show, until the record company decides to release it as a single. Get him to play the song some more and add in the support of various wacky breakfast DJs on local radio. Wait until interest in the single is coming to the boil and then release the record into the shops. Timing is everything, particularly if the Spice Girls also have a single out: if you can't get your copies into the shops quick enough, you may not hit number 1 until after Christmas, even if you shift half a million copies. And no matter how delicious the innuendo in the song, this can leave a bitter taste in the mouth.

Listen Here *Chef Aid* (Columbia, 1999). If Chef's Chocolate Salty Balls aren't enough to satisfy you, there's a bit of Meat Loaf too.

Listen On *Hot Buttered Soul* – Isaac Hayes (Stax, 1969). Isaac's breakthrough album, including 'Hyperbolicsyllabicsesquedalymistic'. That's as long as 'Supercalifragilisticexpialidocious' but somewhat funkier.

Read Further *Cooking with Heart and Soul* (Putnam, 2000). Isaac Hayes 'makes music' in the kitchen. The recipe for Chocolate Salty Balls is included.

Flat Beat Mr Oizo
No. 1 1999

You Muppet
Some time in the late 1990s the French techno DJ Laurent Garnier decided he wanted to buy a car. By chance, he went to Quentin Dupieux's father, and though history does not relate what happened on the automobile front, it was the connection that began Dupieux Junior's long drive towards stardom. First Quentin, a fledgling director, made a promo for one of Garnier's singles. Then Garnier, who also runs his own record label, released one of Quentin's singles. The accompanying video, directed by Quentin, featured his best friend Philippe Petit, driving around with an orange hand puppet, by the name of Stefan, bobbing along to the music . . .

Meanwhile, back at Levi's Towers, things weren't going so well. The glory days of the Kamen Years were a thing of the past: not only were sales down by 13 per cent but Levi's simply weren't as cool as they used to be. The young hip things were all going to Diesel or wearing combat trousers. The people actually buying Levi's were young fogeys trying that little bit too hard to be cool, iconic figures of British counterculture such as the prime minister. In an attempt to be hip again, Levi's started making their adverts a little bit weirder and without giving Jas Mann a bell. There was one with a child trying to bang a square peg into a round hole. Another with a hamster that went round and round on its wheel until the wheel broke and it died from having nothing to do. And then someone at the ad agency saw Quentin's film.

The reason for mentioning all this is that the point of the Flat Eric ads was to continue Levi's crawl back towards credibility. And certainly the music – Quentin's scratchy, minimalist techno – was anything but regulation chart fodder. Rather, it was far more at home on a small, trendy label or as part of the then burgeoning Air Daft Punk Dmitri from Paris French music revolution. The ad itself, meanwhile, echoed Quentin's original film: Philippe ('Angel') was still riding around, going nowhere in particular; his side-kick, Stefan, meanwhile, was replaced by the similar-looking Flat Eric, a puppet made to order from the Muppet-making Jim Henson Studio.

What happened next was that Levi's hip and off-beat ad campaign did not quite go according to plan. Rather than staying small and trendy, Flat Eric became huge. White van drivers would drive around, windows down, doing their best head-nodding Flat Eric impression. Levi's were deluged with calls about where they could buy one. And Quentin Dupieux, under the name Mr Oizo, saw the accompanying single go straight in at number 1. Levi's, after initially resisting the Flat Eric phenomenon, brought him back for a second series of ads, complete with Flat Eric record bag, Flat Eric T-shirt, Flat Eric hat and Flat Eric puppet.

What is interesting looking back is how excited normally sane people got about Flat Eric. Here is the then editor of culture bible *The Face*, which 'interviewed' Flat: 'it's the first time in history that people have tried to be like a puppet. People want a piece of Flat Eric. Women want to have sex with him, men want to be him.' Here is cultural commentator Charlotte Raven: 'Flat Eric is a person trapped inside the body of a gonk . . . in just a few seconds his creators have achieved what few modern dramas have managed: a totally believable character whose life we are only glimpsing.' And here is a not-remotely-up-his-own-bottom writer from the *Guardian* describing how the 'Flatness' of Eric is the very 'antithesis' of the prevalent cultural 'Blobbiness': 'Flatness isn't anything so trite as a back to basics reaction, it's about precision, the epiphany of the essential, and the sparking of embedded, fantastic contexts.' And there was me thinking it was to do with the grubby old business of flogging trousers.

Let's face it. Flat Eric was nothing more than a Muppet, and not even a proper one at that. If Gordon the Gopher had gone on the puppet equivalent of the French exchange, Flat Eric would have been his

> If Gordon the Gofer had gone on a French exchange, Flat Eric would have bee his nonchalant Gallic partner.

nonchalant, knowing Gallic partner. Did he succeed in making Levi's trendy again? Well, at least they're still in business. The next time a puppet ad stole the nation's hearts, his name was Monkey and he was trying to make us tune in to ITV Digital . . .

Listen Here *Analog Worm Attacks* (F Communications, 1999). The album that's more Mr Oizo than Flat Eric.

Listen On 'No. 1' – Mr Oizo (F Communications, 1997). No Levi's ad, no sales.

Puppet Further Go to www.flateric.de and buy yourself your very own Flat Eric.

The Stefan Dennis video reconstruction package

Stefan Dennis's 'Don't It Make You Feel Good' left behind one of the iconic video images of the age. It's the sort of image that once you've seen it you can never quite erase from your brain. If you haven't seen the video, or if you would like to relive it, please follow the reconstruction package I've put together below.

Step One Find yourself a leather jacket and white T-shirt to wear. If you haven't got a leather jacket, something you can turn up the collar on will suffice.

Step Two Next you'll need a mirror to walk towards, preferably full length. Position yourself a few metres away and on your face add a Billy Idol sneer.

Step Three Now strut towards the mirror, 'singing' the song title. Punctuate the word 'feel' with a single 'Do The Loco Motion' thrust (the action to 'good time' from Big Fun's 'Blame It On The Boogie' can also be used). On the word 'good', attempt to sneer and smile at the same time.

Step Four Repeat until sullied.

4 Stick to the Day Job
– Celebrity Hits

To adapt the title of a successful television series, these are celebrities . . . we should get them out of here. They're famous for being actors, soap stars, footballers and reality TV show contestants. Their rise to the heady heights of *Hello!* and *Heat* is nothing to do with their musical abilities and quite frankly, it shows.

This isn't to cast aspersions on their original career, at which they generally excel. And certainly, if the tables were turned and pop stars did their jobs, I'm sure they'd be equally bad. Gazza's version of 'Fog On The Tyne' may bring tears to everyone's eyes, but would Jarvis Cocker be able to dribble his way through the opposition's defence? Of course not, he'd wave his bum at the referee and get himself sent off. Or what about Gareth Gates taking Richard Harris's role as Dumbledore in *Harry Potter*? Exactly. And imagine what a fool Peter Andre would make of himself taking part in *I'm a Celebrity* . . . – oh, he did do that, didn't he?

Fortunately, the thing about celebrities and music is that they aren't in it for the long haul. They want the hit single, the appearance on *Top of the Pops*, and then it's back to their day job. We are left with one ropey single and a salutary lesson in how many doors fame will open. Not always fully, it has to be said: Naomi Campbell's 'Love And Tears' struggled to reach number 40, for example. And though Craig and Sid Owen did better, neither exactly set the chart on fire.

MacArthur Park
Richard Harris
No. 4 1968

Cake? In the rain?

Perhaps one of the most incongruous of all pop careers is that of actor Richard Harris, who sadly died from Hodgkin's disease in 2002. In recent years Harris had become known to a whole new generation thanks to his role as Dumbledore in the *Harry Potter* films: a magical world away from his peculiar past. It was a little odd at the time too – the very emblem of hard-drinking, macho fighting actordom, Richard Harris had achieved international success with films such as *The Guns of Navarone* and *This Sporting Life*. In 1967 came the cinematic adaptation of the musical *Camelot*, in which Harris played King Arthur. Blimey, people thought, this guy can sing.

One such person was Jimmy Webb, renowned songwriter and friend of Harris. Webb is one of those writers whose work has been covered by everyone from Glen Campbell to Linda Ronstadt to Joe Cocker to Art Garfunkel and includes such hits as 'Wichita Lineman' and 'By The Time I Get To Phoenix'. In the late 1960s he wrote a twenty-two-minute cantata, which was designed to take up the whole side of an LP. When the band he was working with, the Fifth Association, turned it down for their concept album *The Magic Garden* Webb took the seven-and-a-half-

minute coda – yes, that's seven and a half minutes – and got Richard Harris to record it instead.

'MacArthur Park' does not do things by halves. Bob Dylan's 'Like A Rolling Stone' may have altered all perceptions about how long a single should be, but when songs like 'MacArthur Park' started coming out, its six and a half minutes started looking the essence of brevity. And then there's the lyrics – perhaps only Duran Duran's line about someone being as 'easy' as (you won't get this if you don't know it) a 'nuclear war' comes close to the chorus of this song. We'll sidestep the bit about MacArthur Park 'melting' – it was the sixties and one or two people, I believe, took acid – and move on to *that* metaphor: some dastardly person has left Richard Harris's cake in the pouring rain. I'm summarising slightly, but the poor chap is gutted: it took an age to bake and he hasn't got the recipe any longer.

> Why would anyone put a cake outside in the first place?

My question is this: why would anyone put a cake outside in the first place? Obviously if you do that, there's a chance that the cake might get wet. That's why cakes are generally kept indoors, normally in a tin to keep them moist. And considering poor old Richard has clearly spent hours putting the thing together, that would seem to be the decent thing to do. Still, full marks for Jimmy Webb getting hellraiser Richard to come over all upset about soggy baking: that's such an achievement, it almost excuses him leaving his metaphor out in the rain and rhyming 'cake' with 'take' and 'bake' in successive lines. Almost, but not quite.

More Richard Harris and Jimmy Webb collaborations ensued: no more hits but successful albums

A Tramp Shining, The Yard Went on Forever and *The Richard Harris Love Album*. Richard seemed forced to sing 'MacArthur Park' on every chat show he went on, until he made the decision to concentrate on his acting. In the late 1970s his heavy drinking threatened to get the better of him, but he made a successful comeback in the 1990s, first with his Academy Award-nominated performance in Jim Sheridan's *The Field* and then with the *Harry Potter* films. 'MacArthur Park', meanwhile, was covered in a slightly shorter form by Donna Summer in 1978. It reached number 1 in the US and number 5 here.

Listen Here *MacArthur Park* (Half Moon, 1997). The songs of Jimmy Webb, as sung by Richard.

Listen On *The Prophet* (Atlantic, 1996). Richard Harris does Kahlil Gibran to music.

Listen Further *The Donna Summer Anthology* (Mercury, 2002). It may be the late 1970s, it may be disco, but the confectionery is as soggy as ever.

If Telly Savalas
No. 1 1975

Lolly pop

If it was New York, 1975, and there was a murder that needed solving, there was really only one detective in town. Sure, what he saved in hairdressing bills he made up for in lollipops, and yes, so he might have to bend the rules if it meant results, but that's how it works on the streets. And you know, so sometimes plain-clothes detective Bobby Crocker or Detective Stavros might help him out, but at the end of the day no one was better than Theo Kojak. And we loved him, baby.

Telly Savalas first played the fictional detective in the 1973 film *The Marcus-Nelson Murders*. It went down so well that a spin-off TV series ensued, though no one could have guessed how big it would become. Savalas's acting career had not been without highlights – an Oscar nomination for *The Birdman of Alcatraz*, a classic slice of Bond villainy in *On Her Majesty's Secret Service* – but with *Kojak*, he suddenly hit the big time. So much so that not only did someone suggest he record an album, but people actually went out and bought it.

The clue really is in the name. Telly. That's exactly where Mr Savalas should have stayed. But with his shirt undone one button too many, the compulsory

> Telly is exactly where Mr Savalas should have stayed.

medallion and not-bald-here chest hair sticking out, the jacket shrugged over the shoulders, Telly went for seduction mode. I don't think it would be unfair to suggest that he couldn't actually sing. Telly obviously agreed, which is why on his 1975 number 1 single he went for speaking the words rather than risk a tune. With an orchestra noodling away in the background in a slightly bored sort of way, Telly tried to do a bit of Barry White, though with his harsher tone, he couldn't quite get the hard-bitten bit out of his voice.

'If' is a curious love song, with Telly running his lady through a number of hypothetical situations in order to show her the depths of his feelings. He starts with a cliché, the one about a picture painting a thousand words. So why can't Telly paint his lady? My guess is, a bit like the singing, that Telly is simply not an artistic sort of guy. Next up is a reference to the ancients, and the question of how a face can launch a thousand ships. Where, Telly asks, does that leave him? And just while you're pondering that one, Telly decides to get all confused over spatio-temporal matters. Imagine a situation, he asks, where someone could be in two places at once. If that was him (you might need a sick bag at this point) he'd be with his lady today *and* tomorrow. Yeah, Tel, but that's two different times, not two different places. My theory is that he started the thought with seductive intentions, but halfway through realised he'd set himself an elephant trap – a scenario where he could be with his lady and someone else at the same time – and tried to get round the problem with the schmaltzy today and tomorrow line. I wonder if she bought it?

Telly's first album, *Telly*, was followed by the not remotely cashing-in *Who Loves Ya Baby*, but with his cover of 'You've Lost That Lovin' Feeling' only reaching number 47, he returned to catching criminals instead. *Kojak* continued until 1978, with sporadic specials and TV movies throughout the 1980s. In 1994 Telly sadly died following a brief battle with cancer.

Listen Here   *Telly* (MCA, 1974). It's not a Telly, it's an album.

Listen On   *Who Loves Ya Baby* (MCA, 1975). Telly does the Righteous Brothers.

Listen Further   *Decksanddrumsandrockandroll* – Propellerheads (Wall of Sound, 1999). The Big Beat boys update Telly's Bond moment covering 'On Her Majesty's Secret Service'.

Anyone Can Fall In Love Anita Dobson
No. 4 1986

Not so permanent after all
Unlike *Neighbours* and *Home and Away*, British soaps have on the whole been less successful when it comes to pop stars, and *EastEnders* has disappointed in particular. Maybe it's the succession of dreary ballads they've trotted out over the years – Nick Berry and 'Every Loser Wins', Martine McCutcheon and her 'perfect' moment – in keeping with the misery of life on the Square, maybe, but not the sort of thing to make you rush down the record store. Other attempts have just been, frankly, poor – but we'll get on to Sid 'Good

Thing Going' Owen in a minute. None, though, in my opinion has grated as much as this contribution from the former landlady to the Queen Vic herself, Anita Dobson.

The idea behind this single is so simple it is sinister. Everybody likes the theme tune to *EastEnders* so why don't we write some words to go along with it? No, Mr Songwriter, why don't we write some *good* words to go along with it? 'Mine's a pack of pork scratchings' fits the tune, but I wouldn't rush out and release it as a single. And just before you get cosy thinking that this is a love-is-for-everyone sort of number, here's the gist of the second line. Falling in love is the easy bit: now you've got to work at it. They might as well have gone the whole hog and got that woman with the stick from *Fame* to start talking about paying in sweat. You think you've got life all sorted now you're in love? Oh boy, are you in for a shock.

One of the reasons that the song might have been so successful was that although it was sung by and credited to actress Anita Dobson, the words actually fitted her *EastEnders* character of Angie Watts, long-suffering wife of Dirty Den. It's been said before, but it's worth saying again: maybe people thought it was Angie who was singing and that buying the single would help her out. What the single does show is that a ten-second introduction to a TV show does not stretch out into a three-and-a-half-minute pop song. Especially when the arrangement screams *Pebble Mill at One*. There's only one good bit in the entire exercise, which arrives one minute fifty-five seconds in: in order to get into the unnecessarily squealy guitar solo, the song shifts up a key via those cliffhanger drums. Duh! Duh! Duh Duh Dududuh!

Anita, of course, fell in love with fellow poodle

perm, Queen guitarist Brian May. Unfortunately, rather than keep their feelings to themselves, they seemed keen to show the world just how much they loved each other. Anita's debut album, *Talking of Love*, featured three Brian songs, and includes 'To Know Him Is To Love Him'. Brian went on to choose this song as one of his Desert Island Discs. And although in 1992 Brian claimed that 'Too Much Love Will Kill You', he is still very much alive, and the couple finally tied the knot in 2000. Angie Watts, meanwhile, died of cirrhosis of the liver in 2002, which I guess rules Anita out of an *EastEnders* return, though Den returned, so you never know.

> Maybe people thought it was Angie who was singing, and buying the single would help her out.

Listen Here   *Chegger's Choice* – Various Artists (Global TV, 1999).

Listen On   *Talking of Love* (Parlophone, 1987). Anita sings, Brian produces.

Listen Further   'Every Loser Wins' – Nick Berry (BBC, 1986). He's only not here because his theme tune for *Heartbeat* got to number 2.

Diamond Lights
Glenn and Chris
No. 12 1987

No one could stop them

Football and pop music are not good bedfellows, it would have to be said. Normally, though, the charts are sensible enough to resist footballers' charms. When Kevin Keegan released 'Head Over Heels In Love' in 1979, it only got to number 31. When the then Manchester United sitter-misser Andy Cole released the call-trading-standards-entitled 'Outstanding' in 1999, it only got as far as number 68. But somehow, in 1987, the Tottenham midfield duo of Chris Waddle and Glenn Hoddle found a way through and scored themselves a hit.

There's one basic problem that runs through the whole 'Diamond Lights' debacle in my opinion, and that is this: the lads took it all far too seriously. Take the name. Glenn and Chris have the opportunity to use one of the great pop partnership names of all time – Hoddle and Waddle – but like Chris with that penalty in the World Cup semi-final, they hoof it over the bar. The only possible reason for opting for Glenn and Chris, which is about as unmemorable as, say, Charles and Eddie, is that the duo didn't want the football thing to get in the way, didn't want the whole celebrity thing hanging over the music. I think they wanted – and if true then you've got to admire their footballs – the tune to be taken seriously.

Big mistake. Because the interesting thing was that as talented and creative as Glenn and Chris may have been on the pitch (and let's be fair – they were bloody great to watch), this brilliance did not transfer on to vinyl. 'Diamond Lights' is not so much a mazy dribble in the Maracana Stadium as it is a nil–nil draw in soggy Darlo. It's a dirge: plodding power pop that is the sort of thing you might expect on a Mr Mister B-side, or if you played an A-Ha single at the wrong speed by mistake.

But if the lads haven't got it musically, maybe they could save the day by becoming fashion icons? Um, not quite. Appearing on *Top of the Pops*, Glenn and Chris were both members of the mullet school of hairdressing. They both had been watching their *Miami Vice* videos because they thought it was cool to roll up the sleeves of their jackets. Actually, we should give a special mention to Glenn's jacket, which was white (this was complemented with a lovely white belt). And finishing off the jackets/jeans look, both Glenn and Chris had a shirt whose buttons were done up right to the top. Nice.

There was apparently a second single, appropriately enough called 'Goodbye', but the Spurs management clearly got wind of it and Glenn was transferred to Monaco before it could be released. Glenn and Chris returned to dazzling people on the pitch instead.

These days, of course, Tottenham would be delighted to get as high as twelfth.

> There's one basic problem that runs throughout the whole debacle: the lads took it all far too seriously.

Listen Here 'Diamond Lights' (Record Shack, 1987). The single with the hold-my-sides catalogue number KICK 1.

Listen On *Diamond Life* – Sade (Epic, 1984). What you got instead if the sales assistant didn't hear you right.

Listen Further 'Fog On The Tyne (Revisited)' – Gazza and Lindisfarne (Best, 1990). Another Spurs footballer. Another terrible record.

Don't It Make You Feel Good Stefan Dennis
No. 16 1989

In a word, Stefan, no

In the late 1980s it seemed as though the transition from *Neighbours* to the pop charts was the simplest thing in the world. There was Kylie, of course. Then Jason Donovan. Even Craig 'bog brush' McLachlan. It got to the point where the show's übersuccess among school kids and students could guarantee music stardom for any actor who felt like having a stab. And then along came Stefan Dennis. Stefan played bad(ish) guy Paul Robinson, whose sharp business acumen led to him running the Daniels Corporation and Lassiter's Hotel. He did dastardly things like getting married to impress Japanese businessman Mr Udugawa and getting involved with a pair of identical twin sisters, Caroline and Chrissie, purely to confuse the viewer (Caroline was the one with the wonky mouth. Or was that Chrissie?). But perhaps the most dastardly thing he did of all was to release this single.

While Kylie and Jason and Craig were bouncing around and doing fluffy-bunny pop rubbish, Stefan decided he wanted to do something a bit more *rock*. Over backing music that on close inspection sounds suspiciously like a car crash (or is it a career hitting the buffers?), Stefan sang about making you feel good. Somehow he managed to get an 'urgh' into 'good' – 'Go-urgh-d' – which seems about right. I think it was meant to be sexy, in a bad-boy sort of way, but having seen him for so long on *Neighbours*, the thought of Paul Robinson offering you a wild night of passion seemed frankly incongruous. It wasn't so much dirty as, well, grimy. If anything, Stefan came across as the dodgy bloke in the nightclub your mate told you to avoid.

> It wasn't so much dirty as, well, grimy.

Stefan Dennis left *Neighbours* in 1993, Paul Robinson heading for a new life in Brazil with Chrissie – or was it Caroline? Since then, his acting career has done somewhat better than his music one: he has starred in numerous stage productions as well as appearing in TV shows such as Sky's *Dream Team* and the Scottish soap *River City*. Interviewed by fans of the latter in 2003, Stefan was asked if he'd ever restart his music career. 'Yes I would,' he replied, 'if the timing was right.' You have been warned.

Listen Here 'Don't It Make You Feel Good' (Sublime, 1989). A slightly optimistic choice of record label, there.

Listen On 'This Love Affair' (Sublime, 1989). The follow-up smash that mysteriously stalled at number 67.

Listen Further 'Mrs Robinson' – Simon and Garfunkel (CBS, 1986). Paul and Art's heartfelt anthem to Caroline. Or is it Chrissie?

Good Thing Going
Sid Owen
No. 14 2000

Going, going, gone

It must be a bit harsh, I suppose, if you want to make it as a singer, but your career as an actor gives you an image problem it is all but impossible to get over. Take Sid Owen. For twelve years between 1988 and 2000, give or take the odd month off to deal with his £200-a-day cocaine habit, Sid played the character of Ricky Butcher, Frank's son, Bianca's husband, car mechanic and all-round general spanner. Daft, I think, is a polite way to describe the character; 'Thickie' Ricky is the less polite tabloid phrase. And when everyone knows you as a plonker, it's a bit difficult to persuade them that suddenly you possess all the sex appeal and rock-god status that goes with the pop music territory.

'Good Thing Going' wasn't in fact Sid's first crack at the charts. That happened in 1995, when Sid and Patsy 'Rick-kaaaaaaaaaaay' Palmer cashed in on their on-screen relationship for Children in Need. I hope the children weren't that needy in 1995, because 'Better Believe It' only got as high as number 60. Sid clearly had the bug, though, and when he left *EastEnders* (for the first time) he felt it was time for another go. Buoyed by singing 'Let It Be' on TV show *Stars Sing the Beatles*, cheered by karaokeing his way through Channel 5's *Night Fever*, he made what can only be described as a brave choice for his solo single.

Reggae.

I'll be honest with you at this point. Reggae is not my favourite type of music. UB40, with the notable exception of 'Rat In Mi Kitchen', have never done it for me. But even I can hear that Sid makes Ali Campbell sound like Bob Marley. 'Good Thing Going' was originally a Michael Jackson song and covered with great success by reggae ledge Sugar Minott in 1981. His version got to number 4. Sid's version, which ended up ten places lower, didn't so much lilt as list. On the single sleeve Sid went for suave: a white leather jacket, leaning against a wall, looking moodily into the distance. By the time he appeared on *Top of the Pops* he just looked faintly embarrassed.

Sid Owen soon returned to playing Ricky in *EastEnders*. He has since left again. 'Sid is a fine actor in his own right, who deserves to be remembered for more than his Ricky persona,' said a BBC person. This time, though, he is concentrating on his property and restaurant businesses rather than his singing.

Listen Here 'Good Thing Going' (Mushroom, 2000). Like Peter Andre. But worse.

> Even I can hear that Sid makes Ali Campbell sound like Bob Marley.

Listen On 'Better Believe It' – Sid Owen and Patsy Palmer (Trinity, 1995). Well, it was for charity.

Listen Further *Good Thing Going* – Sugar Minott (Bianco, 2001). Belated compilation of Mr Sweet Reggae.

At This Time Of Year
Craig
No. 14 2000

Nasty Nick made him a star. Saint Nick took it away again

In 2000, hard though it is to believe now, reality TV was a new and fledgling concept. No one was actually sure whether or not the first series of *Big Brother* would actually be a success, whether it would last its ambitious ten-week run. People questioned the ethics of the programme, whether or not it was an infringement of the contestants' rights.

And then came Nick Bateman.

Nick Bateman made *Big Brother* for Channel 4 and Endemol and made them a lot of money in the process. He lied. He cheated. He broke the rules. He played *Big Brother* like he wanted to win the cash rather than for some self-discovery life experience. Forgot Saddam. Osama Bin who? For a couple of months 'Nasty' Nick, as the tabloids dubbed him, was the most hated man in Britain. The only place he wasn't loathed was in the *Big Brother* house itself, and

that's because they didn't know what he was up to. And then they found out.

Enter Craig Phillips. Cheeky scouser. Builder. Said 'Errrrr'. That was about it, really. He hadn't really lit the TV screens up in the previous weeks. Oblivion, surely, was his. But as the housemates gathered round the table to confront Nick and his cheating, it was Craig, consciously or otherwise, who seized the chance. Craig, like Darren (gormless, 'tache, chickens), wasn't so bothered about the fact that Nick had been cheating. What really got his goat was less to do with justice and more to do with male pride: Nick had duped him and he didn't like that. While Darren's blank-face response had runner-up written all over it, Craig articulated what the nation thought. Nick, he said, had made him look 'like a cunt'. There were still many weeks to go, but that, I reckon, was the precise moment he won.

When *Big Brother* finished the contestants and the media were in uncharted territory. How far would their fame and celebrity carry them? Was the outer reaches of cable TV their limit or was everything there for the taking? As the offers came flooding in, it was Nichola (The skinhead punk? The lesbian nun? It all slips so quickly, doesn't it?) who should have warned the others. Her debut single, 'The Game', hit the dizzy heights of number 72. The *Sun*, in an editorial, put it thus: 'Please leave our lives immediately. Your fifteen minutes of fame are well and truly up. You are not celebrities, you just happen to be part of a TV freak show which is now over . . . Go home and go back to jobs. We don't care about you anymore.'

> Cheeky scouser. Builder. Said 'Errrrr'. That was about it, really.

WEA Records, however, don't appear to read the *Sun*. A couple of weeks later, they signed Craig on a five-album deal and were telling anyone who would listen that they had a Christmas number 1 on their hands. Here's John Reid, a man whose acumen and insight in the record business had got him to the dizzying heights of managing director: 'I do not make novelty records. And I do not sign people to five-album deals just because they were in a popular TV series. I have signed Craig because he is a very talented singer and people will buy his records because of that. Not because he won *Big Brother*.'*

To be fair, John was right about the second thing: people didn't buy Craig's debut single because he won *Big Brother*. Unfortunately, they didn't buy his single because he was 'a very talented singer' either – because he wasn't. 'At This Time Of Year' had cash-in written all over it: it takes quite a discerning listener to be able to distinguish between the sleigh bells and cash tills ringing in the background. Ironically, a TV builder did get the Christmas number 1 that year: Bob the Builder fixing it – it being Craig's continuing musical career.

Oddly enough, a second single, a solitary album, let alone the full five, failed to materialise. Craig took a leaf out of Bob the Builder's book and started banging nails into things on daytime TV. And DIY, not DI-SCO remains his thing. On a webchat hosted by the *Sun* before the start of *Big Brother 4*, John from Hull asked him whether the pop career would ever be revived. Craig, thankfully, replied thus: 'No chance. You can all safely return to HMV now!'

Listen Here 'At This Time Of Year' (WEA, 2000). In places it almost sounds likes the Bee Gees. I'm being serious here.

Listen On 'The Game' – Nichola Holt (RCA, 2000). The *Big Brother* single that did even worse than Craig's.

Listen Further 'Big Brother UK TV Theme' – Element Four (Channel 4 Music, 2000). If you really need a musical reminder of the show, this is probably the one.

* *BBC News*, 13 November 2000.

Five celebrities who failed to break the twenty

'Floral Dance'
Terry Wogan (No. 21)

'Love And Tears'
Naomi Campbell (No. 40)

'Close Every Door'
Phillip Schofield (No. 27)

'Are You Lookin' At Me?'
Ricky Tomlinson (No. 28)

'Outstanding'
Andy Cole (No. 68)

5 No Words for These
– Gibberish and Instrumental Hits

Words, F. R. David so poignantly sang in 1983, don't come easy. The only way he could get across his feeling to his loved one was through the power of song. Hits didn't come easy for F. R. David either – this number 2 smash proved his only contribution to the charts – but his theory brings us neatly to this next chapter. As Ronan Keating sort of puts it, sometimes the best way of saying things is not to say anything at all.

There are different strands to this chapter. There are those songs indebted to classical music, a popular composer funked up or rocked out to appeal to modern tastes. There are the instrumental virtuosos – the Kenny Gs of this world (though Kenny, sadly, never breached the top twenty and is absent). And then there are those who eschew words for what can only be described as gibberish: strange 'words' that always cause an argument in a game of Scrabble.

The problem for all these people, and why the charts generally remain immune to their charms, is that we like our songs to *mean* something even if it is as banal as not being a girl any longer and yet – strangely – not quite being a woman either. Having nothing to say is fine the once: careerwise, it's not so good. We like to 'connect' with our performers and not many of us speak sax solo.

Nut Rocker B. Bumble and the Stingers

No. 1 1962

Oh, bee hive

The best thing about this song is that it is less than two minutes long. The worst thing about it is the band name: Pun Bad and the Groaners might be more suitable. There was, though, some justification: the band's first single was 'Bumble Boogie', a rock and roll version of Rimsky-Korsakov's 'Flight of the Bumble Bee'. Now I say band – you might have to pay attention here – because as music sometimes was in them days, the record company house band recorded the music, while another group of young things went out on tour and pretended to be the band.

Behind all the shenanigans was Kim Fowley, an up-and-coming pop Svengali, whose long career would go on to take in P. J. Proby, Mothers of Invention, Cat Stevens, Soft Machine and Jonathan Richman and the Modern Lovers. Having put 'Bumble Boogie' together and seen them storm up the American charts, Fowley saw the follow-up, 'Boogie Woogie', falter and the Stingers begin to lose their, well, sting. With the record company losing interest, Fowley approached another label for his next song, a Jerry Lee Lewis-style adaptation of the March of the Wooden Soldiers from Tchaikovsky's *Nutcracker Suite*. Taking the same house band as before, Fowley recorded 'Nut Rocker' under the name Jack B. Nimble and the Quicks. But when

the original record company heard the song, they knew it could be a hit and persuaded Fowley to bring the band back to them and rerecord the song with B. Bumble.

With one small change. When the day of recording came, Ernie Freeman, the pianist who'd played on the original recordings, couldn't make it. So in stepped a young songwriter and musician called Al Hazan, who just happened to be hanging around the studios. Given half an hour to learn the song, Kazan took his moment, or rather his thirty moments, and did the business. So much effort did he put in that he cut his finger on the piano keys, and the ivories were covered in blood by the end of the recording. The Jack B. Nimble record company, as you could imagine, weren't too chuffed and could only watch as the B. Bumble version was put out first and became the bestseller.

> Like any proper buzzy thing, B. Bumble, it transpired, could only sting the once.

The single hit number 1 in Britain, and another 'band' (B. Team and the Stingers?) were sent out to promote the record. Hazan got his own record contract, though perhaps didn't make the most of it by recording an arrangement of 'Chopsticks'. Fowley, meanwhile, looked for more bits of classical music for Bumble to plunder to diminishing effects: the *William Tell* Overture became 'Apple Knocker', Rachmaninov's *Prelude* in C sharp minor became 'Rockin' On 'N' Off'. And then 1963 arrived, and so (thank the Lord) did the Beatles, and classical music boogie became a thing of the past. Like any proper buzzy thing, B. Bumble, it transpired, could only sting the once.

Listen Here *The Best One Hit Wonders in the World . . . Ever!* (Virgin, 2003).

Listen On *Ballet Suites* – Tchaikovsky (Deutsche Grammophon, 1996). The Berlin Philharmonic do the Wooden Soldiers thing ever so slightly differently.

Listen Further *Impossible But True: The Kim Fowley Story* (Ace, 2003). All Kim Fowley's best bits, including Cat Stevens, Gene Vincent and Soft Machine.

Also Sprach Zarathustra Deodato

No. 7 1973

Two thousand and funk

There aren't many great philosophers who can claim a foothold in the annals of rock and roll. Descartes found himself updated by Prince in his groovesome 'I Rock Therefore I Am'. Various Hi-NRG dance acts have performed under the influence of a Karl Popper or two. Which leaves the nineteenth-century German thinker, Friedrich Wilhem Nietzsche, and this early-seventies near-nine-minute funkathon.

Nietzsche's *Also Sprach Zarathustra* concerns this bloke called Zarathustra, who takes himself off to the mountains to think for ten years or so. One morning, he gets up, heads back down the mountain path to explain to the world what he's learned. I'm condens-ing one of the great works of philosophy a little, I'll admit, but the important point is that it tickled the thought buds of classical composer Richard Strauss. His *Also Sprach Zarathustra* (1896) is a half-hour musical poem based on Nietzsche's book, starting with the triumphant and familiar dawn sequence.

Skip forward to 1968 and Strauss's piece is rediscovered all over again, thanks to Stanley Kubrick's cinematic classic *2001: A Space Odyssey*. It wasn't the only piece of classical music used in the film – 'The Blue Danube' is also memorably used – but there was just something about the combination of Kubrick's iconic images and Strauss's brooding brilliant build-up – daah, daaaah, daaaaaaah . . . DA-DAAAH! – that just said space. So etched was the music in the public consciousness that the piece soon became – and remains – shorthand for all things galactic.

Enter Eumir Deodato. Born in Rio de Janeiro, the Brazilian pianist, composer and arranger moved to New York in 1968, where he quickly made a name for himself, working with the likes of Frank Sinatra, Roberta Flack, Aretha Franklin and Wes Montgomery. In 1972 he released his debut album, *Prelude*, from which this single is taken. Strauss wasn't the only classical composer reworked on the album – Debussy and Borodin also got the Deodato treatment – but 'Also Sprach Zarathustra', with its *2001* connotations, was the one that caught the public's imagination. The first time you hear it, you can't quite believe he's doing it. The main theme is so familiar

> What keeps the song on this side of Wensleydale is its rhythm section of Stanley Clarke and Billy Cobham.

that hearing it funked up borders almost on the cheesy. But what keeps the song on the right side of Wensleydale is its rhythm section – Stanley Clarke (bass) and Billy Cobham (drums) drive the groove along, allowing others to noodle away on top.

'Zarathustra' made Deodato: the single shifted five million copies worldwide, won him a Grammy and turned him into a star. And though he's never quite captured those intergalactic heights again, his guiding hands continue to pop up all over the place. First up were Kool and the Gang, with Eumir adding funky production touches to 'Celebration', 'Ladies Night' and 'Get Down On It'. More recently he produced the Björk albums *Post*, *Telegram* and *Homogenic*. And as for 'Zarathustra', its lengthy jam credentials found a home with Phish, the nineties answer to the Grateful Dead, for whom it became a live favourite.

Listen Here   *Prelude* (CTI, 2002). The debut album. Missed a trick by not reissuing it a year earlier.

Listen On   *Deodato 2* (CTI, 2002). This time it's *Rhapsody in Blue* that gets the funky treatment.

Listen Further   *The Best of Kool and the Gang* (Mercury, 1994). You might not want to admit it in public, but let's be honest, 'Celebration' is a great song.

Mah Na Mah Na
Piero Umiliani
No. 8 1977

Muppet porn

Towards the end of the first series of *The Muppet Show* a new puppet appeared with what can only be described as a somewhat limited vocabulary. Attired in green fur, a shock of red hair and sunglasses, said creature may sound like Chris Evans on a particularly boozy night out but in fact was called Mahna Mahna. And accompanied by a pair of Snowths – sort of a cross between a cow and a Clanger – he sang his eponymous song. Mahna Mahna went mahna and then, yes, mahna again. Then he did some sort of improvisation, which is best described as scat kazoo, before mahnaing all over again. And when the Muppets decided young Robin (see Chapter 3) needed a little assistance up the charts, Mahna Mahna did the decent thing and provided his services for the B-side.

In fact, though, 'Mah Na Mah Na' was not originally a Muppet song at all. Enter Piero Umiliani, legendary Italian film composer and cult hero of those who like all things lounge and easy listening. Back in 1968 Piero had written the soundtrack to a Swedish film called *Svezia*

In 1997, a particularly rough-looking girl group called Vanilla adapted the song again.

Inferno E Paradiso (Sweden Heaven and Hell). Now I hope you're not resorting to some sort of lazy nudge-nudge-wink-wink national stereotype and assuming that a Swedish film made in the 1960s was most likely, in some way, a little bit rude. This was a documentary concerning itself with the shifting morality of a nation. Ok, so there may have been a couple of lesbian nightclubs in it. And all right, so maybe there's a bit of wife swapping thrown in too. So it's soft to the core. That's ethics for you.

But whether the film is deemed pornographic or serious documentary, it still begs the question of what the hell 'Mah Na Mah Na' was doing there, as it doesn't really fit in with either. Apparently, the soundtrack was five minutes short, Piero had these three notes that, as he put it, 'worked at the time', and there you go, 'Mah Na Mah Na' was born. Piero didn't even put it on his recording of the soundtrack. But the Americans did, and the song was rediscovered. Which is presumably – let's be charitable here – how Jim Henson heard it.

The Muppets' cover may have made the song famous and may have led to Piero's one and only UK hit, but they were not the only people to get their hands on those three little notes. French crooner Henri Salvador added his own words for his 1969 version, 'Mais Non, Mais Non'. The Gallic theme continues with its use in the advertising for French smiling-face biscuits BN (BN, BN as the advert goes). In 1997 a particularly rough-looking girl group called Vanilla adapted the song again, on their don't-mess-with-me Essex anthem, 'No Way No Way'.

Sadly, Piero passed away in 2001. 'Mah Na Mah Na', however, looks set to linger on for a while yet.

Listen Here   *The Best One Hit Wonders in the World . . . Ever!* (Virgin, 2003). Don't play it. Believe me, you won't get it out of your head for days.

Listen On   *Easy Tempo* – Various Artists (Eighteenth Street Lounge, 1999). The best of Italian film music, Piero included, though not 'Mah Na Mah Na'.

Drink Further   Visit the Mahna Mahna bar in Tokyo. 2-9-26 Taishido, nearest tube Sangenjaya Station, if you're passing.

Toccata Sky
No. 5 1980

Baroque and roll

In the late 1970s the renowned classical guitarist John Williams decided he wanted to set up a band: a little bit rock, a little bit classical, a little bit jazz. The two most damning words that a rock critic has in his armoury, 'progressive' and 'fusion', could also be applied. Anyway, John got in Tristan Fry, timpanist for the Royal Philharmonic Orchestra, Francis Monkman, harpsichordist and founder member of Curved Air (what *is* Curved Air when it's at home?), Australian guitarist Kevin Peek and Herbie Flowers, tuba player, bassist and responsible for 'Grandad' by Clive Dunn. But let's go into that in a later chapter.

After toying with the name London Pride, the band settled on Sky (the name, not the island). But as impressive as the line-up was, the combined record labels of London looked at the project and said no to the new Yes. Three years after punk, the next Emerson, Lake and Palmer were not at the top of any A&R man's shopping list. Not to be defeated, the band signed to a small European label, Ariola, and proved everybody wrong. Helped partly by John Williams's fan base and also his single 'Cavatina' (the theme music to *The Deer Hunter*), the debut album, *Sky*, was a roaring success. And though the music critics may have agreed with the record companies – the classical ones thought it trashy, the rock ones thought it too poncey – the band's Sky at Night tour was a sell-out.

'Toccata' was the single off Sky's follow-up, the double album *Sky 2* (chosen, for some reason, ahead of the side-long 'rock symphony' 'FIFO'). Originally a piece of organ music written by Johann Sebastian Bach (readers of a certain age may be scratching their chins at this point) and rocked up by the band, 'Toccata' lives up to its definition – 'a piece in free form designed partly to show off the instrument and the technique of the player'. It kicks in with *that* Halloween organ riff, the 'da*da*DA!' that launched a thousand Hammer horror films, builds up with a bevy of keyboard pyrotechnics and then in come John Williams and the band. It's virtuoso to the point of pointlessness, late-seventies keyboards wobble around like they're lost on their way to a *Dr Who* convention, and suddenly, Jeff Wayne's *War of the Worlds* didn't seem so bad after all.

> Late seventies keyboards wobble around like they're lost on their way to a *Dr Who* convention.

But what do I know? Hitting number 5, Sky did their stuff on *Top of the Pops* and continued to sell. They played a gig in Westminster Abbey, complete with dry ice and flashing lights. And though harpsichordist Francis Monkman left to write film soundtracks, the band followed *Sky* and *Sky 2* with, er, *Sky 3*, *Sky 4 Forthcoming* and *Five Live*. When John Williams left in 1984 it signalled the start of the end of the band, and though there were more albums and new line-ups to come, they would never recapture the heights of the original line-up.

Listen Here   *The Best of Sky* (Music Club, 1994). 'Toccata' is here. Likewise 'Gymnopedie No. 1' and 'Ride of the Valkryries'.

Listen On   *The Essential John Williams* (Metro, 2000). The fretwork fireworks without the prog rock pyrotechnics.

Listen Further   *Bach: Toccata in D* (Solstice, 2000). The Johann Sebastian mix.

Da Da Da Trio
No. 2 1982

Daftwerk

By contrast to Sky's pomposity, this next hit is about as stripped down as popular music gets. Trio were a minimalist German dance trio, Stephan Remmler (Da), Gert 'Kralle' Krawinkel (Da) and Peter Behrens (Da). Stephan and Gert had actually been together on and off since the late 1960s, but it was only with the arrival of Peter that the duo fulfilled their destiny and became a Trio. Da Da Da without the third Da, after all, is just Dada, and though a little bit odd at times, the band were never that surreal.

There is one other person worth mentioning, however, and that is Klaus Voorman. A long-time Beatles stalwart, Klaus had got to know the band in their Hamburg days, and their friendship led to his greatest claim to fame: designing the album sleeve for arguably the Fab Four's greatest album, *Revolver*. His association continued into the seventies, playing bass for both George Harrison and Ringo Starr, as well as John Lennon's Plastic Ono Band, and he was still recording with John when Lennon was killed in 1980. Following that, Klaus fancied a change of direction, and decided to return to Germany to try his hand at a bit of production. Which was when he came across Trio.

'Da Da Da', by far the band's most successful song, is little more than a Casio keyboard blipping away like a car indicator and Stephen Remmler mumbling a sort of multilingual monotone over the top. There's a touch of Alan Partridge to the verses, too, with every line finished with a clipped aha. Aha. And then there's the chorus, all da this and da that, with the boat well and truly being thrown out and a touch of guitar added in the background. Sounding like some sort of squiffy Kraftwerk, 'Da Da Da' may have been a meaningless chorus, but meaningless choruses cross linguistic barriers, and it was a huge hit across Europe.

There followed a series of 'Da Da Da'-based albums. Their debut album *Trio* was rereleased with 'Da Da Da' added. This was followed by a live album, complete with 'Da Da Da', which proudly boasted of being the first cassette-only album (cassettes: so ubiquitous, now so defunct . . .). This was followed by *Trio and Error*, with another version of . . . Ja Ja Ja, Ja ahead of me here. The band then released a final album, *Bye Bye*, and split up. And that was it, until fifteen years later in 1997, when the song was used in a Volkswagen advert in America, and became a hit there all over again.

> There's a touch of Alan Partridge to the verses, with every line finished with a clipped aha.

Listen Here *The Best One Hit Wonders in the World . . . Ever!* (Virgin, 2003). They've missed a trick by putting the track at number five on CD 2.

Listen On *Triologie* (Polygram, 2000). All Trio's greatest, remastered for the twenty-first century.

Listen Further *Man Machine* – Kraftwerk (Cleopatra, 1978). The original and the best. Includes 'The Model'.

Mmm Mmm Mmm Mmm Crash Test Dummies

No. 2 1994

Today's chorus is brought to you by the letter M

Misheard and forgotten lyrics have been a blight on the rock and roll landscape. How many times have you found yourself stood next to someone at a concert, suffering their out-of-tune, loose approximation of the band's lyric? Maybe it's because it's dark that people have no inhibitions in blaring out 'Wooh hoo la la roads are winding'. And arguably worse than people singing any old thing are people who have misheard the lyrics as something else. In the early 1980s Bruno Brookes used to have a popular feature on his Radio One teatime show where listeners would send in their hilarious mistakes. Typical of the calibre of entry was someone mistaking the line in 'Reward' by the Teardrop Explodes, the one about Julian Cope blessing his cotton socks. But where he sings about being 'in the news', it actually sounds like (hold your sides now) 'in the nude'. How the nation did chuckle.

But worry no more. For in 1994 Canadian band the Crash Test Dummies found a way round this problem by coming up with a chorus that was both hummable and hmmable. Genius. Even people whose teeth had fallen out could sing along. What no one could quite do, of course, was completely replicate singer Brad

Roberts's voice, which, to give it its proper name, is a rich sort of baritone and, to put it another way, is low enough to make a foghorn seem high pitched. A funny voice going 'Mmmm'? It had hit written all over it.

The irony is that for a band whose only proper hit had such a nonsensical chorus, Crash Test Dummies are actually pretty smart. Too smart, in fact, for any sort of sustained mainstream success. The follow-up to 'Mmm Mmm Mmm Mmm', 'Afternoons And Coffeespoons', boasted references to T. S. Eliot, a feat not achieved in pop music since verse nine of Bob Dylan's 'Desolation Row'. Even 'Mmm Mmm Mmm Mmm' is pretty thoughtful: each verse offers a vignette of a child not fitting in – a boy who had an accident and his hair turned white, a girl covered in birthmarks, a boy taken to church by his parents and doesn't get it. What does it all mean? Hmmmmmmm ...

For a brief moment the Crash Test Dummies achieved fame. Weird Al Yankovic recorded his own version, 'Headline News', replaced the original verses with tales of ice-skater Tonya Harding and penis-loser John Bobbitt and added the sound of a whip at the end of the Mmms. The song was overplayed on radio stations everywhere, and even the band got bored of it. They started changing the words at concerts because, as they told one audience, 'you've had to endure this song a million fucking times already'. Sometimes they even – gasp – swapped the 'Mmm' for other sounds. Then they started putting words in their choruses again and

> Even people whose teeth had fallen out could sing along.

went back to being big in Canada and culty else-where. Very much worth checking out, though, their late-nineties foray into drum and bass and falsetto singing aside.

Listen Here   *God Shuffled His Feet* (Arista, 1993). The albummm.

Listen On   *Puss 'N' Boots* (Cha-Ching, 2003). A recent return to form.

Listen Further   *Jingle All the Way* (Diesel Motor, 2002). A Christmas album by the Crash Test Dummies. Yes. Really.

Scatman (Ski-Ba-Bop-Ba-Dop-Bop)
Scatman John
No. 3 1995

Skiddly biddly di poo poo

The story goes that jazz legend Louis Armstrong was all set to sing along to the tune 'Heebie Jeebies' when his sheet music fell to the floor – one could almost say scattered – and, unable to remember what the words were, he improvised a load of nonsense, scat bat biddly diddly boo ha, and thus scat was born. It is per-haps not the greatest innovation ever to hit music, nestling in the nether regions of the scale between boy bands and waving cigarette lighters in the air, but somehow it endures. Will Young, first winner of *Pop Idol*, sets off his extinguishable version of 'Light My Fire' with a touch of the skibbly dibblies. But a couple of years earlier, this fine gentleman had made a whole career out of it.

Scatman John, or John Larkin to give him his proper name, had, until the early nineties, enjoyed a pleasant if not exceptional life as a jazz pianist; he may even have played the occasional hotel bar. Until, that is, the day he decided to scat. John's scatting style was unique for one simple reason: he suffered from a stut-ter. But rather than see this as a hindrance, John had worked out how to utilise his stutter into the non-sense notes and repetitious sounds that make up the joys of scat. The Scatman was born.

For reasons one finds hard to fathom, several record companies listened to a fifty-something pianist scat-ting over a dance beat and decided it was not for them. Except in Germany (it's almost predictable isn't it?), where a deal was signed. 'Scatman' the song took Scatman the Scatman's stutter as its subject: the mes-sage was simple – don't let a stutter, or anything else for that matter, hold you back. But hey. No one was listening to the words, it was the bits in between where Scatman was scatting and your radio sounded like it was having a seizure that counted. As the record rocketed up the charts all over Europe, the listening expe-rience changed quickly from curios-ity to 'not again' to putting your foot through the speaker as Scatty started revving through the gibberish gears. And as quickly as it had arrived, scat was that.

> And as quickly as it had arrived, scat was that.

Now I'm all for people with stutters having role models, and when Scatman John sadly died of cancer in 1999, the many tributes listed on the Internet were heartfelt and poignant. But really, can't music do any better? Gareth Gates might be annoying, and his version of 'Suspicious Minds', not to mention 'Unchained Melody', might be, in my humble opinion, a bloody awful record, but at least he doesn't suddenly go 'widdly doo dah'. Roger Daltrey may have been putting it on, but 'My Generation' did show how stuttering can be used to sound like f-f-swearing. Basically, what I'm saying is, it may be a way out, but it's still bad jazz. Having an interest in shit isn't called scatology for nothing, you know.

Listen Here   *Scatman's World* (RCA, 1995). 'Scatman', 'Scatman's World', 'Welcome To Scatland' and 'Song Of Scatland' all included.

Listen On   *Listen to the Scatman* (Stunt, 2003). 'The Jazz Vocal/Piano of John Larkin' according to the record sleeve.

Listen Further   *Hot Fives and Sevens* – Louis Armstrong (JSP, 1999). Includes 'Heebie Jeebies', where it supposedly all began.

Not one hit wonders. People often think they are. But they aren't

Nick Berry
'Every Loser Wins' *and* 'Heartbeat'

Bob the Builder
'Can We Fix It' *and* 'Mambo No. 5'

Dexy's Midnight Runners
'Come On Eileen' *and* 'Geno'. And numerous other great songs. And great albums. And great live performances. I could go on

Right Said Fred
'I'm Too Sexy' *and* 'Deeply Dippy'

Aqua
'Barbie Girl' *and* 'Doctor Jones'

6 Laughter Tracks
– Comedy Hits

Here's the basic problem with comedy singles: they're funny once. If at all. Normally the bits that are used at the end of a sketch show to pad it out to half an hour, left on their own with no preceding twenty-seven minutes of sketches, they tend to look a bit thin. In the same way that sitcoms seldom translate to the big screen with much success, so comedy records don't, on the whole, enjoy a triumphant career in the charts.

The master of the comedy record, in many ways, is Weird Al Yankovic, who has made a career out of parodying other people's records. You know when a song has reached a certain standing when Weird Al turns up with a wacky version of it (witness, for example, his hilarious Michael Jackson spoof 'Eat It' or his rib-tickling Kurt Cobain tribute 'Smells Like Nirvana'). It is a tradition that has been copied on this side of the Atlantic too: Billy Connolly's take on Tammy Wynette's 'D.I.V.O.R.C.E.' or Morris Minor and the Majors' Beastie Boys spoof.

Other comedy records rely on the popularity of the programmes or acts or characters – the same sort of spur for success as our collection of celebrity singers in Chapter 4. The Young Ones, for example, made hay in the early 1980s with hits for both Neil ('Hole In My Shoe') and Alexei Sayle (''Ullo John Got A New Motor?'). Maybe they should be included here, though I think the words 'Cliff' and 'Living Doll' make them just too successful for this book. This latter song is perhaps the daddy of the third kind of comedy hit: the Comic Relief charity record. I guess if it's for a good cause, it doesn't matter how funny they are.

Funky Moped/ Magic Roundabout
Jasper Carrott
No. 5 1975

Zebedee doo dah

I have a soft spot for Jasper Carrott. He might not be the most cutting-edge comedian around, and that police comedy series he did with Robert Powell wasn't that great, and maybe the less said about sitcom *All About Me* the better. But in the late 1970s and early 1980s, his assorted TV shows such as *Carrott's Lib* and *Carrott Confidential* deservedly pulled in the punters with his Brummie take on zits, bantam cocks, 'genuine' car insurance claims and supporting Birmingham City. Born Robert Davies, the name Jasper was a nickname at school, with Carrott added when he started doing the clubs. A resident performer at the Boggery Folk Club in Solihull, Jasper's reputation as a comedian was already mushrooming in the mid-seventies, when this record boosted his profile still further.

'Funky Moped', if truth be told, is not the greatest song ever written. And while we're being honest, it's not even very funny. Recorded with the helping hand of various members of the Electric Light Orchestra ('Searching!'), Jasper tells the sad tale of how having spent the night charming a young lady, he sees her ride off into the night on a long-haired lout's motorbike. If only, Jasper sighs, his 'funky'

moped was fixed. Then no one could stop him. Go funky moped, yeah!

The truth as to why the single was so successful probably lies in its B-side, which was not a song at all, but a very rude sketch about *The Magic Roundabout*, which, of course, was promptly banned and thus attracted the interests of punters everywhere. It's actually all fairly tame by today's standards, a bit of swearing, a couple of cheap jokes about whether or not Florence is a virgin, and Zebedee going 'boing!' at various intervals. But it's still quite funny nonetheless, and in 1975 was enough to tickle the nation's funny bone.

> The single's success lies in its B-side, a very rude sketch about *The Magic Roundabout*.

Jasper saved his 'funny' songs for his stage show after that, but has maintained his appeal as a stand-up ever since. In 2002 he was awarded the OBE for his services to charity. Either that, or the Queen found a copy of 'Funky Moped' in the attic and thought, *that* deserves a gong. He's rich too: a shrewd investment in the TV company Celador – makers of *Who Wants to be a Millionaire?* – has made him a cool £50 million. And if you fancy a game of 'Spot the Likeness', dust down your DVD of *The Office*. Lucy Davies, who plays receptionist Dawn, is his daughter.

Listen Here 'Funky Moped'/'Magic Roundabout' (DJM, 1975). Forget the A-side. Laugh at the B-side.

Listen On 'Twelve Days Of Christmas' (DJM, 1977). Carrott does the Christmas chart. The Christmas chart doesn't do Carrott.

Laugh Further *Carrott in Notts* (DJM, 1976).
Carrott doing funny in the Midlands.

D.I.V.O.R.C.E.
Billy Connolly
No. 1 1975

P.A.R.O.D.Y.

If it was 1975 and your girlfriend was listening to
country singer Tammy Wynette, the chances were
that your relationship had seen better days. If you
were lucky, the focus was on Tammy's first hit, and
whatever the misdemeanour, your partner was going
to stand by her man. If things had reached the point
of no return, then if need be, Tammy was there to
spell the situation out for you. It's D.I.V.O.R.C.E. time.

Tammy's relationship-ending anthem hit number 12
in the summer of 1975. Lacking the tune of 'Stand By
Your Man' (a number 1 song), it relied instead on an
irritating little G.I.M.M.I.C.K. for its success. The reason
for this ever so slightly creaky device was that in the
song the singer has a S.O.N. who can hear things but
can't spell them. So Tammy can say things like
C.U.S.T.O.D.Y. without alarming little J.O.E. Personally, I
reckon Joe (aged four) probably doesn't know what
'custody' means and would be more alarmed by his
mum wandering in the house talking in some slightly
wacko code. But there you go.

Enter Billy Connolly to put the B.O.O.T. in. Back in the
1960s Billy had started out as part of a folk act called
the Humblebums. Another of the group's members
was Gerry Rafferty, who would later go on to form
Stealer's Wheel and get Bob Holness to dust down his
saxophone for 'Baker Street'. Not. With Billy writing
comedy songs and Gerry leaning towards music to
cut people's ears off to, a split was inevitable. And
while 'Stuck In The Middle With You' hit number 8 in
1973, Billy eventually went seven places better with
his Tammy pastiche. In his version of 'D.I.V.O.R.C.E.'
it's all to do with the 'wee' D.O.G., who bites the V.E.T.
and causes a relationship-finishing argument.
G.U.F.F.A.W.

For a while, it looked as though Billy's parody had
successfully killed off this annoying spelling gimmick.
Bands turned their attention to
counting instead. XTC on 'Senses
Working Overtime' went for the
basic '1,2,3,4,5'. Tom Robinson was
a bit smarter, showing off his two
times table on '2-4-6-8 Motorway'.
But then came Ottowan and
'D.I.S.C.O.' Not far behind were
Freeez with their we-know-all-the-vowels classic
'I.O.U.' And on into the nineties the gimmick went,
with a curious resurgence at the height of Britpop.
Blur went for 'T.O.P.M.A.N.'; Pulp sang about a
'F.E.E.L.I.N.G.C.A.L.L.E.D.L.O.V.E.'; and Oasis went
for . . . actually, Oasis decided not to take any chances.

> Enter Billy
> Connolly to put
> the B.O.O.T. in.

Listen Here *The Pick of Connolly* (Spectrum,
1993). Cover features a picture of Billy picking his
nose.

Laugh Further *Billy and Albert* (EMI, 2000). Definitive Billy gig at the Royal Albert Hall.

Listen Further *The Definitive Collection –* Tammy Wynette (Columbia, 1998). There's 'D.I.V.O.R.C.E.' There's 'Stand By Your Man'. And there's 'Kids Say The Darndest Things'.

Convoy GB
Laurie Lingo and the Dipsticks
No. 4 1976

Trucking awful

It's hard to imagine now, in an era of mobile phones and photo messaging and texting and the like, but in the 1970s the big new thing in communication was the CB radio. The craze had originally taken off thanks to the American president Richard Nixon. He'd imposed a speed limit of 55mph to help the US through the oil crisis, whereupon truckers across the land bought themselves a CB radio and warned each other of radar traps up ahead. There may have been no such restrictions here, but CB radio still crossed the Atlantic, and truck drivers here too started speaking in 'lorry lingo' and calling each other by silly names or 'handles'. 'Breaker one-nine, this is the Hairy Cornflake. Drop the hammer, Funky Gibbon, or I'll never make the flip-flop.' 'No can do Hairy Cornflake,

check out the Christmas lights in your mirror: I don't fancy getting a driving award!'*

In 1973 an American advertising campaign for bread featured the trucking character C. W. McCall, created by Bill Fries. The character was so popular that it led to a recording career: 'The Old Home Filler-Up And Keep On A-Truckin' Café' and 'Wolf Creek Pass', a touching song about brake failure, were both country hits. But it was the song 'Convoy' that crossed over into the pop charts. All about the joys of trucking and dodging the police, it was littered with CB references and interspersed with radio dialogue between Rubber Duck, Pig Pen and Sodbuster. It was an American number 1 and almost incomprehensibly, number 2 in the UK. But that wasn't quite the end of the story . . .

Enter Radio One DJs Dave Lee Travis and Paul Burnett. Paul was sort of the Gary Davies of the seventies, making the lunchtime show his own. His previous biggest claim to fame had been working on sixties pirate station Radio 270, broadcasting from a boat just outside Bridlington. Paul had felt so seasick doing the breakfast show that he had thrown up live on air. Dave Lee Travis, meanwhile, had begun his musical career as tour manager for Herman's Hermits. After a similar pirate radio route, by 1976 he was doing the nation's teatime slot.

Under the pseudonym Laurie Lingo and the

> Time has not served the jokes well. Some of them, one feels, were probably old in the seventies.

* 'Speed up Steve, or I'm never going to get back.' 'Sorry Chris, can't you see the police lights in your mirror? I don't want a speeding ticket.'

Dipsticks, DLT and Paul released 'Convoy GB', a theo-retically humorous parody of the C. W. McCall song, shifting the 'action' from the Interstate 44 to halfway up the M1. I say theoretically, because time has not especially served the jokes well. Some of them, one feels, were probably old in the seventies; there's a particularly weak pun about changing gear, for example. Others show how attitudes have changed: there's a rather dodgy West Indian accent, at one point; a search for 'nice chicks' at another; not to mention the effeminate trucker who drives a 'camper' van. DLT adopts the handle of 'Super Scouse' and sings the song in a grating Liverpudlian accent, which I can only guess must have been funny at the time. Paul Burnett is 'Plastic Chicken' and is responsible for setting up perhaps the worst joke on the entire record. He asks Super Scouse what a 'suicide jockey' is (CB slang for a driver with a load of explosives). DLT responds with a dreadful impression of Jimmy Savile followed by a loud bang.

'Convoy GB' hit number 4 in the charts and didn't seem to do either DJ much harm. DLT went on to don the mantle of the 'Hairy Cornflake' and host the Radio One breakfast show. He later invented 'snooker on the radio' on his weekend show and now appears on BBC Three Counties Radio and the army's very own station Garrison Radio. Paul Burnett went on to work for several local stations, including Capital Gold, and has most recently been involved in *Making Waves*, the feature film of life back on Radio 270.

Listen Here 'Convoy GB' (State, 1976). The truck stopped with the single.

Listen On *The Best of C. W. McCall* (PSM, 1998). Yee and if you must, haw.

Look Further *Convoy* (DVD, 2001). Sam Peckinpah made the definitive film. DLT didn't get the call.

Jilted John
Jilted John
No. 4 1978

The one about a chap called Gordon

Once upon a time, a long long time ago (well, the late 1970s) there lived a nice chap called John. John had a girlfriend called Julie. John loved Julie. Julie loved John. Then along came another chap called Gordon. Gordon loved Julie too. Julie decided she loved Gordon more than John. Julie jilted John. John called Gordon a moron. John become a pop star.

A love spurned has always been a rich topic for rock music, and in the late seventies I don't know if girls were being particularly flighty, but spurning was the new going out. There was poor Sting, who couldn't, who couldn't, who couldn't stand losing his girlfriend. There was Joe Jackson, who asked 'Is She Really Going Out With Him?' But the gilted Jilted was undoubtedly John.

One group of people probably remember the song better than others: people who were called Gordon.

John was in real life Graham Fellows, and inspired by a song by John Otway (younger readers: ask your folk-loving uncle), he wrote and recorded 'Jilted John'. Musically at least, the song is a sort of punk parody, though there's enough real life in the lyrics to twinge our former teenage selves (the name of the girl who did the same to me has been expunged to save myself embarrassment).

But what everyone remembers about the song is the chorus where John repeatedly calls Gordon a 'moron'. And one group of people probably remembers it better than others: people who were called Gordon. I'm not called Gordon so can only imagine what it must have been like to be eight years old when the song came out. Poor sods. And if you think they had a tough time, spare a thought for Bernard Kelly, Graham's mate, who appeared on *Top of the Pops* as 'Gordon' and has the 'moron' tag chucked at him by every hilarious builder ever since. I can't vouch for whether the moron tag is valid or not, but I do wonder if Jilted John has thought his accusation through. If Julie is going out with a moron, what does that make Julie? And if Julie used to go out with John, what does that make him? Is he a moron by association?

One person who most certainly isn't a moron is Graham Fellows. Anyone who got his sister to write to John Peel requesting the record (which he then played) is clearly some sort of pop genius. Anyone who goes to Christian Youth camps not because they are Christian but because the camps are full of attractive young things (where Graham was when the song became a hit), well that's the sign of a higher mind too. And though the nation tired quickly of Jilted John (we don't like moaners – see Orville), they have

continued to be seduced by Graham in other guises, most notably his comic character John Shuttleworth. In fact, Jilted John is probably in this section the wrong way round: rather than being a comedian who had one hit, he is a one-hit wonder who became a comedian. But I had to squeeze him in somewhere, so don't complain. Honestly. Some people. Morons.

Listen Here   *True Love Stories* (Essential, 1999). Includes both LP and single versions of 'Jilted John'.

Listen On   'Paperboy Song' on the same album – for anyone who has ever had a paper round.

Listen Further   *The Yamaha Years* – John Shuttleworth (Chicken, 2003). What Graham did next.

Stutter Rap (No Sleep Til Bedtime)
Morris Minor and the Majors
No. 4 1987

Still a one hit wonder in my book

In 1987 the most notorious band in Britain were American rappers the Beastie Boys. Fighting for their right to party, the band's debut album *Licensed to Ill* mixed heavy metal riffs with New York know-how and a stage show designed to offend: women in cages, inflatable penises, that sort of thing. And as much as the kids liked them and stole the VW badges from cars to prove it, it was the tabloids that really loved the band. Whipping them up as some sort of latter-day Sex Pistols, there seemed nothing this 'sick' band would not stoop to. Made-up stories about hurling abuse at disabled children? All in a day's work.

The parody was quick to arrive. Up-and-coming comedian Tony Hawks was the creator of a spoof rap band, Morris Minor and the Majors, and had already gone down a storm on *Saturday Live* when the idea for a single came up. Backed by his Majors of Phil Errup (geddit?) and Rusty Wing, Morris launched 'Stutter Rap' on an unsuspecting public. Here's the joke: he's a rapper, but he's got a stutter. That's pretty much it. There's then a bit of top and tailing with some Beastie Boys jokes (no sleep until bedtime, rather than Brooklyn, etc.), which, truth be told, don't have that much to do with the 'Stutter Rap' bit. They do the bit from Chaka Khan's 'I Feel For You', except it's all about chucking cans. The whole thing sounds as if it was knocked together for next to nothing, which it proba- bly was. Someone must have found it funny, though, because it ended up at number 4 and shifted 200,000 copies. In Australia it got to number 1.

That was pretty much it. There was a follow-up single, a Stock, Aitken and Waterman spoof called 'This Is The Chorus', but this one really did stutter. The band's career ended up being not so much Morris Minor as, well, mini. Tony Hawks went on to be one of those people who are always on Radio Four quiz pro- grammes and who have a lucrative career as a writer. Having travelled round Ireland with a fridge and played the Moldovans at tennis, his next project was *One Hit Wonderland* and his quest to lose his solitary- single status (though not, it has to be said, in this country). Personally, I think Tony protests slightly too much about his one hit wonder status: if he didn't bang on so much about 'Stutter Rap' no one would ever have known it was him.

Listen Here *More Greatest Hits of the Eighties* (Disky, 2000). 'Stutter Rap' is joined by another 142 songs that didn't make it into volume one.

Listen On *Licensed to III* – Beastie Boys (Def Jam, 1986). What the Majors were parodying.

Read Further *One Hit Wonderland* by Tony Hawks (Ebury, 2002). Tony has a Morris Minor hit in Albania.

> Here's the joke: he's a rapper, but he's got a stutter.

Loadsamoney (Doin' Up The House)
Harry Enfield
No. 4 1988

Bish bosh zoom zoom wallop. Dosh

In the late 1980s, following the success of *Saturday Live*, the comedy and music show presented by Ben Elton, Channel 4 decided to do it all over again, except on a different day. *Friday Night Live* featured among its regulars comedian Harry Enfield, who had built up a following for his character Stavros, a Greek kebab-shop owner who said things like "Allo matey peeps' and 'Up the Arse', a reference to his beloved Arsenal football club. But for the new series Harry added a new character, created with Paul Whitehouse. Loadsamoney was a satire on everything that was wrong with the 1980s: a flash London plasterer who loved Mrs Thatch, was absolutely raking it in and wanted everyone to know about it. Waving his stash of cash, he'd shout things like 'Shut your mouth and look at my wad!' and, of course, 'Loadsamoney!' He proudly wore a T-shirt that read 'Bonk Aid – I Bonked The World'. There wasn't much, in fact, that Loadsamoney wouldn't brag about.

So much for satire. In a not dissimilar way to Mr Blobby on *Noel's House Party*, Loadsamoney quickly began to take over *Friday Night Live*. Enfield added another character to try and balance things a bit – the completely broke Geordie Buggerallmoney, who smoked a lot of tabs – but it was Loadsamoney everybody wanted to see. Soon the character was taking hold far beyond the traditional Channel 4 audience, with one small difference: somewhere along the way, the satire got lost. The people who Loadsamoney was mocking wanted to be him. They copied him and got wads of their own to wave about.

In the summer of 1988 Harry released this cash-in single. What with Loadsamoney being a plasterer, there were lots of hilarious 'house' puns to tie in with

> Somewhere along the way, the satire got lost. The people who Loadsamoney was mocking wanted to be him.

the prevalent dance music. That and all the catchphrases and compulsory wad-waving. It's not a great work of art, but it's a shrewd and carefully crafted package: its catalogue number, for example, was DOSH1. And there was also a fairly useful producer behind the controls: future dance guru and Madonna acolyte William Orbit.

The joke quickly wore thin, and Loadsamoney didn't last much longer. Heartily sick of his creation, and I would guess worried about his career becoming defined by it, Harry killed him off in a car crash on the following year's Comic Relief. Even so, in a funny sort of way Loadsamoney lives on, for ever capturing the essence of the time.

Listen Here 'Loadsamoney (Doin' Up The House)'. The catalogue number was DOSH1. There wasn't a DOSH2.

Listen On 'Big Girl' – Precocious Brats featuring Kevin and Perry (Virgin/EMI, 2000). Last time William Orbit. This time Judge Jules.

Listen Further *Ray of Light* – Madonna (Maverick, 1998). Some American singer or other that William also went on to produce.

The Stonk Hale and Pace and the Stonkers
No. 1 1991

It didn't stonk. It stank

Since its inception in the mid-1980s humour fund-athon Comic Relief has done a multitude of good things and raised approximately oodles of cash for worthwhile causes both in this country and abroad. Part of the cash has always come from the accompanying singles, among which there have been eleven top-ten singles, including seven number 1s. One successful formula has been to combine a comedy act with a pop star or group: witness Cliff and the Young Ones, Mel (Smith) and Kim (Wilde), Bananarama and La Na Nee Nee Noo Noo (French and Saunders and Kathy Burke), Gareth Gates and the Kumars. The other approach has been for a straight song: Cher, Chrissy Hynde, Neneh Cherry and Eric Clapton on 'Love Can Build A Bridge', the Spice Girls with 'Who Do You Think You Are', Boyzone and Westlife with 'When The Going Gets Tough' and 'Uptown Girl'. Only twice, in fact, has a fully fledged comedy single been attempted. In 1992, to tie in with the general election, Mr Bean found his voice to sing '(I Want To Be) Elected' with Iron Maiden frontman Bruce Dickinson. And a year earlier, there was this.

1991 was the Comic Relief where the red nose had arms. It was the one when Theophilus P. Wildebeest went groin to groin with Tom Jones, when French and Saunders and Raw Sex did their Abba medley, and when Hale and Pace invited everyone to, for want of a better word, stonk. I've always felt slightly sorry for Hale and Pace, a middling comedy duo who were a touch too mainstream for alternative comedy, a touch too alternative for the mainstream, and always seemed to fall somewhere between the two. Similarly with this song. Stonk is one of those words that is almost rude but not quite: a stonker is in some places slang for an erection, so that means to stonk you dance like what? Stiffly? I don't know, but cue lyrics about your granny stonking, people stonking in the offices and suchlike. I think people thought, well it *is* for charity, bought it anyway and listened to Victoria Wood on the B-side.

Hale and Pace had one further stab at the music industry. In their 1998 BBC series *Jobs for the Boys* they attempted to write a song to represent Britain in the Eurovision Song Contest. Perhaps appropriately called 'More Than Enough For One Life', their entry failed to make the final eight.

Listen Here 'The Stonk' (London, 1991). It *is* for charity.

Listen On The B-side by Victoria Wood. It is for charity. And it's funny.

Donate Further www.comicrelief.com. Spare your record collection and feed the world with one swift click.

Always Look On The Bright Side Of Life
Monty Python
No. 3 1991

Jesus

Monty Python, with or without the Flying Circus, have over the years had the effrontery to break the golden rule of comedy records and record the occasional song that is *actually* funny. 'The Lumberjack Song'? Funny. 'Sit On My Face'? Still brings a smile to mine. 'Every Sperm Is Sacred'? I rate. 'I Like Chinese'? Well ok, so nobody's perfect.

In 1979 the team got together for their second and arguably finest film, *Monty Python's Life of Brian*, which quickly became a firm favourite of churchgoers everywhere. Alongside the other classic scenes – blessed are the cheesemakers, the stone-throwing women with beards, the People's Front of Judea, the 'very naughty boy' call-and-answer session and so on – is the film's iconic end. Having failed to escape crucifixion, Brian finds himself being treated to a rousing version of 'Always Look On The Bright Side' by his new cross friends. It's a cheery song, with a simple message: you might be about to die, but chin up, it's not *so* bad.

Over a decade on, the song's gallows humour was still striking a chord with another institution known for being long suffering: football fans. And as well as being sung on the terraces, Radio One breakfast DJ

Simon Mayo started spinning the song himself. Following the success of 'Donald, Where's Yer Troosers?' and 'Kinky Boots', Simon Mayo achieved a memorable hat-trick by getting this song into the charts as well. I guess the reason the song endures unlike other comedy records is that first, its humour is gentle rather than full on (and thus doesn't wear so quickly) and second, its theme has a touch of the universal rather than the specific. Everyone can relate to it.

The song also boasts that oft-neglected part of the pop repertoire: the whistle. Much maligned by the dreary work of Roger Whittaker over the years (if you don't know who he is, ask your dad), just putting your lips together and blowing is, in fact, crucial to a song's success. If you can whistle the tune in the bath, so the legend goes, you've got yourself a hit on your hands. Otis Redding memorably sat on the dock of a bay, whistling away. Bryan Ferry showed whistling could be suave on his version of 'Jealous Guy'. And Eric Idle's song got a whole new generation puffing away too.

> Simon Mayo achieved a memorable hat trick by getting this song into the charts.

Listen Here *Monty Python Sings* (Virgin, 1989). Does exactly what it says on the tin.

Listen On 'The Spam Song' from the same album. All together now . . .

Listen Further *The Rutles* – the Rutles (Rhino, 2003). Eric Idle's spoof of some band from Liverpool or other.

They don't always hit number 1

Five Levi's songs that didn't chart

'Mannish Boy'
Muddy Waters (No. 55)

'Can't Get Enough'
Bad Company (No. 88)

'Mad About The Boy'
Dinah Washington (No. 41)

'Heart Attack And Vine'
Screamin' Jay Hawkins (No. 42)

'Novelty Waves'
Biosphere (No. 51)

7 We'll Be Right Back after This Break – Advert Hits

In the mid-1980s model Nick Kamen began an advertising revolution by taking all his clothes off in a launderette. The accompanying music, 'I Heard It Through The Grapevine' by Marvin Gaye, was released as a single and found itself shrinking to fit nicely in the top ten. Suddenly, the music in an advert went from being an important component to a potential money-spinner. And it was classic American brands, such as Levi's and Coca-Cola, that were leading the way.

The Levi's strategy has gone through several changes over the years. To begin with it was all about classic soul: Sam Cooke, Ben E. King, Percy Sledge and so forth. Then they went through a seventies rock period: Bad Company, Marc Bolan, the Clash. And then, in the mid-nineties, they decided to go all modern and try for new music: the results – Stiltskin, Babylon Zoo – are clear for all to see. I guess that while a great old song has already proved its worth over the years, a new song by a new band is tainted with commercialism. And as well as it being a tag difficult to remove, it creates a level of exposure the band is never going to enjoy again: the advert is a glossier, more expensive version of any video the band might record. Its saturation showing on TV and at the cinema beats a flyposting campaign hands down.

It's not just one hit wonders who suffer from being involved in adverts. Before the Spice Girls sacked their manager, they seemed to be advertising everything under the sun and looked all the tackier for it. Madonna and Missy Elliott doing the Gap thang seemed misjudged on every level. Justin 'loving it' for McDonald's felt a solitary mistake in an otherwise perfect pop year. Moby's dance credibility took a hammering by the apparent leasing of virtually every song from *Play*.

In essence, rich companies are paying pop stars for a slice of their credibility: the money may be good, but it's a dangerous career move I would advise all musicians against. And for an unknown act, the risks are even higher: because they're new, they haven't got any credibility in the bank in the first place …

The First Time
Robin Beck
No. 1 1988

Even wetter than the real thing

In 1971 Coca-Cola launched one of the seventies' iconic adverts, a veritable Benetton of children on top of an Italian hillside, all singing in perfect harmony how they'd like to buy the world a Coke. Then someone had the brainwave of rewriting the lyrics and *voilà*! The New Seekers had a number 1 hit with 'I'd Like To Teach The World To Sing'.* It seemed such a brilliant idea – all that airplay was basically free advertising – that in the late 1980s Coca-Cola decided to see if everyone would fall for it all over again. And guess what? We did.

Robin Beck began her musical career by dabbling in disco in the late 1970s. As well as being a backing singer for Chaka Khan, Cher and, um, Leo Sayer, she recorded an album, *Sweet Talk*, with contributions from Luther Vandross and Irene Cara. Fame, though, seemed reserved for someone else until Coke came calling. It was a case of goodbye glitter and hello guitars: Robin now offered up the soggiest of soft rock: think Starship, think Heart, think Tiffany's mum.

The lyrics of 'The First Time' swaps the 'Coca-Cola is it' lines of the advert for a fittingly saccharine take on falling in love. Put it this way, it's not quite the 'very

* In 1994 Oasis had a similar brainwave and released the not-dissimilar-sounding 'Shakermaker'. Their royalties went on a different brand of coke.

first time' that Madonna sings about in 'Like A Virgin'. Robin's best line comes in the middle eight, when she reflects (and I paraphrase) that there are no words to describe her feelings. It's an excellent point, but one that, sadly, arrives about two verses too late. Dipping heavily into the *Hallmark Book of Bad Metaphors* (Cheese and Unwin, 1983), Robin goes for a 'more is less' strategy in describing falling in love: it is variously a 'break in clouds', an 'uncharted sea', the 'first ray of the sun' and an 'unopened door'. There's electricity too, apparently, flowing from each kiss. Though if you will go around snogging Robocop, what do you expect?

> Robin goes for a 'more is less' strategy in describing falling in love.

'The First Time' was huge and spent three weeks at number 1 in November 1988. But the accompanying album, *Trouble or Nothing*, did, well, nothing. It all ended in tears as 'Save Up All Your Tears' and 'Tears In The Rain' failed to do the business. A couple more albums led to modest chart success on the European mainland (ok, Germany), but even another advert single – 'Close To You', used by McDonald's – was not enough to propel her back up the charts. Robin married a member of the House of Lords (the hard rock band, not the posh bit of Parliament) and left the 'biz' to bring up their daughter, Olivia. An attempted comeback came and went in 2000, leaving Robin's debut hit her first, and only, time.

Listen Here *Hot City Nights* (Sony, 2003). 'Massive Rock Anthems to Take Your Breath Away' is the shoutline. Can you guess which other one hit wonder is also featured here?

Listen On *Wonderland* – Robin Beck (Sony, 2004). Considering it is being released in Germany, should that be Wunderland?

Listen Further *The Very Best of the New Seekers* (Spectrum, 1996). The original fizzy pop.

Inside Stiltskin
No. 1 1994

Inside. Then outside

In the early nineties, of course, grunge was everywhere, Kurt was king and Courtney his queen. Stiltskin, along with Bush, were a sort of British reaction. Bush made it big in America but not in Britain, but then they didn't have a Levi's jeans commercial behind them. A lavishly shot black-and-white affair, the advert starts off with an Amish family out for a quiet serene country picnic, when the two teenage daughters amble off to discover – gasp – a pair of jeans by a lake. Cue Stiltskin and their humdinger of a guitar riff and a Nick Kamenesque model emerging from the water. The camera pans down, but just as the girls are hoping for a bit of an eyeful, goddammit, the hunk has only gone and got his Levi's on, shrunk to fit (do you see what they've done there?). But hang on. If he's got his jeans on, then whose trousers are the girls holding? Cue aching sides as doddery old bloke with white beard appears, swimming the doggy paddle.

'Inside' steamrollered its way to number 1 in May 1994, a month after Kurt Cobain died. Was this symbolic? Was the nation after anything that smelt ever so slightly of Teen Spirit? Was this simply another example of our old favourite, the Jean Genie? Who knows. A top-ten album, *The Mind's Eye*, followed, but 'Inside' was as inside the top twenty as Stiltskin were going to get. With Nirvana no more, and Blur and Oasis Britpopping their way up the charts, as quickly as Stiltskin had arrived, their moment had gone. In 1995 the band split up.

Singer Ray Wilson's calling, however, was not yet over. Genesis, who now even Phil Collins had had enough of, were in need of a new singer and Ray was their man. The new line-up recorded an album, *Calling All Stations*, but this time their touch really was invisible,* and Tony Banks and Mike Rutherford endethed the book of Genesis for good. Ray, meanwhile, abacabbed** his way to a solo career. In 2001 he played thirteen sell-out nights at the Edinburgh Festival, for his Live and Acoustic set, including a stripped-down version of, of course, 'Inside'. As for his fellow band members, guitarist Peter Lawlor does very nicely out of writing music for TV – those silly dancers in the red on BBC1? That's him. James Finnigan (bass) set up a guitar institute, and Ross MacFarlane has both twirled his drumsticks for the Proclaimers and turned his attention to acting.

> Was the nation after anything that smelt ever so slightly of Teen Spirit?

* A very bad Genesis pun, for which I can only apologise.
** This one, though, there really is no excuse for.

- **Listen Here** *The Best Air Guitar Album in the World . . . Vol. II* (Virgin, 2002). Halfway down disc 2. Which kind of says it all.
- **Listen On** *The Mind's Eye* (White Water, 1994). The album that includes the appropriately titled 'Rest In Peace'.
- **Listen Further** *Live and Acoustic* – Ray Wilson (Spv, 2002). The acoustic version of 'Inside' you've always wanted to hear.

Spaceman Babylon Zoo
No. 1 1996

The 501 song that spent five weeks at number, oh, 1

It's the future. In a galaxy far, far away, in a space suburban house in a suspiciously sixties-looking space suburb, mom and pops are pacing around the room. The goldfish bowl may float around, the dog may have become a K-9esque toaster on wheels, but some things don't change: their daughter has vanished, and in a future where mobile phones have apparaently been disinvented they don't know where she is. But wait, what's that noise? Yes, yes, the thumping bassline is Babylon Zoo, but we'll come to them in a moment. I'm talking about the full-throttle warp-speed jet engine that is roaring in from out back. Pops pops into the space garden, just in time to see the family spaceship return, and his space babe daughter,

the Russian supermodel Kristina Semenovskaia, rematerialise. Guess where she's been? That's right. She's only gone and gone back to Earth* to get herself a pair of figure-hugging Levi's – 'the only jeans in the universe cut from 01 denim'.

No, I haven't the foggiest what '01 denim' is either.

In the mid-1970s, so the concert review went, we saw the future of rock and roll, and its name was Bruce Springsteen. In the mid-1990s we saw the rock and roll of the future, and it came from, well, Wolverhampton. Jasbinder 'Jas' Mann was born in Dudley at the start of the seventies, before spending his childhood in India, the Himalayas and back in sunny Brummie. In the early 1990s he was lead singer with big in Birmingham baggy groovy indie things the Sandkings, and though they supported the likes of the Wonderstuff and the Happy Mondays, they never quite got their big break. Goodbye Sandkings, hello Babylon Zoo.

Freed from gazing at his shoes and hiding behind a big, floppy, indie fringe, Jas began experimenting with his love for all things science fiction. In a disused building in Wolverhampton he created his very own art/video/music cross-genre playground. In 1995 he made a short 'B-movie' film in the style of cult director Roger Corman** called 'Spaceman Sub-Organic

> As Bucks Fizz so rightly said you speed things up, but then you've go to slow them down.

---

* I say Earth. I believe there is also a Levi's outlet in the shopping centre just off Saturn. You know, the one on the rings road.

** Jas's interest in the director continued with the Zoo's debut LP, *The Boy with the X-Ray Eyes* – a nod to Corman's 1963 cult classic *The Man with the X-Ray Eyes*.

Mutation', and it was the music from this that would become his international smash-hit single. Minus the sub-organic mutation bit, of course.

Enter Arthur Baker. The legendary dance remixer, who'd twiddled everyone from Afrika Bambaataa to New Order, was brought in to sprinkle his magic. His contribution was simple but devastatingly effective: just as Stock, Aitken and Waterman were alleged to have done to Rick Astley's vocals to get Kylie Minogue's, Arthur sped 'Spaceman' up. For thirty-five seconds or so – the length of, say, a Levi's 501 jeans commercial – Babylon Zoo sounded absolutely out of this world. With Jas singing 'Spaceman' over the top like some sort of demented Luke Smurfwalker, the bass funked and the drums grooved like they was *so* tomorrow.

And then 'Spaceman' came out of light speed. As Bucks Fizz so rightly said many years before, you speed things up, but then you've got to slow them down. And for me, this is where you can hear Babylon Zoo's flirtation with fame grind to a halt. Thirty-five seconds into the song out went the fabulous futuristic dance groove and in came sub-Bowie eighties goth rock. The first line of the first verse was all about 'pungent smells' consummating Jas's home: that was the odour of one-hit wonderdom, and no matter how much Glade Jas bought it wasn't going to go away. Jas may have sung about not being able to 'get off the carousel', but the fact was, the carousel stopped pretty quickly.

Jas did his best. He predated David Beckham in the sarong school of fashion (a silver number made by his mum, bless). He gave good interview. But as big as the single was – and it was huge, half a million copies shifted in the first week, the then fastest-selling debut single of all time, five weeks at number 1, a chart topper in twenty countries – none of the follow-up singles had the zip of 'Spaceman'.* But maybe this is what you get from advertising jeans with a button fly.

Or maybe, at the height of Britpop, Babylon Zoo were just a little too straight. There was no discernible irony, no winks to the camera, none of that dextrous feat of sticking your tongue both firmly in your cheek and up the Beatles' backsides at the same time. In the mid-nineties, when everyone knew you had to be knowing, Jas went around talking about his 'five dimensional music'. Arthur Baker, interviewed a few years later, said: 'I think he was really talented, he just had no sense of humour.'** And nowhere was this more obvious than on Jas Mann's appearance on Chris Morris's *Brass Eye*, in which the interviewer fires off a number of vicious questions: You've sung all the notes from A to G, have you ever sung an H? You write the lyrics, who writes the words? Have you ever written a spherical song? Has Michael Nyman? Jas ('I think he's getting close') didn't know how to respond.

Listen Here *The Best TV Ads ... Ever!* (Virgin/EMI, 2000). In between the music from the CGU ad and the one for Tango.

Listen On 'All The Money's Gone' (EMI, 1998). Haven't heard it myself, but the solitary review on amazon.co.uk describes it as 'mousy and whiney'.

Listen Further *Perfecto Presents Arthur Baker*

* OK, I should fess up here. 'Animal Army', the follow-up, did scrape its way to number 17, so technically he shouldn't be here. But Jas does admit to the label ('It's like I always say, it's better to be a one-hit wonder than a no-hit wonder') so let's leave him in.
** Burnitblue.com, October 2001.

Breakin' (Perfecto, 2001). Not Arthur Baker literally breaking. That wouldn't be very nice, and it probably wouldn't sound great either.

I Just Want To Make Love To You
Etta James
No. 5 1996

Fewer calories, more sauce

In 1990 the KLF asked one of rock's, nay life's, great imponderables: what time is love? It is a question that many musicians have attempted to answer over the years: Wilson Pickett suggested it was the midnight hour; Simon and Garfunkel made their bid for Wednesday Morning, 3 a.m.; Craig David, well, he widened it out to pretty much seven days a week. But in the mid-1990s the female vote came swinging in. Wilson Pickett, it transpired, was about twelve and a half hours out. Love time was set at 11.30. Or, as it was alternatively known, 'Diet Coke Break'.

In one of those oh-so-clever switch-around adverts, the Diet Coke ad swapped builders leering at secretaries for secretaries leering at builders. The former, you see, is the worst kind of boorish male sexism; the latter is an irony-rich, postmodern play on gender stereotyping, and most certainly not a thinly disguised excuse for women to ogle at some beefcake with his kit off. Said 'builder', bum-crack-free model

Lucky Vanous, celebrates his 11.30 breather by stripping down to the waist and glugging a can of the low-cal fizzy stuff. Meanwhile a giggle of women drool on from the office window above, each daydreaming about getting Lucky.

In the background, meanwhile, is a soundtrack that is anything but fat free. Etta James's sultry accompaniment puts the 'oohs' into blues, her version of the Muddy Waters classic ditching the guitar licks and replacing them with a serious amount of horn. The basic thrust of the song is thus: Etta will do whatever you like, wash your clothes, make your bread, anything you want. In return, she doesn't want her man heading out and working long hours, doesn't really want him to do anything. Just as long as whenever Etta is, as Glenn Miller put it, 'In The Mood', then her man is, as Prince once sang, 'Rock Hard In A Funky Place'.

Etta James was actually born Jamesetta Hawkins in Los Angeles in 1938. (You *did* see what she did there?) A gospel child prodigy, by the 1950s she had teamed up with bandleader Johnny Otis and took no time at all in getting raunchy. Her debut single, 'Roll With Me Henry', was considered too risqué for the fifties and had to be renamed 'Dance With Me Henry' before it could be released. By the 1960s Etta had signed up to Chess Records and took her place on the rock and rollercoaster. On the upside were classic blues and soul numbers such as 'Something's Got A Hold On Me' and 'I'd Rather Go Blind'; on the downside there were

> The Diet Coke ad swapped builders leering at secretaries for secretaries leering at builders.

abusive relationships, financial problems and heroin addiction.

But if Etta has more than paid her dues over the years, then she has been handsomely rewarded with an amazing voice: one capable of switching from purring like a pussycat to giving it some serious wild-cat growling. Put it this way: if Etta had you in her sights and her thoughts were honing in on your ring-pull, it would take an exceedingly brave man to resist.

Listen Here *Blues Brother Soul Sister Classics* (Polygram, 1999). Track one. Side one. Nuff said.

Listen On *The Best of Etta James* (Spectrum, 2000). Track one, side one, too.

Listen Further *This Note's for You* – Neil Young (Reprise, 1988). Title track finds Mr Young dissing those who take the adman's shiny penny.

Underwater Love
Smoke City
No. 4 1997

Portishead meets *Splash*

Mermaids, those mysterious half-female-beauty, half-fish creatures, come in all shapes and sizes. They can be 'little' as in Disney or Denmark, or they can be 'large' as in Daryl Hannah, Tom Hanks's 1984 aquatic amour. But be warned: if you ever find yourself over-board at sea, don't take it as given that the mermaids will save you from Davy Jones's locker. Take the poor chap who found himself drowning in a 1997 jeans commercial. His brief delight at the thought of rescue quickly went down the plughole, as they fell in love with his Levi's instead.

After Stiltskin and 'Spaceman' 501s went all sultry with Smoke City. The band started in the early 1990s with singer Nina Miranda and DJ whiz Mark Brown, with the line-up later completed by guitarist Chris Franck. The Smoke City in question is London town, where Nina and Mark went to school together, though Nina, you may be unsurprised to hear, spent part of her childhood in Brazil. After various indie-label singles, the band's break came when 'Underwater Love' was chosen as the opening track of *The Rebirth of Cool Volume Six* – a nineties series of acid jazz and trip-hop compilations that the words 'post' and 'club' were invented for. The phone call from Levi's happened soon after.

'Underwater Love' is a fantastic song, or, more specifically, it has a fantastic *feel*: the hypnotically plucked guitar, the funky drum loop, a judicious mix of Brazilian beats and sonar bleeps, wafts of organ and hints of Herbie Hancock, all topped off by Nina's mesmeric vocals. It's the voice that really makes the record, two parts Brazilian Beth Gibbon to one part Björk, sultry yet somehow spooky at the same time. And if that wasn't enough, Nina goes on to use the simple trick that always gets the British going: speaking in another language.

It doesn't matter if you're Jane Birkin going all

> What was the point of the mermaids stealing the Levi's? It's not as if they've got legs.

French with Serge Gainsbourg or John Cleese speaking Russian to seduce Jamie Lee Curtis in *A Fish Called Wanda*, a little bit of something foreign can work wonders. Nina effortlessly switches between singing and speaking Portuguese and English, all drawing the listener in. If only everyone could translate this well. Trawling the Internet for information on Smoke City, one search engine mangled a German article about the band as follows: 'Smoke Town Centre, those of "Underwater Love", the song from the Levi's advertisement with the type, that from the boat tilts and the nixen. Oh so, those.' Quite.

More Little Mermaid than big splash, Smoke City's chart career sank after this single, though they did record two extremely well-received albums before disbanding, *Flying Away* and *Heroes of Nature*. Nina's bewitching vocals, meanwhile, remain much in demand. She has sung with, among others, Nitin Sawhney, Robert Miles, Bebel Gilberto and Arkestra One.

There's one thing I don't understand, though. What was the point of the mermaids stealing the sailor's Levi's? I mean, it's not as if any of them have got legs.

Listen Here   *Rebirth of Cool, Volume Six* (4th and Broadway, 1996). Where it all began.

Listen On   *Flying Away* – Smoke City (Jive, 2001). They may have only one hit, but this album shows they had more than one song.

Listen Further   *Dummy* – Portishead (Go, 1994). Despite the inevitable dinner-party overdose, this is still a great record.

Ooh La La
The Wiseguys
No. 2 June 1999

The Frog Chorus for the big beat generation

It must have been a great day at Budweiser's advertising agency. 'Hey guys, how about this? There's this frog in a swamp, right, and he goes "Bud". Then we get another one and he goes "Wise". And then we get a third one, and goes, er . . . "Er"! Put 'em together, and what have you got? Bud. Wise. Er. It's like, subliminal. But here's the best bit: they hitch a ride on the back of a crocodile, go into a bar and order themselves a drink.' 'Jimmy, that's genius. All we need now is some music . . .'

In the late 1990s Budweiser, the self-styled 'King of Beers', saw what Levi's had done and decided they'd like a piece of that too please. Enter the Wiseguys, a British big beat duo who by the late 1990s had become one Wiseguy, Theo Keating, also known as D J Touché. Keating chose his moniker because he was a big fan of the classic A-Ha single 'Touchy!' and would end his set with it every night. Actually, that's a lie, he decided on the name in fact as a big fan of the cartoon

Advertising at its most postmodern, or popular culture disappearing up its own backside?

musketeer Touché Turtle. Actually, that's a lie too. I've no idea why he's called Touché at all. Let's move on.

Anyway, Theo has always been a big fan of hip-hop, and this fed into his music, giving his choons a bit more of a kick than his rivals'. His big beat* credentials are impeccable: he played the Boutique in Brighton and Fabric in London; he did Manumission in Ibiza with Fatboy Slim. He toured the world with the Propellerheads. In June 1998 Wall of Sound released 'Ooh La La', the first single from Theo's album *The Antidote*. It went the same way as his 1994 EP, the gone and frankly forgotten 'Ladies Say Ow!'.** But one year and several beer commercials later 'Ooh La La' was rereleased and leapfrogged its way to number 2.

Pay attention, here comes the irony part. The title and main refrain for this advert-cum-chart-hit is, in fact, a sample from another, earlier advert. 'Ooh La La, Sasson' was the catchphrase for then trendy American jeans Sasson, who along with Jordache were *the* label to have on your butt as you mooched around downtown Stateside in summer 1981. The original advert was penned by songwriter Ellie Greenwich, who co-wrote such hits as 'Da Doo Ron Ron' and 'Do Wah Diddy' and (thanks for this, Ellie) discovered Neil Diamond. So successful was the advert that Ellie was put forward for a Clio (the advert award, not the car). If you would like to pause at this point to consider the heady implications of all of this, whether the use of 'Ooh La La' is advertising at its most piquantly postmodern or just popular culture disappearing up its own backside, please feel free to do so.

As for the (bud)Wise(er)guys, the follow-up single 'Start The Commotion' sadly did nothing of the sort. Big beat became small beer, and Theo became 'Touché' full time. Rumours of him teaming up with DJ Dum Dum are sadly completely fabricated, though in 2003 he was offered the next best thing: to master-mind the solo career of former S Club 7 popster Tina Barrett – the one who wasn't Rachel, or Hannah, or the one who could sing.

Listen Here *The Best TV Ads . . . Ever!* (Virgin/EMI, 2000). In between the one from the Caffreys ad and the one for Carling Premier.

Listen On *The Antidote* (Wall of Sound, 1998). The album with 'ooh', 'la' and 'la' again.

Listen Further *Decksandrumsandrockandroll* – the Propellerheads (Wall of Sound, 1998). As big as big beat gets.

* Big beat (n.) A popular form of dance music from the late 1990s, so called because its 'beat' was extremely 'big'.
** And that *is* true, in case you're doubting me.

Make Luv Room 5 featuring Oliver Cheatham

No. 1 2003

He likes to party. Well. Everybody does

A man walks into a bar. This may sound like the start of a joke, indeed it is one word short of being one of the world's shortest jokes,* but here the last laugh is with him. A tall, gangly, moderate-looking guy called Tom (it could have been me), he is sat there sipping his drink when the jukebox starts up some funky disco beat. Suddenly Tom is off his stool and strutting his stuff, kind of John Travolta meets Hofmeister Follow the Bear (less likely to be me). Before he knows it, and to the jealous stares of his fellow drinkers, two saucy females are up and dancing with him (now it's definitely not me). And all because the ladies love Lynx Pulse.

Following the success of such brands as Gravity, Africa, Dimension, Phoenix and Voodoo,** in 2003 Lynx launched Pulse, the world's first-ever vegetarian deodorant. Its essence, according to the website, is 'spontaneous, uninhibited dance, something that women find irresistible'. Speaking from personal experience, whenever I dance in a spontaneous and uninhibited fashion, women are quite capable of controlling themselves, but maybe that's what you get for using Slazenger Sport. The website goes on to claim that eight million men use a Lynx deodorant 'at least once a week'. Sometimes, less is pwoar.

The soundtrack to this spraying seduction comes from Room 5, also know as Belgian DJ Junior Jack, with vocals from Oliver Cheatham, a sort of poor man's Errol Brown. Cheatham had a blink-and-you'll-miss-it hit in 1983, the number 38 'smash' 'Get Down Saturday Night', which with music's great art for reinvention at some point stopped being a scraping-the-forty failure and started being talked up as a 'lost disco classic'. Room 5 sampled 'Get Down' into 'Make Luv', and after an underground hit in Belgium, Oliver got the call to rerecord the vocals for the release proper. The Lynx effect was soon apparent, and 'Make Luv' hit the number 1 spot for four weeks.

Though Oliver is well into his funky fifties, he still 'likes to party'. It's good to see that he can still 'make luv', even if he can't spell it. He's clearly a smarter guy than me, because not only can he 'make luv' but at the same time he can also 'listen to the music'. Be careful: while women may be clever enough to do more than one activity at once, men's one-track minds do not normally allow for such multitasking. Listening to the music and simultaneously 'luvving' can lead to shouts of 'Oh Kylie!' at inappropriate moments.

This dual theme was continued in the Room 5/Cheatham follow-up, 'Music And You', but this time the can was empty and the single 'got down' in a different way from its predecessor. Still, maybe a

> Well into his funky fifties, Oliver can still 'make luv', even if he can't spell it.

* The only word missing is the punchline. Ouch.
** The bizarre thing is, I didn't make any of those up.

precedent has been set: a hip-hop version of the theme from Old Spice, anyone?

Listen Here   *Music and You* – Room 5 (Positive, 2003). Four out of the ten songs include the word 'u', though interestingly not the title track.

Listen On   'Get Down Saturday Night' – Oliver Cheatham featuring Jocelyn Brown (Hallmark, 2003). The lost classic.

Listen Further   *The Best of Linx* (Disky, 1996). Classic eighties pop duo with David Grant on vocals. Best moment, of course, the top-ten hit 'Intuition'.

Just say no

The worst five rap performances of all time

John Barnes
for 'World In Motion'

Mmoloki Chrystie
for 'Just Say No'

John Barnes
for 'Anfield Rap'

Victoria Aitken
on that telly programme about being posh and stupid

Duran Duran
for their cover of Public Enemy's '911 Is A Joke'

8 Too Much Too Young
– Child Star Hits

Children should be seen and not heard. Whoever came up with that may well have been listening to some of the following songs. Just thinking about putting the words 'child' and 'star' together brings up a little nausea in my stomach. The words 'precocious' and 'brats' also spring to mind. How can someone be allowed on *Top of the Pops* when they have no concept of what such an honour means?

Child stars fall roughly into two camps. They are either all pure and innocent – think various school choirs or Aled Jones – which is all a little nauseating. Or they are dressed up like adults singing about things they don't understand, which is all a bit paedo-friendly. And if that wasn't a bad enough base from which to start, their chart careers are hampered by a further in-built difficulty: they grow up.

It's not just in music, of course, where child stars suffer. Macaulay Culkin is just one of many young actors facing the rest of their acting career with a cute kid image to shift. But whichever field the success is in, the result is the same: cuteness will only get you so far . . .

There's No One Quite Like Grandma
St Winifred's School Choir
No. 1 1980

An a-choir-ed taste

St Winifred's Roman Catholic Primary School in Heaton Mersey, Stockport, may bob up and down those school league tables, but in terms of chart supremacy their position is unsurpassed. You might groan at the memory, you might cringe as the song rolls away inside your mind, but credit where credit is due: how many times has your old school got to number 1?

In 1978 the choir got its first taste of the rock and roll lifestyle when they sang on Brian and Michael's Lowry-inspired number 1 'Matchstalk Men And Matchstalk Cats And Dogs'. But rather than enjoying a triumphant appearance on *Top of the Pops*, difficulties with union clearances (well, it *was* the seventies) saw the choir banned from appearing and their place taken by a load of London stage-school replacements. Not to be defeated, the choir went 'solo' and, guided by choir leader Terri Foley, released this saccharine hit.

I wonder how many grandmas got this record for Christmas in 1980. I wonder how many times she had to open the wrapping paper and do that forced smile of surprise (ever so difficult with her dentures), holding the grin as little Jimmy insisted it be played imme-

diately. Sweeter than a Werther's Original, 'There's No One Quite Like Grandma' is another example of that most deadly of twin-pronged chart attacks, the assault of the six- and sixty-six-year-old brigade, the 666 formula: children too young to know better, grandparents who've lost their taste along with their marbles. And just in case grandma is being bathed in too much of a warm glow by her loving grandchildren, the song does have an oft-overlooked sting in the tail. Verses two and four see the choir looking into the future, a time when they're 'older' and, by a mixture of implication and the use of the past tense, a time when grandma is no longer around. That's got to hurt: one minute grandma has a bit of a cough, the next they're already preparing for life without the old dear. And suddenly, too, the line about thanking grandma for helping the grandchild 'on their way' is all a little loaded: if you ever need me to do the same for you, little Jenny is saying with a wink, you know where I am.

So what was it like being a member of St Winifred's choir? In two words, hard work. There were auditions, there were three rehearsals a week, and it was all taken quite seriously. The choir had been going since the early 1970s and had already sung and recorded a lot by the time 'Grandma' was a hit. It was, according to choir member Tara Daynes, far from their best song: covers of Abba, Buddy Holly and the Carpenters made up the rest of their set. But 'Grandma' was the hit, and Tara remembers a group of choir members sneaking off to listen to the chart on the radio. The whole gamut of television appearances followed: *Top of the Pops* alongside the Boomtown Rats, Dana's *Wake Up Sunday*, *Jim'll Fix It* (yes, someone really *did* write in asking if they could sing with the choir) and

Tiswas – some teacher with a glint in her eye agreed to allow the choir to be, I think the word is flanged, with blue gunge.

So how much did the choir make from their number 1 hit single? Tara got a fifty-pence book token. The money, they were told, was to be pumped into the school, though Tara didn't notice any huge changes while she was there. And despite not having another hit single, they remain the school choir of choice. Rival choir the Ramblers (the Abbey Hey Junior School) peaked at number 11 with 'The Sparrow'; in March 1981 the children of Tansley School could reach only number 27 with their not-remotely-bandwagon single, 'My Mum Is One In A Million'. For St Winifred's, the gigs kept coming: when the Pope visited Britain, they recorded the official UK song; in 1986 they sang backing vocals on the Housemartins' second album, _The People Who Grinned Themselves to Death_; and in 1993 they did similar duties on 'One Voice', a top-twenty hit for Bill 'Jack Duckworth' Tarney.

The _Coronation Street_ connection, meanwhile, continues. By far the most prominent member of the choir is Sally Lindsay, a firm Corrie favourite for several years as barmaid Shelley Unwin. By contrast, then lisping lead vocalist Dawn Ralph worked as a proofreader after leaving school, before marrying and settling down in the Stockport area. Tara, now somewhat more gothically minded, has come through the other side. To start with, especially when starting secondary school, it was all a bit embarrassing and the jokes would come flying in. Then, at about university time, things started to turn. The whole experience became acceptable and now, finally, is rather cool.

Listen Here   _Chegger's Choice_ – Various Artists (Global, 1999). The filling in a Rolf Harris and Clive Dunn sandwich.

Listen On   _The People Who Grinned Themselves to Death_ – the Housemartins (Polydor, 1992). St Winifred's and Fatboy Slim on the same record?

Listen Further   'The Sparrow' – the Ramblers (from Abbey Hey Junior School) (Decca, 1979). Close, but no 'Grandma'.

Just Say No
Grange Hill Cast
No. 5 1985

Ok. No

If a common moan among drug aficionados is that their substances ain't what they used to be (cue long and boring story about some half-remembered holiday in Morocco), then anti-drug campaigns by contrast have gone in the opposite direction. In the 1980s there was some really bad shit going around. First, there was the 'Heroin screws you up' campaign (nice sledgehammer shoutline there), with some cocky bloke telling us 'I can handle it' while his body slowly warped into Keith Richards after a night on the town. And then there was this.

The 'Just Say No' campaign, with its simplistic moralising, black-and-whiting of the issues and handy-to-remember slogan originated (where else?)

in the United States, with Nancy Reagan its cheer-leader. In the UK it piggybacked perhaps *Grange Hill*'s finest hour: the drug addiction of Zammo McGuire. A gritty, urban and compelling storyline (especially compared to other drama offerings of the time such as, say, *Heidi*), it was the school soap at its best: annoying the parents, engrossing the children and getting some sort of point across at the same time.

But if only someone had said no to this accompanying single. Sure, it raised money for charity (the acronymically challenged SCODA – don't people think these things through?), but in three and a bit minutes it unstitched all the subtlety and credibility the series had created. Compare it to another contemporary anti-drugs song – 'White Lines' by Grandmaster Flash. There's just no competition. While Flashy was shouting 'free!' and 'rock!', the *Grange Hill* song went 'slap!' and 'bass!' chunking it along with some third-rate Mark King on the four-string. There's a sax solo that goes on long enough to make the most anti-drugs person think about jacking up, if only to get through the rest of the song.

And nestled in among all those keyboard 'stabs' are the cast themselves. Put it this way, if they turned up for a *Pop Idol* audition, I'm not sure they'd get into the final fifty. And if their limited singing ability wasn't enough, the lyrics don't exactly give them much to work with. You don't have to swan around like some sort of 'star' apparently – though the cast did their best by indulging in that charity single staple, the holding the headphones to the ear routine in the video. Instead, you can be a 'hero' by simply being 'who you are'. It's almost brilliant in its blandness. Things only get marginally more interesting with the middle eight rap, 'by courtesy of Mmoloki Chrystie',

according to the record sleeve. Mmoloki, who played Kevin Baylon, clearly fancies himself as a bit of an MC, which is a shame as he ended up in the top five worst raps of all time (see page 89).

Mmoloki delivers what is meant to be a wake-up call, which after the preceding sax solo is perhaps no bad thing. Addressing someone with 'no need' to dabble, Mmoloki describes how the 'taste' turned to 'craving' and then to 'greed'. And what does Mmoloki say to any such person who wants to be his friend? I'll give you a clue. One word. Two letters. Rhymes with woe.

The *Grange Hill* cast were rewarded for their sterling efforts with a visit to the White House. According to Erkan Mustafa, who played Roland, some of the cast were not exactly saying 'no' at the time. And would it be churlish to mention John Alford (Bobbie), later done for dealing cocaine? You're right, it probably is. As for Lee MacDonald, who played Zammo, he acted like a 'hero', had 'faith in himself' and saw his 'dreams' come true. Well, as long as his dreams were all about running a key-cutting shop in central London.

> The sax solo goes on long enough to make the most anti-drugs person think about jacking up.

Listen Here 'Just Say No' (BBC, 1985). The 12-inch features an extended rap. Just don't.

Listen On *Schooldisco.com – The Album* (Columbia, 2001). It's got the theme from *Grange Hill* on it.

Listen Further 'White Lines (Don't Don't Do It)' – Grandmaster Flash and Melle Mel (Sugarhill, 1983). The correct way to do a drugs song.

Walking In The Air
Aled Jones
No. 5 1985

There's no business like snow business

In the early 1980s, in the days before global warming turned the festive season soggy, sometimes it used to snow. When this happened, little boys would rush out all excited, and build themselves a snowman. And if the little boy was incredibly lucky, either that or he found himself part of an animated version of a Raymond Briggs story, the snowman would come to life and take him for a flying trip over snow-capped hills: walking, as it were, in the air. Of course, the snowman would melt and the boy would be incredibly sad, but hey, that's life. And it's a barrel-load happier than what normally happens in *EastEnders* on Christmas Day.

The Snowman was first shown on Channel 4 in 1982, and like some sort of cartoon *Great Escape*, quickly became a Christmas television staple. In 1985 Aled Jones took 'Walking In The Air' into the charts. It wasn't his first single – his version of 'Memory', the theme from the Andrew Lloyd Webber musical *Cats*, had stalled in the summer at number 42. This time,

though, the Anglesey-born soprano hit paydirt. With a badly judged pink bow tie, hair cut by his mum and a voice that, frankly, made him sound a bit of a girl, Aled was not exactly Ozzy Osbourne, but that didn't stop him hitting number 5.

Sharper readers may have noticed a discrepancy of three years between the first showing of *The Snowman* and Aled's hit record. Had Channel 4 cottoned on to Jones the Voice before anyone else? Er, not exactly. The interesting thing is that Aled never actually sang on *The Snowman*. That honour went to another young chorister, Peter Auty, who was paid a mere £300 for his version. If that wasn't bad enough – does anyone feel like a conspiracy theory coming along? – in the rush to finish the film on time, his name was left off the credits. Don't get too upset on the poor lad's behalf just yet – there's more to come. While Aled was getting all the glory and doing *Top of the Pops* and snorting fat lines of coke off the tanned thighs of a bevy of supermodels (I'm guessing a little here), Peter's own version of the song – the real thing – peaked at a miserable 42. Interviewed on the twentieth anniversary of the film (when his name was finally added to the credits), Peter claimed that he wasn't that bothered at the time, though his parents were 'quite miffed'.

> Aled never actually sang on *The Snowman*: that honour went to another young chorister.

So what happened to Aled? Well, not to put too fine a point on it, his balls dropped. Told not to sing for five years, Aled had that nervous wait to see whether his soprano warblings would mature into something more fruity. Sadly, they didn't. Actually, I'm joking; they matured very nicely indeed by all accounts, and in 2002 Aled finally released a new album, *Aled*, followed by 2003's *Higher* – so called, Aled slightly *Spinal Tap*-ishly explains, because it is four notes higher than the last one. With programmes on BBC Radio Wales and Classic FM, not to mention presenting *Songs of Praise*, Aled is a busy bunny. He's also married and has a daughter called Emilia. Aw. And what does he think now of his one hit single? 'Sheer class, man. My vocal pissed all over the other guy's: anyone who says otherwise I'll have them.' Ok, so I made that bit up as well. 'I was just a little kid who had a decent voice and was in the right place at the right time,' he actually told a BBC web chat.

Listen Here   *The Best Christmas Album in the World . . . Ever!* (Virgin, 2002). It wouldn't be the 'best' without it.

Listen On   *Higher* (UCJ, 2003). Given the way Aled's voice has gone, 'lower' might have been a more appropriate title.

Listen Further   'Walking In The Air' – Peter Auty and the Sinfonia of London (Stiff, 1985). All the jokes about choirboys could have been his.

It's 'Orrible Being In Love (When You're 8½) Claire and Friends
No. 13 1986

'Eally 'ather 'errible

Saturday-morning children's television has had its highlights and lowlights over the years. For every Ant and Dec, there has been a Mark Curry. For every *Tiswas*, there has been an *It's Wicked*. For every Posh Paws there has been a Gordon the Gopher. And while the programmes have offered their fair selection of great pop moments – the phone-in on *Going Live!* when the caller asked Five Star just why they were so fucking crap – they have also dealt the charts a comparable number of clangers.

The missing link between Noel Edmonds's *Swap Shop* and Phillip Schofield's *Going Live!*, *Saturday Superstore* matched the commercial mood of the eighties by being a TV show spuriously posing as a shop. Mike Read, Radio One Deej and big fan of Frankie Goes to Hollywood, was general manager, Sarah Greene was the Saturday girl, Keith Chegwin the delivery boy and David 'They laughed at Jesus too' Icke ran the 'sports department'. The comedy puppet

> An unappealing mix of Oliver Twist-style dropped aitches with a world-weariness about all things smoochsome.

character was a crow called Crow, and the not-remotely-cheap-TV slot was a talent competition called The Saturday Superstore Search for a Superstar.

As such, and I don't think I'm being unnecessarily cruel here, that project was a failure. A more accurate title might have been The Saturday Superstore Search for an Icky Child Star Whose Brief Foray into the Charts was Promptly Forgotten. Admittedly not quite as snappy a title. First up was three-year-old Natalie Casey, whose rendition of 'Chick, Chick Chicken' did not exactly lay her a golden egg (number 72, 1984), though she did go on to star many years later in *Hollyoaks* and *Two Pints of Lager and a Packet of Crisps*.

Two years later eight-and-a-half-year-old Claire Usher did better, going all the way to number 13 with 'It's 'Orrible Being In Love (When You're 8½)'. Claire was a pupil at a certain St Winifred's School in Stockport, and the guiding hands of Kevin 'Brian' Parrot and Michael 'Michael' Coleman of Brian and Michael fame were involved. A winsome little ditty about youthful romance, the song combines an unappealing mix of Oliver Twist-style dropped aitches with a world-weariness about all things smoochsome. Quite what being eight and a half has to do with it I'm not completely sure. Except that it rhymed with 'scarf'.

Maybe by the time she got to nine everything was sorted out. Which is more than can be said about her pop career. The follow-up, 'My Boy Lollipop', made no one's heart go 'sugardypop'. Claire went on to focus on her first love, dancing, and would go on to become a *Riverdance* regular.

Listen Here 'It's 'Orrible Being in Love (When You're 8½)' (BBC, 1986). The single.

Listen On 'Big Sister', the B-side to the single. Well, at least there's no letter dropped.

Listen Further 'Chick Chick Chicken' – Natalie Casey (Polydor, 1984). Another winner. Another career launched.

Hey Matthew
Karel Fialka
No. 9 1987

Pop meets *Points of View*
However awful you might have thought your parents were as a child, just imagine how much worse life would be if they were pop stars. If Michael Jackson was your dad, one minute you might be happily minding your own business, the next you're being dangled out over a hotel balcony. If Bill Wyman was your father, your wedding would be somewhat complicated by the fact that your dad has already married the bride's daughter. And then there's the sniggers in the playground as the full horror of what your parents have called you is revealed: Peaches, Satchel, Zowie Bowie. So Matthew Fialka, whose pop father Karel sat him down in front of the telly, must have felt he had escaped such treatment.

How wrong he could be.

Karel had a Czechoslovak mother, a Scottish father, and thus was born, as logic would dictate, in Bengal, India. In the late 1970s and early 1980s he attempted to wow the UK as a poet-cum-street performer. It didn't quite come off: his debut album, a new wavey collection called *Still Life*, which contained the single 'The Eyes Have It', was well received but didn't quite set the charts alight. For reasons not quite clear, his second album, *Human Animal*, was not released until 1988, a gestation period that made the Stone Roses seem like fast workers.

While dad was slaving away on that difficult second album, Matthew was watching television. And as he was doing so, Karel started to worry: just what effect were all these programmes having on his son's young and impressionable mind? All those bombs and guns and violence. The 'cat' and indeed the 'mouse'. The 'beauty', the 'beast', the 'famine', the 'feast', the press on a 'witch hunt', the politician doing a 'publicity stunt'. Was Matthew becoming addled before his father's very eyes?

So which programmes was Matthew watching? We are fortunate to have a list of them, which Matthew intones in a Haley Joel '*Sixth Sense*' Osment 'I see dead people'-style voice, in between his father's long list of Mary Whitehouse concerns. In alphabetical order, Matthew watches the following: *Airwolf*, *The A-Team*, *Blue Thunder*, *Daffy Duck*, *Dallas*, *Dynasty*, *The Dukes of Hazzard*, *He-Man*, *Rambo*, *Road Runner*, *Silver Hawks* and *Tom and Jerry*. Now certainly, if that was young Matthew's only knowledge of the outside world, problems could arise. He'd be under the impression that dead people can come back to life (Bobby in *Dallas*). He'd have the mistaken belief that in order to get into a car, one had to jump in through the window (*The Dukes of Hazzard*). And most disturbingly of all, he would be under the illusion that with a couple of spare hours, a blow torch and an escaped patient

from a mental hospital for help, a watering can, a tin of beans and a pair of garden shears could be turned into an armoured tank (*Tom and Jerry*. I'm joking, of course, I mean *The A-Team*.)

If Karel is worried about Matthew's addled mind, the answer is perfectly simple. Switch the television off. Communicate with your son. Take him to the zoo or something. Put the second album on hold for an afternoon – I mean, it's been seven years already, what difference is another couple of hours going to make? Karel worries about what his son is going to end up as – and Matthew tells him: a soldier, a street fighter, a policeman, a cowboy, a train driver, a fireman, a pilot. All I can say is Karel, relax: no one has a clue what they want to be when they are eight. I wanted to be a professional footballer, and here I am writing about one hit wonders. I got over it. Matthew hasn't ended up, as far as I'm aware, as a mass murderer or a child killer or something. So maybe watching television isn't *all* bad, after all.

> Switch the television off. Communicate with your son. Take him to the zoo or something.

Listen Here   *Human Animal* (IRS, 1988). Tonight, Matthew, I'm going to record a quirky pop album.

Listen On   *Still Life* (Blueprint, 1980). Tonight, Matthew, I'm going to do things a little more new wave.

Listen Further   *Hey Jude* – the Beatles (Apple, 1968). A song for another pop star's son, this time the young Mr Lennon.

I'd Rather Jack
The Reynolds Girls
No. 8 1989

A bit of an albatross

In the late 1980s, a decade before *Pop Idol*, when Simon Cowell was nothing more than Sinitta's boyfriend (and *so* macho), young pop wannabes had to use their own initiative to get themselves noticed. For two young Liverpool sisters, Aisling (sixteen, A levels) and Linda (seventeen, hairdresser), their plan of campaign consisted of pestering Pete Waterman when he came to Liverpool to record his weekly radio show. And you know what? It worked.

In the Stock, Aitken and Waterman scheme of things the Reynolds Girls were definitely second division: if there was Kylie and Jason and Rick Astley at the top, with Sonia and Mel and Kim somewhere behind, then Linda and Aisling were bumping along the bottom with Princess, Big Fun and Halo James. No great lookers (like Kylie), no great vocals (like Rick), no Aussie soap stardom (like Jason), their appeal boiled down to their straight-talking, telling-it-like-it-is lyrics – a stirring clarion call to the then youth of today. And what was getting the Reynolds Girls' goat? The poll tax? Mass unemployment? Um, not exactly.

'I'd Rather Jack' is a musical manifesto for a new sort of radio station, one that the kids actually want to listen to, and in no way whatsoever a dig by Stock, Aitken and Waterman at radio stations that won't play their records because they value their eardrums.

Their argument, distilled concisely in the song's chorus, is that given a choice between Fleetwood Mac and 'Jack', a then popular form of asinine dance music, the girls would go for Jack every time. Or, failing that, Yazz. What they wouldn't put up with, however, were golden oldies. Along with Fleetwood Mac, also singled out for their scathing scouse criticism were the Rolling Stones, Pink Floyd, Dire Straits and heavy metal. And it was more than just the music: they were also unhappy that DJs were, by some curious mathematical twist, always twice as old as them, and thus depriving their 'generation' of their own 'identity'.

Let's be fair, briefly, to Linda and Aisling. First, Fleetwood Mac being past it: if you were growing up in the late 1980s and all you knew of the band was Mick Fleetwood's car-crash presentation of the Brits with Sam Fox, this might be considered a reasonable deduction. Second, the bit about the DJs being too old: again, the Girls got it about right – the Radio One clearout of the Smashy and Nicey generation was just around the corner. And third, not wanting to hear Dire Straits on the radio: who would argue with that?

In every other way, though, the Reynolds Girls have ended up on the wrong side of history. Whither Jack and Yazz? Whither Stock, Aitken and Waterman? Whither the girls' bouffant hair, denim jacket and stripy top combo, and their funny hitching-a-ride dance routine? How Fleetwood Mac, the Stones and the Floyd must sleep easier at night. And what happened to the Reynolds Girls? What happened was, after this one hit single, the puppets – poppets? – fell out with the puppet masters. 'I don't believe anyone should consider themselves bigger than the public that buys their records,' Pete Waterman rather cattily told *Number One* magazine. 'We are one big happy family,' he added, 'and they didn't fit in.' And though the girls put up a creditable show of bravado – 'nobody will get rid of the Reynolds Girls that easily' – life was ever so chilly outside the Hit Factory tent. Managed by their dad (never a good sign), released on their own record label (what more can I say?), the follow-up single 'Get Real' saw the nation say just that to the duo.

Listen Here   'I'd Rather Jack' (PWL, 1989). A one-off single from the Hit Factory production line.

Listen On   The B-side to 'I'd Rather Jack' is the must-have-taken-them-hours 'I'd Rather Jack (Instrumental)'. It really is just the single without any words.

Listen Further   *Say You Will* – Fleetwood Mac (WEA, 2003). Fifteen years on, the band continues to give the Reynolds Girls two fingers and go from strength to strength.

Trouble Shampoo
No. 11 1994

They invented girl power, you know

At the wild-child end of this chapter are two young things from Plumstead, East London, Jacqui Blake and Carrie Askew whose brief foray into the pop world was all about, like, staying up, you know, really late. And you know what? They're going to be in such trouble when they get home, but *they don't care*!

Like Neil Tennant from the Pet Shop Boys, Carrie and Jacqui started out in music journalism before becoming musicians themselves. While Neil worked his way up the hallowed pages of *Smash Hits*, Carrie and Jacqui ran *Last Exit*, a fanzine dedicated to the Manic Street Preachers. Deciding to prove themselves 4 Real, the girls got a little help from Bob Stanley of Saint Etienne and released their debut single, 'Blisters And Bruises', which *Melody Maker* made their single of the week. This was followed by 'Bouffant Headbutt', described by *Select* magazine as 'rambunctious', before this third single gave them the breakthrough they were looking for.

All this indie point-scoring is important because Shampoo were no industry-conceived gimmick. Their bratty, brassy, Julie Burchill meets the Reynolds Girls persona was very much themselves and it didn't take long for their attitude to divide opinions. Those music journalists who hated rock bands who took themselves seriously, and liked all things pop and bubblegum and ephemeral, thought they epitomised everything they stood for. Others just didn't get them at all. 'Trouble', with its infectiously irritating chorus ('Uh-oh!') and shouty-shouty verses, not to mention the Manics PR people working their magic behind the scenes, was expected to be an absolute smash. But however much the girls stamped their feet, the door to the top ten stayed shut. The line in the chorus about bubbles being burst was proving ominously prescient.

Telling lyrics continued on the stalled follow-up, 'Viva La Megababes', with the girls asking whether

> However much the girls stamped their feet, the door to the top ten stayed shut.

anyone actually gave 'a fuck'. The answer, it was turning out, was not many. All of which was a shame, because their debut album, *We Are Shampoo*, contained some sparky and original songs. Will Coldplay ever write a song like 'Shiny Black Taxi Cab', all about vomiting on your way home from the boozer? Would Travis come up with something like 'Dirty Old Love Song', which discusses just how bad Whitney Houston and Mariah Carey are? I think not.

In July 1996 Shampoo released a new single – 'Girl Power'. Their definition of this consisted of staying out late and getting drunk, looking 'sweet' but being 'sour', partying, driving the neighbours mad and doing things, if they so wanted, that made your hair curl. With the music press enjoying a Shampoo backlash, no one was interested. Not only did it once again stall in the twenties, but a week later, a new five-piece called the Spice Girls released their debut single 'Wannabe'. The rest, as they say, is pop history.

But as much as both the charts and the music press had turned their backs on Carrie and Jacqui, there was one place where their shouting and moaning and their love of bubblegum pop felt right at home. Yes, if ever there was a band for whom the words 'big', 'in' and 'Japan' were invented, it is Shampoo. In the same way that Shed Seven kept Take That off the number 1 spot in Thailand, so 'We Are Shampoo' sold over a million copies in the land of the rising sun. Even the follow-up album did a healthy 500,000. The girls couldn't go out in the street without being mobbed, and the money rolled in. So successful were they that one newspaper survey placed them as the twenty-third highest-earning women in the UK. The only people the girls might be in trouble with now, I suppose, is the taxman.

Listen Here *We are Shampoo* (Food, 1994). The wash-and-go debut album.

Listen On 'Girl Power' (Food, 1996). They were ahead of the Spice Girls. The Spice Girls quickly left them behind.

Listen Further *Generation Terrorists* – Manic Street Preachers (Sony, 1992). The band the girls went gaga about in the first place.

Not just Men at Work

Some other Australian one hit wonders

'Live It Up'
Mental As Anything

'Beds Are Burning'
Midnight Oil

'Chains'
Tina Arena

'Waiting For A Train'
Flash and the Pan

'Love Is In The Air'
John Paul Young

'You're The Voice'
John Farnham

9 Reach for the Remote
– TV and Film Hits

Television and film have gone different ways in recent years. Television, *the* medium of the twentieth century, has gone from a small smattering of terrestrial channels into a multi-option world of satellite and cable and digital and Freeview. The result has been the decline of 'event' TV, those television moments when the whole nation is glued to the same programme, moments that become a shared part of the national experience. Like the fragmenting radio audience, its influence on producing, say, one hit wonders, I think, has somewhat waned.

By contrast, cinema-going in a land of multiplexes has continued to grow at a great rate, the big films getting bigger, the theme tunes getting all the more important. It's depressing to think of music as subordinate to another medium, but in this case it is, the spin-off single little more than a marketing tool for a greater Hollywood good. For unknown acts, again, it is the problem of exposure: the sudden arrival of the sort of coverage that their record company would never give them. The result is a lot of pressure and a difficult question: where do you go from there?

I Wanna Be A Winner
Brown Sauce
No. 15 1981

Noel, Maggie and Cheggers played pop

If you weren't watching St Winifred's School Choir get flanged on *Tiswas*, your early-eighties Saturday mornings were most likely spent with Noel Edmonds, Keith Chegwin, Maggie Philbin, John Craven and a purple dinosaur called Posh Paws. *Multi-Coloured Swap Shop* was the children's show based on, um, swapping things. If you'd been given a space hopper for Christmas but really fancied a slinky, this was the programme for you!

As well as filling up Saturday mornings, Noel and the team branched out with the annual Swap Shop Star awards, a glitzy ceremony where the stars gathered to see if they'd won an 'Eric' in such exciting categories as Favourite Expert. The show contained a musical interlude: I'm not saying it was the perfect time to nip to the bog, but one year it was Keith Chegwin on vocals, then it was Keith Chegwin and Maggie Philbin duetting, and on a third occasion it was Keith and Maggie *and* Noel. Appearing as the band Brown Sauce (because that's what Noel liked with his fish and chips), the trio also called upon the dubious talents of Scottish songwriter B. A. Robertson (who had enjoyed hits such as 'Bang Bang' and 'To Be Or Not To Be'). The song he wrote, 'I Wanna Be A Winner', went down so well that this single soon followed.

Now I'm not saying that Brown Sauce didn't hang together as a group, but image-wise each seemed to belong to a different band. Maggie Philbin, in short red dress and Rickenbacker bass, looked like a prototype Bangle. Keith Chegwin, strumming guitar and wearing a dark jacket, black shirt and bright yellow tie, would have been more at home in Showaddywaddy. Noel, banging on a drum in a red striped rugby shirt, was Phil Collins with a lot more hair. As for the song itself, it was all about wanting to win an award, 'a little Oscar' said Eric. Anything else didn't come close, whether it was hosting *Nationwide* with Frank Bough or riding like Willie Carson. It's fairly cheesy pop rock 'n' roll of the Dire Straits 'Twisting By The Pool' variety, with the only distinguishing feature being an impressive attempt to rhyme Ronald Reagan with Kevin Keegan.

> Keith Chegwin continued with the sauce, but i a slightly different way.

Backed by B. A. Robertson's 'Hello Hello' *Swap Shop* theme, 'I Wanna Be A Winner' eventually rose to number 15 in the charts. There was a failed follow-up single, 'Spring Has Sprung', but with Noel absent the band was renamed the Saucers. Noel went on to *The Late Late Breakfast Show* and later Mr Blobby; Maggie found her way on to *Tomorrow's World*; and Keith, well, he continued with the sauce, but in a slightly different way.

Listen Here   'I Wanna Be A Winner' (BBC, 1981). The single that didn't win any awards.

Listen On   'Hello Hello', the *Swap Shop* theme on the B-side.

Listen Further 'Bang Bang' – B. A. Robertson (Asylum, 1979). Before Baracas, there was only one B. A. in town.

Footloose
Kenny Loggins
No. 6 1984

Everybody did indeed cut

I blame *Grease*. Without the rip-roaring success of the late-seventies mid-fifties musical, we might never have suffered the subsequent glut of eighties dance films. Some stayed true to *Grease*'s retro formula – the sniggeringly titled *Shag*, the gruesome twosome of dirty dancers Patrick Swayze and Jennifer Grey. (Is it just me, or was he just a little too *old* for her?) Others just were weird. *Flashdance* featured Jennifer Beals in that famous career move of welder by day, dancer by night. But as barking as this may have been, it didn't come close to the sheer unbelievability that was 1984's *Footloose*.

Imagine you're a film mogul and this guy comes in with the following pitch: so there's this small town, right, in Middle America – just like every other town, staunchly religious, but with one exception: dancing is banned. Now suppose there's this new kid in town, bit of a hot shot, who likes to move his feet. Not only that, but he falls in love with the preacher's daughter. He's going to show the town the power of dance – and he wins because, goddammit, dancing is an American right. If it was me, I'd have shown the guy the door, maybe told him he's been working too hard, perhaps even offered him the phone number of a doctor friend of mine. But not this film mogul: he signs the film off and says yeah, and gets that Kenny Loggins to write the title song.

Kenny Loggins is the sort of soft rock artist that the letters M, O and R were invented for. Recording since the early 1970s, he specialised in ballads and had some pedigree when it came to film soundtracks. The one from *Caddyshack*? That was his. Given the script he had to work with, *Footloose* is not a bad effort – a sort of southern boogie with a gulping guitar line. And hell, at least it's upbeat rather than some soppy smooch-fest.

Kenny's film career was not quite finished. When *Top Gun* turned up, he recorded 'Danger Zone', a hit in the US, though it failed to chart here. Then it all started getting a little weird. In the early 1990s Kenny went all eco-friendly. In 1992 he took part in an experiment singing live to dolphins to see how they would react. (Let me get this straight Kenny, they chattered. They banned dancing?) Then he decided to share his love for his wife Julia with the world. Together they wrote the US bestseller *The Unimaginable Life* – a not remotely mawkish mixture of poetry, diary entries and meditations on why their relationship was just so strong.

> The sort of soft rock artist that the letters M, O and R were invented for.

Listen Here *The Hits Album* (WEA, 1984). Original volume of the eighties rival to the *Now* albums.

Listen On *The Essential Kenny Loggins* (Columbia, 2002). I'll leave it to you to decide how essential the theme for *Caddyshack II* really is.

Read Further *The Unimaginable Life* – Kenny and Julia Loggins (Quill, 1998). Kenny and Julia tell you about their love.

Axel F Harold Faltermeyer
No. 2 1985

Music to put bananas up exhaust pipes to

If you ever want a way of measuring just how long ago the eighties was, think of it like this. Imagine, if you will, a time when Eddie Murphy was considered to be funny. It's true. People used to laugh at Eddie Murphy back then. And in all the right places.

All of this is thanks to a triumvirate of early-eighties comedies in which Eddie played pretty much the same character – a brash, cocky motormouth, so quick with the verbal jousting that he was able to distract attention away from the moustache he was wearing under his nose. First up, there was *Trading Places*, in which Eddie did just that with high-flying businessman Dan Aykroyd, Denholm Elliott was rather brilliant, and a private detective on a public telephone delivered perhaps the most perfect 'Fuck off' in cinematic history. Then there was *48 Hours*, in which gang member

Eddie argued the toss with Nick Nolte, the exasperated cop who needs his help (there was a tortuous sequel that felt like it *did* last for forty-eight hours, but that's another story).

With his stock rising, Eddie hit paydirt with *Beverly Hills Cop* – a wisecracking Detroit cop who so much doesn't do things by the book he could have written a book about them. Heading for the Californian hills, in order to uncover the truth behind a murder of a friend, Axel was given two stiff local cops to wind up, taking them (gasp) to strip bars for no particular reason except to bump up the ratings. I haven't got the precise details, but I'm fairly sure he broke the record for the most number of 'fucks' on a film. 'Get the fuck out of here' was his almost camp-sounding catchphrase.

The music for *Beverly Hills Cop* was provided by Harold Faltermeyer, a synthesiser breed of mad scientist, or was it the other way round? A cut-price Casio Jean-Michel Jarre, Harold's polite little ditties were better suited to body-popping or miming being stuck in a box than a fancy light display on the side of a skyscraper. Showing off all the different sounds on his new keyboard, 'Axel F' hasn't really travelled that well through time and indeed, sounds remarkably slight for a major film theme song.

> A casio Jean Michelle Jarre. Harold's ditties were better suited to body-popping or miming being stuck in a box.

If *Beverly Hills Cop* was the moment Eddie Murphy hit the big time, it was also the making of Harold Faltermeyer. for a few years he was the cinematic soundtrack king. *Top Gun*, *Fletch*, *The Running Man*, *Beverly Hills Cop II*, *Fletch Lives* all featured his trademark keyboard sounds. He even won a Grammy for his film music. But as the eighties ended and the charm of synthesiser began to fade, Faltermeyer's star faded too. In 1990 he produced the Pet Shop Boys album *Behaviour* and then, well, I guess someone must have pressed the off switch.

Listen Here *Now That's What I Call Music Volume Five* (Virgin EMI, 1985). The last one with the pig on the front.

Listen On *Harold F* (Universal, 1999). If you give an F, try this best-of compilation.

Watch Further *Beverly Hills Cop Collection* (DVD, 2002). Eddie when he was funny. And when he was less so.

Only Love
Nana Mouskouri
No. 2 1986

The Greek one with the glasses

One of those acts for whom the words 'easy' and 'listening' were invented, Nana Mouskouri fits a Greek-sized hole in an undiscerning record collection between Mantovani and Des O'Connor. Yet curiously for someone with such a long and successful musical career, the only time she got near the British charts was thanks to a novel by one of the champions of modern literature, Judith Krantz.

Born in Crete in 1934, Joanna 'Nana' Mouskouri and her family moved to Athens three years later. It can't have been the greatest place to grow up, what with the German occupation, the Greek civil war and everything, but Nana found solace in singing and a place at the Athens Conservatory of Music. Her talent quickly shone through and her rise to prominence was rapid: a Golden Lion award at the Berlin Film Festival for her soundtrack to a documentary film; an English-language album produced by Quincy '*Thriller*' Jones, not remotely patronisingly called *The Girl From Greece Sings*; an appearance at the 1963 Eurovision Song Contest, representing, er, Luxembourg. There was also a helping hand from Harry 'Day-o!' Belafonte, with whom Nana toured during the 1960s.

A star in all sorts of places, and particularly big in France for some reason, British audiences perhaps know Nana best for her seventies BBC show *Nana and Guests*, which in true Ronseal fashion did exactly what it said on the tin. And though there were best-selling albums – the 1969 *Over and Over* spent over one hundred weeks on the UK chart – the singles market remained immune. Despite her striking image (how many other Greek singers with thick black spectacles can you name?) I guess the record companies thought she just didn't have yoof appeal.

> How many other Greek singers with thick black spectacles can you name?

But then in 1986 help arrived in the form of that sadly missed eighties television phenomenon, the mini-series. *Mistral's Daughter* was based on a Judith Krantz novel and starred Stephanie Powers and Timothy Dalton, the eighties George Lazenby. Stephanie plays a country girl who moves to

Paris to look for love and a modelling career. But Mistral, the artist she falls for (aaw), is more interested in his benefactor (boo), but then a young wealthy American appears (aw) but he's married (boo) and so on. Nana supplied 'Only Love' for the soundtrack – slightly sickly in my opinion, but considering it was the theme tune to a trashy adaptation of an even trashier novel, probably pretty well judged – and that elusive hit record was finally hers.

Nana goes on to sell albums by the bucketload. In 1987 she played a gig at the Olympic Stadium in Athens in front of 100,000 people. She has also done sterling work for UNICEF and as a Greek deputy in the European Parliament. In 1995 she thanked the French for their support over the years by releasing a four-CD collection of her greatest moments. If that sounds eye-watering, spare a tear for the highlight of her 1996 *Nana Latina* album – an easy-listening wet dream duet with Julio Iglesias.

Listen Here *Only Love: The Best of Nana* (Polygram, 1991). Love-ly.

Listen On *Gold: Greatest Hits* (Universal, 2003). No 'Only Love' but a sleeve design that quite breathtakingly rips off the Abba Gold series style. Björn, give your lawyer a ring.

Read Further *Mistral's Daughter* – Judith Krantz (Corgi, 1984). The fiction epic that set the whole thing rolling.

Take My Breath Away (Love Theme From Top Gun) Berlin
No. 1 1986

Ich bin nicht ein Berliner

Chicago. Boston. Berlin. What was it about American rock bands back then and calling themselves after cities? Was there some big musical game of Risk going on that the rest of us were unaware of? At least Berlin chose somewhere out of the United States, to show, presumably, that they were a little bit more cultured, and tap into that whole Lou Reed–David Bowie *Low* vibe thing. But while calling an album *Berlin*, à la Lou Reed, just about makes sense, calling a whole band after it does not. It's too familiar, too well known to work properly.

The interesting thing about Berlin (the band, not the place – you see my point?) is that 'Take My Breath Away', the drippy ballad they recorded for the Tom Cruise movie *Top Gun*, is anything but representative of their style. Berlin were more electro, more pop, an LA Duran Duran, with a line in filth to match Animotion's 'Obsession' or the Divinyls' 'I Touch Myself'. Matching their appalling choice of name, their biggest success pre-*Top Gun* was the equally badly titled 'Sex (I'm A . . .)'. My thoughts

> Terri Nunn appeared to have her hair designed by a badger.

exactly. Lead singer Terri Nunn, who appeared to have had her hair designed by a badger, invited the listener to 'wrap' their legs around hers, and 'ride me'. She went on to announce that she was, among others, a hooker, a slut, a blue movie, a bitch, a slave and 'a little girl'. Tipper Gore must have had a heart attack.

Enter legendary disco producer Giorgio Moroder, the man responsible for both 'I Feel Love' and, um, 'Together In Electric Dreams'. Having worked with Berlin on the band's second album, he gave them the call for the *Top Gun* soundtrack he was working on. 'Take My Breath Away' is his piece of work, and what a piece of work it is: a glossy car advert on vinyl, which, of course, the song was later used on. Its very vacuity summed up the emptiness at the heart of the film it accompanied, if not all those great dogfight sequences which, let's face it, were pretty cool.

Unfortunately, Berlin's career quickly went into tailspin. Follow-up single 'You Don't Know' topped at number 39, and following the band's third album, *Count Three and Play*, the band split up in 1987. Terri went solo for a bit, releasing an album, *Moment of Truth*, in 1991, and then, with a different line-up, reformed Berlin a couple of years ago. Following *Berlin Live: Sacred and Profane* in 2000, 2002 saw the release of *Voyeur*, featuring contributions from former Smashing Pumpkin Billy Corgan.

Listen Here *Top Gun* soundtrack (Sony, 2001).
A veritable feast of one hit wonders: Berlin, Kenny Loggins *and* Harold Faltermeyer.

Listen On *Pleasure Victim* (Geffen, 1996).
The debut album, including 'Sex (I'm A . . .)'.

Listen Further *Berlin* – Lou Reed (RCA, 1998).
Mr Cheery's second-greatest album.

Suddenly Angry Anderson
No. 3 1988

Bald as love

One of the reasons that *Neighbours* took off in the UK in the late 1980s is that unlike its British soap rivals, its stories were not heavy, grim and brooding, but light, fluffy and fun. Nowhere is this as apparent as in perhaps the show's ultimate episode: the wedding of Scott (Jason Donovan) and Charlene (Kylie). If it had been *EastEnders* the occasion would have been marked with some disaster: a last-minute hitch, a blackmail plot, a fight, a death or all of the above combined. When Scott and Charlene got married, the biggest questions were where had Emma's pet mice escaped to and would Lucy be allowed to pluck her eyebrows. It was simple, sentimental, soft-focus TV, summed up by the simple, sentimental, soft-focus song that followed Charlene up the aisle.

> Together with the guy from Midnight Oil, Angry gave the impression that you had to be bald to get anywhere in the Australian music industry.

Angry Anderson's route to champion soap crooner was one arrived at via a succession of hard rock bands. Real name Gary, he acquired the nickname 'Angry Ant' due to a touch of 'small-guy syndrome' in his Melbourne youth. In 1973 he sang in his first band, the hard boogieing Buster Brown, and when they split up, moved to Sydney and formed Rose Tattoo. A bit punk, a bit rock, a bit metal, a bit roll, Rose Tattoo quickly became one of Australia's top hard rock bands, and Angry a spokesperson for disaffected yoof. His profile rising, Angry found extra work on TV ('youth reporter' on *The Midday Show*) and film (he played Ironbar Bassey, one of Tina Turner's henchmen in *Mad Max III*).

In 1986 Rose Tattoo released their final album, *Beats from a Single Drum*. Slightly slicker than earlier efforts, it was produced by Kevin Beamish, whose previous credits included REO Speedwagon and Starship. One of its songs was 'Suddenly', which to my mind echoes another American soft rock outfit, Chicago. First time round the song did nothing, but then came *Neighbours*, and the song took off like Bouncer with a rocket up his arse. Together with the guy from Midnight Oil, Angry briefly gave the impression that you had to be bald to get anywhere in the Australian music industry, a suggestion reinforced by the bald lady who accompanied him in the song's video.

With *Beats from a Single Drum* rereleased as a solo album, Angry got back on the road and in 1990 supported Aerosmith on their Australian tour. In 1993 Rose Tattoo reformed at the behest of Guns N' Roses and supported them. I'm guessing Axl liked the band's early music rather than being a *Neighbours* fan. Since then, Angry has mainly focused on his TV career, though he still plays the occasional gig.

Listen Here   *Beats from a Single Drum* (Food for Thought, 1988). He's not that angry here.

Listen On   *Rock 'N' Roll Outlaw* – Rose Tattoo (Repertoire, 2000). Here though, Angry rocks out.

Watch Further   *Neighbours: Best of Neighbours* (DVD, 2003). 'The Births The Deaths The Weddings', as the strapline reads. Though not necessarily in that order.

Falling Julee Cruise
No. 7 1990

Single peak

With its backwards-talking dancing dwarfs and the girl who could knot a cherry stalk with her tongue and the question of just who *did* kill Laura Palmer, *Twin Peaks* was one of those programmes like *24* that you either fell in love with or missed a key episode and were never quite able to catch up. Actually, even if you didn't miss an episode, you probably didn't quite get was happening either. It remains the quintessential David Lynch experience: slightly disturbing, beautifully shot, a touch surreal and with a suitably evocative soundtrack.

> It's a bit like being seduced by a ghost.

Julee Cruise was the singer whose voice was chosen to capture the mood. Growing up in Creston, Iowa, she'd gained a music degree, specialising in French horn before making her way to New York. Here's where she got a big break, getting a part in a country and western musical directed by Angelo Badalamenti. Badalamenti, a long-time David Lynch cohort, got Julee to sing on the soundtrack for his film *Blue Velvet*. The three of them obviously hit it off, because Julee soon found herself working with them on their ever so slightly bizarre *Industrial Symphony No. 1* – one performance saw her singing in a prom dress while suspended eighty feet above the stage.

Next up was her debut album, *Floating into the Night*, which featured her stunning contribution to *Twin Peaks*, 'Falling'. Again written by Badalamenti and Lynch, it mixed the former's ear for sweeping cinematic music with the latter's touch of spooky oddness. Julee's voice – for which words such as ethereal, haunting and floating were invented – is their perfect foil. It's a bit like being seduced by a ghost. 'Falling' is a love song, but love as an otherworldly experience. In its strange way, it's rather brilliant.

For a while, the David Lynch connection continued. Julee appeared in both *Twin Peaks* the series and later the film, *Twin Peaks: Fire Walk with Me*, for which she also sang the song, 'Questions In A World Of Blue'. Her second album, *The Voice of Love*, was also a Badalamenti/Lynch production, though her third, *The Art of Being a Girl*, saw her stepping out of their shadow. And as well as the moody stuff, there has also been the B-52s. Julee got a call from the 'Love Shack' lot and lead singer Cindy Wilson took a break: she has done several world tours with the band.

Listen Here *Floating into the Night* (Warner, 1990). The quirky, quite wonderful debut album.

Listen On *The Voice of Love* (Warner, 1993). More Julee. More songs from David Lynch projects.

Watch Further *Twin Peaks: Series One* (DVD, 2002). Does it make more sense the second time round?

I'll Be There For You (Theme from Friends)
The Rembrandts
No. 3 1995

The art of making *Friends*

The clue, I guess, is the bit in the brackets. Without the phenomenally popular telly romcom, I suspect most of us would never have heard of the Rembrandts. The small minority who might have would be those with a penchant for early-nineties American power pop, an ugly phrase, I know, but one that denotes jangly bands who didn't really trouble the charts but made perfectly nice-sounding records that sometimes sounded like bits of the Beatles, Badfinger, Crowded House and Squeeze. It could have been Jellyfish (*Bellybutton* – corking album), it could have been Matthew Sweet (*Girlfriend* – in my mind, genius), but instead it was the Rembrandts that tickled producer Kevin Bright's taste buds and got the call.

Phil Solem and Danny Wilde have been working together on and off since meeting in a Los Angeles nightclub back in 1976. Their first band, Great

Building, released a well-received album called *Apart from the Crowd* in the early 1980s. Having gone solo, the duo got back together to form the Rembrandts in 1990. There were a couple of minor US hits – 'Just The Way It Is, Baby' and 'Johnny Have You Seen Her' – and a smattering of albums, before the TV company phoned.

You can tell how quickly the song took off by the way it caught everyone unawares. Originally, there wasn't a song – the band just recorded the 42-second theme tune, but then radio stations made their own version by looping the theme tune back to back to create a whole song. So the Rembrandts went back to the studio and wrote a second verse and a middle bit. The song was hastily tacked on to the end of the band's third album, *LP*. With the sleeves already printed, it didn't even appear on the tracklisting.

The irony about 'I'll Be There For You' is twofold. It doesn't really sound that much like anything else in the Rembrandts' repertoire, yet that is the song they will always be remembered for. And second, for the theme tune to a coffee-house-based sitcom, it doesn't really sound like anything you'd hear in a Starbucks or a Costa. Some dreary piped jazz would clearly have been far more appropriate. And while *Friends* went from strength to strength, the Rembrandts, sadly, went in the opposite direction. Unsettled by the success, the duo split in 1996, with Phil Solem going on to concentrate on his new project, the perhaps-not-greatest-name-ever-for-a-band Thrush. In 2001 the band got back together for a new album, *Lost Together*, which was well received, but didn't really make any new friends.

Listen Here *The Best One Hit Wonders in the World . . . Ever!* (EMI, 2003). Scheduled in between Nena and Deep Blue Something.

Listen On *LP* (Atlantic, 1995). It's not an LP. It's a CD.

Listen Further *Friends: Music From the TV Series* (Reprise, 1995). Toad the Wet Sprockett included. But not 'Smelly Cat'.

> For the theme tune to a coffee-house-based sitcom, it doesn't really sound like anything you'd hear in a Starbucks.

10 Brief Encounters
– Smooch Hits

Love, according to the music, is many different things. It is a battlefield (Pat Benatar), a many-splendoured thing (the Four Aces), a stranger (Eurythmics), contagious (Taja Seville), like a violin (Ken Dodd), stronger than pride (Sade), not to mention being the drug (Roxy Music), the law (the Seahorses), the key (the Charlatans) and the seventh wave (Sting). And if sex is the driving force for more up-tempo music, here is its inspiration when the lights go down.

There have been various master seducers over the years. No right-minded Casanova should ever be without his copy of Barry White's Greatest Hits. But the thing about love is that it can happen to any of us at any time, and when the music stops and it's your turn, you haven't really got much choice as to what 'your song' is. That, I think, explains the success of some of these songs. Other factors include a liking for notes either ridiculously long or unfeasibly high. And then there are those songs that aren't so much about getting together as going away: songs to remind you of your loved one as they disappear to distant lands or university. Again, I think it's easy to be cynical, but we've all been there: getting on with our lives when a song on the radio pulls us up sharp. It's not only guitar strings these people can play.

For the full experience, imagine it is eleven o'clock in the morning, the love theme from *Romeo and Juliet* is playing and Simon 'Simes' Bates is reading out today's Our Tune, a letter from Julie from Crawley about a particularly sad incident involving Jeff and a lawnmower. 'I don't know where Jeff is now,' Simes reads out, 'but whenever I hear this song, it reminds me of the good times we had together . . .'

Without You Nilsson

No. 1 1972

Sadfinger

This is a story that starts with a British band called Badfinger. In a perfect world, you'd have at least one of their records in your collection. Chances are, though, that you probably haven't. Signed to Apple in the late 1960s, Badfinger were one of the Beatles' label's bigger successes, helped in no small part by the fact that (a) they sounded a bit like the Beatles and (b) their first and biggest hit, 'Come And Get It', was written by Paul McCartney.

But it was in 1970, recording their third album *No Dice*, that Badfinger reached immortality. Just as John and Paul's finest three minutes is 'A Day In The Life', so Badfinger's best song, 'Without You', was written separately by Pete Ham and Tom Evans and then pulled together. The verse is Pete's, the lyrics all about letting his girlfriend down by going to the studio rather than, as promised, taking her to a party. Tom, meanwhile, had written a chorus called 'I can't live'. The two put the two together and *voilà*, 'Without You' was written. Not that the song was ever a hit for Badfinger. Indeed, the band didn't even release it as a single.

Enter Harry Nilsson. An American singer, Harry also had a Beatles connection: the Fab Four loved his debut album *Pandemonium Shadow Show*, and at the press conference in the US to launch Apple the band hailed Nilsson as 'their favourite singer and group'.

This kick-start to Harry's career was complemented by director John Schlesinger, who chose his version of 'Everybody's Talkin'' for his film *Midnight Cowboy* – a song which although influential, only reached number 23 in the U.K.*

Then Harry heard 'Without You'. He was convinced it was a John Lennon song and searched the Beatles' archive for a song with such a title to no avail. Eventually, he stumbled across the Badfinger song and felt this was his to own. And own it Harry did: while the Badfinger version stands up in its own right, it meanders in at a minute longer than Harry's version. And more than that, Harry's version adds in the violinists who play on the heart strings as well as their own instruments. And even more than that, Harry's version hits all the high notes. While Badfinger's 'I can't live's are short and almost apologetic, Harry sends his into the stratosphere, a trick repeated by Mariah Carey, who took the song back to number 1 in 1994.

> While Badfinger's 'I can't live's are short and almost apologetic, Harry sends his into the stratosphere.

On the Nilsson fansite www.harrynilsson.com Harry is quoted as saying: 'I burst a gigantic haemorrhoid on that big top note.' It may have been a flippant comment from Harry, but by God, you won't ever let listen to the song in the same way again.

Here, though, is where things get sad. As much money as 'Without You' must have made for Pete and Tom Badfinger as songwriters, their 1975 album *Wish* was pulled by their record company due to 'financial

* Later covered by the Beautiful South, whose version reached number 12 in 1994.

irregularities'. Shortly after, Pete committed suicide. And then, with history repeating itself, further financial difficulties saw Tom committing suicide in 1983. If that wasn't enough, Harry spent part of his royalties on a flat in Curzon Place in Mayfair. Lending it out in his absence, his bed saw first the death of Mama Cass in July 1974 and then, four years later, that of Keith Moon. In 1994, at the age of 53, as Harry was working on a two-disc greatest hits CD, he died of a heart attack.

Listen Here *Greatest Hits* (Heritage, 2002). Includes 'Cuddly Toy', but not the version by Roachford.

Listen On *A Little Touch of Schmilsson in the Night* (Camden, 2002). Harry sings standards anything but standard.

Listen Further *Come and Get It – The Best of Badfinger* (Apple, 1994). Includes the original 'Without You'.

Lovin' You Minnie Riperton
No. 2 1975

Very high fidelity

Different singers have different vocal ranges. For the less gifted, such as myself, the range stretches to one note, and even that, somehow, is flat. For others, an octave or two is comfortable enough for a night down the karaoke or a career in a boy band. And then there are people like Minnie Riperton, seventies soul singer, one hit wonder, and blessed with a wineglass shattering five and a half octaves.

I think you know the note I'm talking about. The song starts with the birds tweeting and twittering romantically in the background.* Then in come the violins and keyboards, the opening verse about beauty making loving you so easy. Then Minnie sings some 'la la la la las'. Then she does some 'do do dos'. And then there is that high note. When I try and sing 'Aaaaaaaah', it comes out more as 'Aaaaargh!', though at least my glass of wine is still in one piece. Imagine having Minnie round for supper. 'Put those away Roger! I don't want our wedding present smashed to pieces. The plastic beakers will be fine.' But should you actually be angling for a new dinner set the technique you need to master is called whistle register. Normally when you sing, the notes come through vibrating your vocal-cord folds. But with whistle notes, you stiffen the cords and 'whistle' with them, the air rushing through and creating the sound. So there.

Minnie had actually been singing for many years before 'Lovin' You' was a hit. In the 1960s she recorded for Chess Records, before joining soul-psychedelia

> Minnie Riperton was blessed with a wineglass shattering five and a half octaves.

* A bitch to record, apparently. The sparrows nailed their section in one take, and the nightingales were fine and professional, but the blackbird, still living it up from singing on the Beatles song of the same name, had to have his part rerecorded several times before it was usable.

outfit Rotary Connection, who supported acts such as Sly and the Family Stone, Santana and the Stones. Then in 1971 came the 'connection' that rotated everything: meeting Stevie Wonder. Minnie sang backing vocals on albums such as *Songs in the Key of Life*, and Stevie returned the favour, co-producing and playing on *Perfect Angel*,* Minnie's breakthrough album that spawned the hit single 'Lovin' You'.

Minnie's career, tragically, was cut short by breast cancer. She underwent a radical mastectomy in 1976 and managed to use her popularity and success to campaign for fund-raising and awareness. In 1977 she was awarded the American Cancer Society's Courage award for her efforts. Still recording, she died in 1979 at the age of 31, but her work is certainly not forgotten. The Minnie Riperton Breast Cancer Fund is still going strong twenty years on; there is also an annual Minnie Riperton 5/10K Run and Walk in Los Angeles. Meanwhile, the Minnie Riperton Legacy Preservation Society has been vociferous in campaigning to keep Minnie's music alive. In 2000 it launched the 'We Want More Minnie' campaign, with the aim of collecting 100,000 signatures to send to her record company, all demanding more of their beloved Minnie.

'Lovin' You', meanwhile, has continued a rich and varied life of its own. It has been covered by the likes of Mariah Carey and Julia Fordham. In 1999 it was used by Burger King in the US to advertise their cinnamon breakfast rolls. (Is this because you go 'aaaaaaah' when you bite into their thermonuclear centre?) And most bizarrely, it became the centrepiece

* To get round his recording contract with Motown, he is credited as the mysterious 'El Toro Negro'.

Just how high Minnie Riperton sings on 'Lovin' You'

$$\ldots Aaa^{a}\quad{}^{aa}{}^{a}{}^{aa}\quad{}^{a}aa\quad{}_{aah}^{a}$$

Lovin' you, easy, beautiful, etc. La la la. Do do do ...

of an early *South Park* episode, 'Big Gay Al's Big Boat Ride'. In this, Stan's uncle Jimbo tries to save a huge bet on the atrocious South Park football team by blowing up the opposition. The bomb is due to go off during the half-time entertainment, a rendition of 'Lovin' You' by Richard Stamos, but Richard can't reach the trigger note, the 'Aaaaaaah!', and so the plan fails.*

Listen Here   *Les Fleurs: The Minnie Riperton Anthology* (EMI, 2001). All the highlights.

Listen On   *Songs/Hey Love* – Rotary Connection (BGP, 1998). Includes the wonderful 'I Am The Black Gold Of The Sun'.

Listen Further   *Songs in the Key of Life* – Stevie Wonder (Motown, 2002). Minnie does the backing vocals thing.

All By Myself
Eric Carmen
No. 12 1976

Raspberries, Rachmaninov and Bridget Jones's Diary

In 1976 Eric Carmen was not a happy bunny. His band, the Raspberries, had just split up after four albums,

* Fortunately for Jimbo, Stan returns from Big Gay Al's Big Gay Animal Sanctuary to fire a last-minute touchdown, thus 'beating the spread' and saving his uncle's arse. Richard, meanwhile, who has been spending all the second half trying to hit the 'Aaaaaaah', finally does, and the bomb explodes.

none of which had broken them into the big time he craved. Not that the albums were bad – far from it; their Beatles and Beach Boys-style power pop and harmonies were up there with the likes of Big Star and Badfinger. Heck, their debut album even had the fantastic wheeze of having a scratch-and-sniff sticker on the front that when you rubbed it smelled of raspberries. But for whatever reason – the gimmicks, the matching suits, dare one suggest it, the name – the Raspberries just weren't taken seriously by the rock media. So Eric decided to record, well, all by himself.

> If you were Eric's mate, would you pick up the phone?

Except he didn't, quite. He started off on his own certainly, working out the interlude, the pretty piano bit that kicks in at about halfway through. But then, as interludes have a habit of doing, he needed a song to go round it. Which is where Eric turned to one of his favourite pieces of music: Sergei Rachmaninov's Concerto No. 2 in C minor for Piano and Orchestra. Interviewed in 1991, Eric argued 'it's a crime that there are some spectacular melodies in classical music that the general public doesn't get exposed to'. Eric thus did the good citizen thing and used one of Sergei's spectacular melodies for his own verse. All he needed now was a chorus, and continuing his theme, he turned to Carmen. Eric rather than Bizet, mind you, and a Raspberries song called 'Let's Pretend': 'I thought, "Let's Pretend" was a nice melody. The song didn't go quite as far as I thought it should have. I'll go back and steal from myself for this.'

'All By Myself' doesn't so much jerk the tears as wrench them out of their ducts. It's the sort of song about being miserable and alone that even if you're not feeling miserable and alone, you can't help questioning your existence by the end of verse two. All the classic insecurity buttons are pressed: verse one, about not being as young as you used to be; verse two, not having any friends to talk to; verse three, about how love might be the answer but it is elusive, 'distant' and 'obscure'. It's only an opinion, but perhaps the reason Eric is all by himself is because he's just so bloody *down* all the time. I mean, verse two, about ringing his friends up and nobody answering. If you were Eric's mate, would you pick up the phone? 'Hello? Hi there, it's Eric.' 'Eric! How are you?' 'Not too good actually. Not too good at all. To tell you the truth I'm feeling a bit old and lonely and could really do with some . . . hello? Hello? Are you still there?'

'All By Myself' quickly 'Rach-ed' up the sales, racing to number 12 in spring 1976. But in the UK at least, it has stayed all by itself as Eric's contribution to chart history. Since then Eric's main successes have been in the movies. In 1984 he wrote 'Almost Paradise (Love Theme From Footloose)', which was a huge hit in the US, and he followed this up in 1987 with 'Hungry Eyes' on the *Dirty Dancing* soundtrack. We'll leave the physiology of whether eyes can be hungry for another time. Instead, let's leave Eric in a fitting place for such a classic songwriter: as a keyboard player for Ringo Starr's All Starr Band.

Not, I suspect that Eric needs the work. In 1996 Celine Dion covered 'All By Myself' on her *Falling into You* album, which sold 26 million copies worldwide, and the single – a pared down, subtle, acoustic version of the song – reached number 6. Actually, I'm just kidding about the arrangement. Celine gave it the usual 'Titanic' treatment. Then, just in case Eric was wonder-

ing about where his next meal was going to come from, up it popped again, sung by Jamie O'Neal at the beginning of *Bridget Jones's Diary*, with Renée Zellweger giving a commanding performance as to how the song should best be enjoyed: alone, in your pyjamas, with a large glass of wine and the volume turned to full.

Listen Here *The Best of Eric Carmen* (RCA, 1996). Includes the is-this-biologically-possible 'Hungry Eyes'.

Listen On *The Very Best of the Raspberries* (Cherry Red, 2002). Eric's fruity first band.

Listen Further *Rachmaninov Piano Concertos Nos. 1 and 2* – Krystian Zimerman (Deutsche Grammophon, 2004). Sergei rather than soggy.

Save Your Love
Renee and Renato
No. 1 1982

Rose above the rest

One of the more disturbing conversations I had in the course of working on this book was with a younger female colleague at work. We'd chatted about Chesney, discussed the pluses and minuses of Oliver Cheatham, when the conversation turned round to the subject of Renee and Renato. At the mention of their name, my colleague's face turned blank. 'Renee and who?' she asked. 'Am I meant to have heard of them?' Reader, I hope you felt as old as I did. There is now a whole generation of adults for whom R&R means something completely different.

For the rest of us, Renee and Renato possess a certain iconic status. For somehow, in 1982 Christmas was dominated by their song, knocking 'Beat Surrender' by the Jam off the top spot. Renato was a singing waiter from Birmingham, whose biggest claim to fame was being the person who sang 'Just One Cornetto' in that TV advert. Renee, meanwhile, was many years younger and not actually called Renee at all, but actually Hilary Lester. And not only was Hilary not called Renee, she also wasn't the Renee in the video.

Ah, the video. Manna to the likes of Kenny Everett and friends. Renee's place was taken by a model with a blonde wig, but not that anybody noticed, they were too busy eyeing up Renato's jumper. Pale blue and shiny, it was clearly made from some manmade fibre that has probably since been proved to be the scientific opposite of wool. It wasn't restrictive, though, as the video's most famous scene proved. In classic *Romeo and Juliet* behaviour, Renato serenaded his loved one looking down on him. And then with an accuracy that would have made Jocky Wilson proud, he threw a rose up for 'Renee' to catch. Which she did. First time. Yeah right.

The song having been a huge hit, the real Renee reappeared for a follow-up single, but she needn't have bothered. 'Just One More Kiss' stalled at number 48. She is now, apparently, happily married in the Midlands, while Renato continues to strut his stuff on the world's cruise ships. A quick glance on the Internet finds plenty of gushing reviews from

the sort of people who (a) go on cruises and (b) put their holiday diaries on the Internet. When he's not sailing, there's always his Italian restaurant, Renato's in Tamworth, to run, or his friend, football manager Ron Atkinson, to see. When Big Ron went on the TV show *Room 101* he tried to put Renato in. He failed.

> Renato threw a rose up for 'Renee' to catch. Which she did. First time. Yeah right.

Listen Here *Greatest Hits of the Eighties* (Disky, 1998). Eight (count 'em) CDs of classic eighties cuts.

Listen On 'Just One More Kiss' (Hollywood, 1983). Number 48 was as high as it puckered up.

Listen Further 'It's Christmas Let's Give Love A Try' – Ron Atkinson (N2K, 2002). Renato's mate fails to score.

Bird Of Paradise
Snowy White
No. 6 1983

While my guitar gently tweets . . .
Birds and classic rock have always gone together, hand in hand – talon in hand? – for as long as, well, as long as there have been cigarette lighters to hold aloft. In the 1960s it was Fleetwood Mac and 'Albatross', Jimi Hendrix and 'Little Wing'. The seventies got Lynyrd

Skynyrd and their 'Freebird', the myriad delights of the Eagles. And then, in 1983, in between nipping out the nest to swoop down and pounce on unsuspecting field mice, it was the turn of a small fluffy owl to fly up the charts.

I'm messing with you. Snowy White isn't an owl at all, but one of Britain's great unsung blues guitarists. Inspired by the likes of B. B. King and Otis Rush, Snowy spent the seventies licking with the likes of Peter Green (jamming on his 1979 *In the Skies* album), Pink Floyd (playing on the *Animals* tour of 1976–7) and Thin Lizzy (joining the band in 1979–82). In 1983 he went solo, and the result was this top-ten hit, which featured on the very first *Now That's What I Call Music* album.*

'Bird Of Paradise' somehow manages the difficult feat of sounding both timeless and eighties at the same time. It is Athena Rock or, perhaps more accurately given the title, Bounty Blues. The song smooches its way through the rock and roll gears. The opening has echoes of 'Wind Cries Mary' Hendrix; the verse offers a nod to Dire Straits – indeed, were it not the fact that the single was released two years earlier I'd say it bore more than a passing resemblance to 'Brothers In Arms'. Then just as you're beginning to think he can't sing 'bird of paradise' *again*, Snowy White becomes Showy White, with a Claptonesque solo of soaring proportions. If you listen carefully, you can almost hear him shut his eyes, lean back, pucker his lips at the sweetness of his twang.

A quick word about the lyrics. I think they're meant to be a metaphor. To give a rough summary, the said

'chick' or 'bird' of the title, distinguishable with its plumage of turquoise blue,** is spotted by Snowy in verse one, with a keen eye Bill Oddie would be proud of. The bird circles around for a bit in verse two and then, well, buggers off in verse three. Snowy ends the song with a lament for the 'bird' to come back, so he can watch it mess about again in the 'pouring rain'. My feeling though, and I hope I'm not shattering Snowy's illusions or anything, is that the beautiful blue 'BOP' had more than enough of the British weather system and is hot-winging it back to Bounty-land, never to be seen again.

> Athena Rock, or perhaps more accurately given the title, Bounty Blues.

Anyway. Snowy's kept himself busy, while he's been waiting for his Bird of Paradise to return. Following the single's success, he had a musical rethink and rather than become a hit artist with those nasty trappings of *Top of the Pops* and sell-out stadiums and love-ins with enthusiastic Swedish twins, Snowy decided to return to his first love, the blues. He spent the rest of the eighties touring with a gigging blues band. Then in 1990 he got a call from an old friend, Roger Waters. The result was Snowy's appearance at Roger's massive *The Wall* show in Berlin, the highlight being his walloping guitar solo for 'Comfortably Numb'. Since then, his career has settled into an equally comfortable groove: a bit of blues, a bit of touring with Roger Waters and a bit of royalties from

---

* The early *Now* albums, volumes one through five, were marked by the appearance of what can only be described as a pig in sunglasses. For some reason, this got ditched.

** Leaving aside the question of what other shades there are knocking about, turquoise was very 'in' in the mid-eighties. I myself had a turquoise-and-grey striped jumper, purchased from the wonderfully named Concept Man, sibling shop to Chelsea Girl.

'Bird' being used on adverts. KLM used it in 1994 – do you see what they did there? – and the song re-entered the charts across Europe.

Listen Here *While My Guitar Gently Weeps* – Various Artists (Universal, 2002). Two CDs of soft rock twiddling.

Listen On *Pure Gold* – Snowy White (Connoisseur, 1999). Snowy's finest fretwork.

Listen Further *The Wall* – Roger Waters (Universal, 2003). The live concert in Berlin, where Snowy goes numb.

Move Closer
Phyllis Nelson
No. 1 1985

Closer than close

Safe sex, as Billy Bragg once sang, is all about 'using your imagination'. And in the 1980s imagination was everything. The threat of AIDS was everywhere, stoked in no small part by 'subtle' government adverts full of big, black, looming icebergs, floating across the sea like discarded furniture from a World of Leather sale. Some people responded with abstinence – Timothy Dalton, who took over from Roger Moore as 007, became the Bond Who Didn't Shag. Others went beyond using condoms to staying fully dressed instead (see Jermaine Stewart's 'We Don't Have To Take Our Clothes Off To Have A Good Time').

And then there was Phyllis Nelson. Number 1 for a solitary week in 1985, nestled between 'We Are The World' and Paul Hardcastle's 'Nineteen', 'Move Closer' offered listeners a double whammy of safe sexuality. For men of a certain age the opening chords still bring back all those school disco nightmares, the moment when the entire school seemed to pair off apart from you. Not so much 'Move Closer' as 'Move Right Away, Spotty'. Many years on my Pavlovian response remains – every time I hear the start of the song, lust dissolves into despondency.

But second – and yes, maybe I've had too much time to analyse on the sidelines – 'Move Closer' suggests that dancing is the perfect alternative to a spot of rumpy-pumpy. It's the equivalent of 'really making love', Phyllis suggested, but without all the awkwardness afterwards. Certainly there's no doubting the song's sultry charm: the slow steady backbeat that wouldn't be out of place on a Barry White record; Phyllis's singing, which is anything but Barry White – light, tender and lingering; the intimacy of the words – striking for the time, especially from a female voice.

All of which is great, except that the more you think about the words, the more meaningless they are. How can dancing feel like you're 'really' making love? However good a smooch-fest you're having on the dancefloor, by definition it can only feel *like* you're making love. The only thing that can feel like you're 'really' making love is (cue Barry White) when you're

> For men of a certain age, the opening chords still bring back all those school disco nightmares.

making love. Consider also this recent description of Justin Timberlake in *Elle* magazine: 'he dances like he'd be good in bed.' If even Justin can only dance *like* he'd be good in bed, let's face it, what chance do the rest of us have?

Phyllis hailed from Philadelphia. In the seventies she was a member of female trio Brown Sugar, who split up in the early eighties to pursue solo careers. Phyllis was the most successful. 'Move Closer' was an international hit, while more upbeat songs such as 'Don't Stop the Train' and 'I Like You' remain popular among soul fans. Sadly, Phyllis died from cancer in 1997, but her son, Marc, is attempting to continue the family tradition. Not with much success, it has to be said: his career highlight to date is being a 'pre-star-dom member' of Boyz II Men.

Incidentally, when I finished the Justin Timberlake article, I asked my girlfriend how she'd describe my dancing. 'Enthusiastic,' she replied.

Listen Here   *Move Closer* (Delta, 1999). Phyllis moves closer in both original and remixed form.

Listen On   'Don't Stop The Train' on the same compilation. Phyllis doesn't just do ballads.

Listen Further   *Love Won't Let Me Wait* – Major Harris (Atlantic, 1975). Mid-seventies soul hit with Brown Sugar on backing vocals.

Promise Me
Beverley Craven
No. 3 1991

Less of a bevy, more of a Bev

Ah. The big charity concert. Charity spelled 'charidee', of course. In the late 1980s and early 1990s they were all the rage. Who can forget Live Aid, Bob 'Give us your fucking money' Geldof, Bono plucking swooning girlies out of the crowd and Bob Dylan offering an almost perversely misjudged and out-of-tune career lowlight? Then there was the Freddie Mercury tribute concert, with Axl Rose having a handy bout of amnesia about his opinions on 'faggots', and David Bowie Lording up the Lord's Prayer. Nelson Mandela discovered prison wasn't *all* bad by missing his Dire Straits-headlining seventieth birthday concert – a concert that provided the launchpad for the then-unknown Tracy Chapman. And on 13 May 1991, at the 'Kurd-Aid' Simple Truth concert, another up-and-coming female singer-songwriter was similarly exposed. The unknown act among the all too well-known De Burghs and Collinses on the bill, Beverley Craven had finally arrived.

Finally, I think, is the key word here. For anyone who believes in pop stars paying their dues, then Beverley's

> Beverley's tour featured one of life's more bizarre sponsorship deals: Tampax.

case is a textbook example. Born in Sri Lanka in 1963, Beverley grew up in Hertfordshire and spent much of her childhood in the swimming pool, competing in the national junior championships against Sharron Davies.* But bored with taking off her pyjamas underwater and blowing them up with air, the teenage Beverley turned her attention to music. The first record she ever bought was 'Telephone Line' by ELO,** but thankfully she soon discovered and was inspired by Kate Bush.

What followed was a long period of getting nowhere in London. Beverley waitressed. She squatted. She auditioned for bands and got a string of 'don't call us, we'll call you's. She went solo and spent four years on the dole, always with a just-in-case demo tape in her handbag. Then in 1988 she signed a 'development deal' with Epic records, who sent her out to Los Angeles for two gruelling, grooming months on the club circuit. Beverley started recording her debut album, but after three songs and £30,000 it was deemed too slick. The West Coast was swapped for Chipping Norton, the Simply Red producer replaced by Fairport Convention musicians, and the sound was finally right.

For a while the promise of 'Promise Me' promised Beverley the world. A pretty if perhaps slight drippy ballad about asking her lover to 'wait' for her, the song, like Jimmy Page plucking his beloved Les Paul, struck a powerful chord. The accompanying album, *Beverley Craven*, did the business ('For those who

believe in the singer and the song,' ran the adverts), and in 1992 Beverley won the Brit award for Best Newcomer. Meanwhile, Beverley had found someone worth 'saving' all her love for: Colin Campsie, sometime Go West-ie and songwriter for the likes of Mel C and Natalie Imbrooglie-wooglie. Beverley met him backstage at – could this *be* more romantic? – a Tears for Fears concert.

And soon the seeds of love were sown. When Beverley accepted her Brit award, she was already eight months pregnant with their first daughter, Mollie. For much of the 1990s her career took second place. Over the next few years this erstwhile Kate Bush fan would hit the mothering heights twice more – Brenna was born in 1995 and Connie in 1996. Meanwhile, Beverley's hitless second album, *Love Scenes* (1993), sold well but not as well as the first, despite a tour featuring one of life's more bizarre sponsorship deals, Tampax. Six years on, her comeback album, *Mixed Emotions* (1999), had a decidedly mixed response.

Interviewed at the height of her success in 1991, Beverley said: 'It feels unreal, as if I'm skimming across the surface of someone else's life.'* Which, sadly, was exactly what happened.

Listen Here *The Love Songs Album* (Universal, 2000). Two CDs of solid smooch.

Listen On *Beverley Craven* (Sony, 1991). The debut album with all the promise.

Listen Further *Love Scenes* (Epic, 1993). Album number two. But no hit number two.

* For those of you wondering what happened to Sharron Davies, please see my earlier work, *One Length Wonders: A Celebration of Swimmers from David Wilkie to Duncan Goodhew* (Dolphin, 1999).
** You think that's embarrassing. My first record was 'Pretty Little Angel Eyes' by Showaddywaddy.

* Q magazine, September 1991.

Get Here Oleta Adams
No. 4 1991

Get her

This is a story that starts in 1985, in the lounge bar of the Hyatt Regency Hotel in Kansas City. Enter Tears for Fears, pretty boy Curt Smith and brooding genius Roland Orzabal, eighties Britrock duo whose psychology-leaning licks were taking the world by storm. 1985 was their year. The album *Songs from the Big Chair* was huge everywhere, and singles 'Shout' and 'Everybody Wants To Rule The World' both hit number 1 in America. But rather that being 'so glad' that they'd finally made it, the boys were 'so sad', concerned that they were, well, faking it. Ruling the world was all about going through the motions, being slick, polished, rehearsed. They worried that they were losing touch with their music.

That night in the Hyatt Regency was a revelation. Playing in the bar on a white baby grand piano, accompanied by the barest of drums and double bass, the sweet soul sounds of Oleta Adams simply blew the boys from Bath away. Here's Roland: 'Running into Oleta showed us the other side of the coin. It brought us face to face with music on a pure level. Here was someone literally singing for her supper but still expressing herself brilliantly.' And Curt: 'There we were with a seven-piece band and an audience of thousands every night and yet there was no soul in what we were doing. And then there was this woman with just a piano who could reduce an audience to tears.'

Tears for Fears was Oleta's ticket out of the Hyatt Regency, though not quite straight away. Curt and Roland spent four years and the best part of a million quid trying to capture the Oleta soul sound, until they eventually realised that the best way of capturing the Oleta soul sound was to get Oleta herself on the record. The result was her vocals on the opening two tracks on *The Seeds of Love* – 'Woman In Chains' and 'Badman's Song'. This was followed by a record deal with Tears for Fears' label and a solo album, *Circle of One*, produced by Roland. It was from this that the smash hit single 'Get Here' came. Written by singer-songwriter Brenda Russell, the title track from her 1988 album of the same name, Oleta's version of 'Get Here' captured a moment: a torch song for the troops sent out to Kuwait for the first Gulf War.

Like many of the songs in this section, 'Get Here' works because it locks on to a simple universal feeling and, like a dog with a bone, just doesn't let go. I don't mind how you make your way over, Oleta pleads again and again and, well, again, but please, just get your arse here pronto. For any long-distant lover not sure of the best way to travel, 'Get Here' positively goes overboard in its range of transport options: by railway (Oleta is clearly not British); trailway (for the American hiker in you); by aeroplane (if you're not R. Kelly); your mind (telepaths ahoy); caravan (subtext: you're not staying over); an 'Arab man'-style desert crossing (hmmm); sail boat (now's not the time for a row); swinging rope to rope through the trees (Baltimora-tastic); sled (if your lover is a little husky); speedy colt (or a little hoarse); windsurf

> Tears for Fears was Oleta's ticket out of the Hyatt Regency.

(go on, blow right over); carpet ride (is there Aladdin your life?); and big balloon (just pop along).

It might just be me, but I can't help thinking that there's more than a touch of Black Lace's 'Superman' to this list. Oleta, if you're listening, get yourself a drum machine, invent some silly actions, and *voilà*! 'Get Here' could be the summer anthem for 2005. She might have to wrest control of the song back from its current owner, though – Justin Gurani, the frizzy-topped singer on the first series of *American Idol*, whose love of 'Get Here' got him to second place behind Kelly Clarkson.

Listen Here *Circle of One* (Mercury, 1991). Get 'Get Here' here.

Listen On *Evolution* (Fontana, 1993). Get more Oleta here.

Listen Further *The Seeds of Love* – Tears for Fears (Mercury, 1999). Oleta sings on 'Woman In Chains' and 'Badman's Song'. I have a disturbing soft spot for this album.

Five further cheesy dance hit wonders

'Band Of Gold'
Freda Payne

'Rhythm Of The Night'
DeBarge

'Let's Go All The Way'
Sly Fox

'I Love My Radio (My Dee Jay's Radio)'
Taffy

'Wiggle It'
2 in a room

11 Remember Me?
– Dance Hits

In a previous life I used to write all the record reviews for Our Price, all those recommended singles of the week stickers you get in store. But here was the catch: it was so last-minute in deciding what the titles were, that every week I would write the record reviews without having heard the records themselves. Quite often you could guess. The new Steps single, for example, was likely to sound pretty much like the last one. But with the dance music, it'd all be more problematic. Each week would be another anonymous DJ or MC, remixed by an even more obscure producer. And so I quickly developed a winning formula, a mythical place called 'Clubland' where the tune in question was 'filling the floor', and a focus on what any half-decent dance had, rhythm and a bit of bass. The drums would be 'big' or 'pounding', the bass would be 'fat' or 'funky' and I'd get away with the whole thing for yet another week.

The point of this anecdote is to emphasise how quick the turnaround of new dance acts is and how an unheard-of dance act can push their way towards the top of the charts in a way other genres can't. The possibilities for one hit wonders are enormous. For this chapter, I've tried to choose songs that reflect different types of dance. Some (Stardust) are great. Others (The Weather Girls) just grate.

Sweet Soul Music
Arthur Conley
No. 7 1967

Does exactly what it says on the tin

For all the experimentation and the psychedelia and the Beatles and the Beach Boys and Bob Dylan winding up the folkies and everything else, it's easy to forget just how great soul music was in the late 1960s. I'm not talking about Motown, which personally I've always found a little syrupy, a little too production line. No, I'm talking about soul with *soul*, labels like Atlantic and Stax, singers like Otis, Aretha, Wilson Pickett, Carla Thomas, musicians like guitarist Steve Cropper, unassuming king of the clipped, clean stab. It's a feel that's as fresh as the day it was recorded, and in two minutes and twenty seconds, one song summed the whole scene up.

Born in Atlanta, Georgia, in 1946, Arthur Conley started out singing gospel and in church, before becoming lead singer in local band Arthur and the Corvets. I don't know how little or red they were. A handful of singles on a local label did nothing commercially, but attracted the attention of one Otis Redding, who got Arthur to rerecord one of the songs for his Jotis label. Although that didn't sell, their next collaboration did: a rewriting of Sam Cooke's 'Yeah Man' in homage to sixties soul.

'Sweet Soul Music' begins with a brass fanfare, supposedly pinched from the theme to *The Magnificent*

Seven. Then in comes Arthur with a question: do you like good music? If the answer is yes, listen on. 'Sweet Soul Music' rattles along like a record in a hurry as Arthur namechecks the soul-singing great and the good. If you don't own any classic soul, Arthur's suggestions serve as a great starting point for any collection. First up is Lou Rawls (Arthur's comment: 'tall') – try 'Love Is A Hurtin' Thing'; then there's Sam & Dave – 'boss' – I'd recommend 'Soul Man'; next up is Wilson Pickett – 'wicked' – Arthur suggests 'Mustang Sally'; fourth is Otis – included in the song at Arthur's behest – for my money you can't beat 'Try A Little Tenderness'; finally, there's James Brown, and if he is the 'king' as Arthur suggests, 'Cold Sweat' is the crown jewels. No mention, however, of Sam Cooke, which is perhaps a little harsh, especially as he wrote the song in the first place.

It was a hit on both sides of the Atlantic, and Conley found himself part of the infamous Stax-Volt tour that hit Europe later in 1967. But his rise to fame was to stop almost as soon as it had begun. When Otis died in a plane crash later in the same year, Arthur lost his mentor, cheerleader and friend. With the hits drying up, Arthur left America for a new life in England, Belgium and eventually the home of soul, the Netherlands. Keen to escape the 'Sweet Soul Music' tag, he started recording under the pseudonym Lee Roberts and also ran his own small label. Sadly, he died of cancer in November 2003.

> In two minutes and twenty seconds, one song summed the whole scene up.

Listen Here *Blues Brother Soul Sister Classics* (Polygram, 2000). Find Arthur between Aretha Franklin and John Lee Hooker.

Listen On *Sweet Soul Music* (Rhino, 1996). More of the sweet soul stuff.

Listen Further *The Very Best of Otis Redding* (Atco, 2001). Arthur's mentor, soul's master.

Play That Funky Music
Wild Cherry

No. 7 1976

Honky tonked

Some people, it has to be said, don't look like they sound. Rick Astley, for example, glossy quiff, funny dancing, from Warrington, should not have the sort of deep soul voice that got eighties teenagers all aquiver. Similarly, Joss Stone, surely a big soul momma from the Deep South with at least a decade of tortured relationships behind her, surely not a sixteen-year-old schoolgirl from Devon? And then there were all those seventies funk bands who turned out to be white. Some, like the Average White Band, gave a helpful clue in their name. Others, like Wild Cherry, left the hints to the lyrics.

The original line-up of the band was formed by singer and guitarist Rob Parissi back in 1970, with a little help from a cherry-flavoured cough sweet. But despite a record contract with a small label, their rock sound did nothing, and in 1975 the band split up. Indeed, he was so hacked off with the whole thing that he sold all his instruments and got a job managing a local steakhouse. Eventually, he decided to continue and re-formed the band with an entirely new line-up and a new sound. With dance and disco beginning to bite, Wild Cherry found their original rock not going down as well as before and decided to adapt. Depending on who you believe, Rob enjoyed a Damascus moment when either the punters at a gig told him to play more funky music or the drummer backstage reported the same thing. My gut instinct is for the punters – whoever heard of a drummer with a decent musical idea? – whichever, Rob got a classic out of it, a song that was going to be the B-side to a single, until the sound engineer spotted its potential.

'Play That Funky Music' is a fantastic slab of Sly and the Family Stone-style funk that still sounds as fresh today as it did almost thirty years ago. With no pictures of the band on any of the record sleeves (instead, the band had a penchant for female lips sucking on a cherry), coupled with the music's grinding funk sound and the goading cry of 'white boy', the assumption was that Wild Cherry were black. This helped in getting the song on R&B radio, but led to surprise when the band turned up to play gigs. Rob chose this as the theme to the band's follow-up single, 'Baby Don't You Know', baby not knowing that the 'suckers were white' and that it was perfectly possible for said 'honky' to have 'soul'.

The problem for Wild Cherry was that much of

> With the grinding funk sound and the goading cry of 'white boy', the assumption was that Wild Cherry were black.

white America didn't like disco. Indeed, rock fans proudly showed their hatred for dance, wearing T-shirts that said things like 'Disco Sucks' and burning such records at football matches. And with black music fans now suspicious, the group ended up falling somewhere in the middle. Which is not to say that they didn't go on to make some fantastic music. Hit-free second album *Electrified Funk* grooves, in my opinion, like a bastard. Sadly, the band did not see the decade out, but the funky music lives on, even surviving a massacring by Vanilla Ice in 1990.

Listen Here   *Super Hits* (Epic, 2002). Lots of funky music here.

Listen On   *Electrified Funk* (Epic, 1977). Includes the frankly hot-to-trot 'Hot To Trot'.

Listen Further   'Play That Funky Music' – Vanilla Ice (SBK, 1991). Personally, the cover leaves me cold.

It's Raining Men
The Weather Girls
No. 2 1984

Hi. *Hi!*
I don't know which channel you watch, but personally, I have never seen a weather girl who looks like Izora Armstead or Martha Wash. Sometimes they can be a bit naff and gawpy, like Wincey Willis. Sometimes they are blonde and Swedish, like Ulrika Jonsson.

Occasionally they're posh and condescending, like Sian Lloyd. But the big momma version? Doesn't really work. I don't want to be sizeist, but let's be honest: you can't have a weather person who blocks out half the country.

Things are not looking good with 'It's Raining Men' even before the Weather Girls turn up. First, it thunders. And then it starts up uncannily like it's going to turn into Bonnie Tyler and 'Holding Out For A Hero'. But Bonnie this is not. With a 'Hi' and a '*Hi!*', Izora and Martha announce that tonight, they're *your* weather girls – which I don't know about you, but reminds me of a bad dream I once had. I don't want to diss their credibility still further, but they go on to announce that they've got some 'neeeeeews' we might like to hear. Call me picky, but weather girls don't do news; that's for the newsreader to deliver. If the weather girls start doing news as well, then Huw Edwards is going to be out of a job.

> With a 'Hi' and a '*Hi!*', Izora and Martha announce that tonight, they're *your* weather girls.

Anyway. The news is this. At approximately 10.30 this evening, it's going to start chucking it down with blokes. The girls sing 'Hallelujah!' and appropriately 'amen!', though then go on to confuse the issue by thanking not God but Mother Nature for this freak turn of events. Having suggested elsewhere that 'I Eat Cannibals' could be construed as being rude and having had my claim rubbished by a member of Toto Coelo, I am not going to make the same mistake about the line in the chorus about the girls getting 'wet'. I'll leave that to your sordid imagination. What I would say, and I don't want to dampen the girls' excitement or anything, but lots of men appearing out of nowhere at 10.30 at night? They're not about to hook up with the Weather Girls – they're off to the pub to get a round in before last orders.

Izora and Martha started off together as backing singers for Sylvester, seventies disco groover with hits such as 'You Make Me Feel (Mighty Real)', later covered by Jimmy Somerville. The girls then set out on their own as Two Tons of Fun, before switching record company and name. It's always a danger linking the band name to a song, and it was a theme that the record company exploited to the full. On the duo's *Super Hits* collection, 'It's Raining Men' is followed by 'I'm Gonna Wash That Man Right Outa My Hair', which in turn is followed by 'Big Girls Don't Cry'. In the late 1980s Martha left the duo to go solo and was quickly replaced by Dynelle, Izora's not-that-skinny-either daughter. They are still going. Martha, meanwhile, has recorded with the likes of Black Box and C&C Music Factory, though her rerecorded version of 'It's Raining Men', with help from RuPaul, achieves the miracle of making Geri Halliwell's version seem almost competent.

Listen Here *Super Hits* (Columbia, 2001). The big numbers are here.

Listen On 'I'm Gonna Wash That Man Right Outa My Hair' on the same album. Come on, it's funny.

Listen Further 'It's Raining Men' – Geri Halliwell (EMI, 2001). Lightweight by comparison.

Love Can't Turn Around Farley 'Jackmaster' Funk

No. 10 1986

Now *that's* Chicago

According to Matthew Collin's *Altered State* (Serpent's Tail, 1997), the origins of house music can be traced back to New York's black gay clubs of the late 1970s. Ostracised by society twice over, the result was an atmosphere of togetherness that would infuse club culture over the coming years. It was at one of the scene's most notorious clubs that DJ Frankie Knuckles, not I suspect his real name, spun his stuff, until he got an offer to go to Chicago and join a new club, the Warehouse, from which the resulting scene would take its name.

At the same time as Knuckles moved to the Windy City, advances in technology were starting to have an effect on dance music. People were adding drum machines, cut and pasting records into something new, all the time stripping dance music away from the high gloss of disco into something rawer: bass, drums and precious little else. As well as Knuckles in the clubs, there was a dance show on Chicago radio doing the same sort of thing, the Hot Mix 5 DJ quintet, five guys with a penchant for nicknames: Kenny

> Farley's version featured heavyweight singer Darryl Pandy, a sort of gospel Renato.

'Jammin" Jason, Mickey 'Mixin" Oliver, Scott 'Smokin" Seals, Ralph 'The Razz' Rosario and Farley 'Jackmaster' Funk.

As well as the radio show, Farley enjoyed a DJ residency at Chicago's Playground (the club, not where the kids hung out), later the Candy Store (likewise). And with the scene burgeoning, Farley turned his hand to making records as well as playing them. After a couple of early singles, 'Jack The Bass' and 'Funkin' With The Drums Again' (I hate it when people do that), he hit upon the song that would become the breakthrough house hit. There is some debate as to who came up with the idea of a house cover of Isaac Hayes's 'I Can't Turn Around'. Steve 'Silk' Hurley, who would take 'Jack Your Body' to number 1 the following year, suggests that Farley lifted the idea from him. Whatever, Farley's version, which featured heavyweight singer Darryl Pandy, a sort of gospel Renato fresh from the Greater Tabernacle Baptist Choir, was the one that broke the mould.

As house music's popularity grew in the UK, so did Farley's reputation. But further crossover hits were not forthcoming, and by the end of the late 1980s his radio show was dropped and it was his career that was turning round. Out of favour in Chicago, Farley has since mainly turned to the still appreciative global DJ circuit, with the occasional exploration into R&B and hip-hop.

Listen Here *The Original Chicago House Classics* – Various Artists (Music Club, 2002). Jackmaster, Frankie Knuckles, Mr Fingers and more.

Listen On 'Love Can't Turn Around' (4 Livery, 1996). Ten years on and totally remixed.

Listen Further 'Jack Your Body' – Steve 'Silk' Hurley (DJ International, 1987). Jack, jack, jack, etc.

Pump Up The Volume
M/A/R/R/S
No. 1 1987

Warning: Roadblock ahead

Pump. Not immediately the most obvious musical word, but nevertheless one of the great ones. Elvis Costello used it on his 1978 single 'Pump It Up', a song that could (I'm sure mistakenly) be taken as a paean to all things 'Turning Japanese'. Supergrass used it on their 1999 hit 'Pumping On The Stereo', primarily to rhyme with 'humping'. Technotronic perhaps win the award for best pronunciation, pronouncing 'pump' as 'pawmp' on their 1989 'Pump Up The Jam'. But it was M/A/R/R/S more than any other who really got things pumping with this solitary 1987 single.

In 1987 the pop of Planet Earth was being left behind and the future was M/A/R/R/S. A mixture of advances in technology and someone with the nous to utilise it came together to produce one of the decade's definitive dance singles.

> With more samples than the carpet department of John Lewis, M/A/R/R/S cut and spliced, scratched and sniffed, hiphopped and grooved.

With more samples than the carpet department of John Lewis, M/A/R/R/S cut and spliced, scratched and sniffed, hip-hopped and grooved, James Browned and Public Enemied and Eric B. and Rakimed and Stock, Aitken and Watermanned. Stock, Aitken and Waterman weren't too happy actually: the bit the band used from 'Roadblock' led to all sorts of legal difficulties and copyright problems. But that was for the lawyers; for everyone else, 'Pump Up The Volume' and Bomb the Bass's 'Beat Dis' paved the way for how music would be made for years to come.

'Pump Up The Volume' wasn't the only part of the whole project that was made up of different bits. M/A/R/R/S itself was similarly composite, consisting of 4AD band Colourbox and Rough Trade duo A. R. Kane, together with DJs C. J. Mackintosh and Dave Dorrell. The man who had the idea for the funky collaboration was 4AD boss Ivo Watts-Russell, a surprising suggestion perhaps from the label chief of the Cocteau Twins and the Pixies, but there you go. Then as soon as the group had come together, they quickly returned to their separate ways, leaving behind a load of legal work and old school types talking about the end of 'real music'. There followed a comedy single by the eighties answer to the Barron Knights, Star Turn on 45 (Pints), whose 'Pump Up The Bitter' subsequently reached number 12.

Listen Here *Now That's What I Call Music 1987* (EMI, 1993). Single's greatness enhanced by being surrounded by the likes of Wet Wet Wet and Hue & Cry.

Listen On *The Best of Colourbox 1982–1987* (4AD, 2001). The US 12-inch version of 'Pump Up The Volume' is also included.

Listen Further *69* – A. R. Kane (Rough Trade, 1988). Eclectic doesn't begin to describe their debut album.

Groove Is In The Heart
Deee-Lite
No. 2 1990

We didn't ask for another

If you're anything like me, just reading the words in the title will have set off one of the best bass lines of the nineties in your head. Guest fretman Bootsy Collins, that erstwhile parliamentarian and the man who put the get-on-up into James Brown's 'The JBs'. Now add in some drums, a funky little beat, nothing too heavy now, maybe perhaps a bongo or two. Over the top, let's stick in a silly noise that goes from high to low, then low to high again: wee ... ooooh. Ooooh ... wah! A little bit of sax, now. Why don't we try Maceo Parker, horn blower for everyone from Prince to Funkadelic.

> What, precisely, does 'de-lovely' mean, beyond going nicely with 'delicious'?

All we need now are a few vocals, preferably of the certifiable sex kitten variety. Best not to listen too closely because title aside, the words don't really make much sense. Do *you* know what a succotash wish is? Or how deep a hula groove actually needs to be in order to move one to the nth hoop? And what precisely does 'de-lovely' mean, beyond going nicely with 'delicious'? Answers on a postcard to the usual address please.

Deee-Lite, along with the singer from Imagination and Brian from East 17, are one of those acts with perhaps more e's than is strictly necessary. Though at least theirs serves a purpose – without it, people might have been expecting a Kiki Dee tribute act. The group was formed in New York in 1982, when Ohio-born Lady Miss Kier (real name Kieren Kirby) met Russian émigré Super DJ Dmitry (real name Dmitry Brill), and the two did their bit to thaw Cold War relations. The addition of Japanese boy Jungle DJ Towa Towa (Doug Wa-Chung from Tokyo) completed the trio. The band's cosmopolitan origins were reflected in the pop-culture patchwork of their music: funk, jazz, soul, rap, house, retro, the kitchen sink, you name it, it got thrown into the mix. With a love of retro fashion, and Lady Miss Kier doing an excellent impression of a seventies Betty Boo on speed, 'Groove Is In The Heart' quickly became irresistible.

More resistible, unfortunately, were the band's subsequent singles. Following their debut number 2 smash, the follow-ups peaked at 25, 52, 53, 45 and 43. There are three albums worth checking out: *World Clique*, the environmentally friendly *Infinity Within* and the Towa Towa-free *Dewdrops in the Garden*. The band split properly in 1996, with assorted solo projects and remix and greatest hits albums following in their wake. In 2003 Lady Kier filed a lawsuit against computer games manufacturer Sega, claiming Ulala, a character in *Space Channel 5*, was based on her

and people might get confused. Let's face it, there's nothing worse than trying to zap a space alien and he's going, 'Hang on, didn't you used to be in that band…?'

Listen Here *World Clique* (Warner, 1990). Groove is in the debut album.

Listen On *Dewdrops in the Garden* (Elektra, 1994). More grooves.

Listen Further *Doin' the Do – Betty Boo* (Camden, 1999). Pop is in the heart.

Music Sounds Better With You Stardust
No. 2 1998

Deft punk

To 1998 now, and a modern summer-holiday classic. The trajectory of Stardust's 'Music Sounds Better With You' followed what has become a well-worn dance hit route. At the start of the year there was the Miami Winter Music Conference, where hip types gather to sample the latest musical wares. Having been a roaring success here, the song spread out like some funky virus across the Balearic club scene, until finally it reached its natural resting home: the British charts.

The main man behind the project was Thomas Bangaltar, erstwhile stalwart of French dance duo

Daft Punk. Between albums Bangaltar got together with producer Alan 'Braxe' Queme and vocalist Benjamin 'Diamond' Cohen to record the song. Sampling a Chaka Khan song, 'Fate', 'Music Sounds Better With You' is a superior slice of dance music. Clipped guitar, fluid bass, hypnotic beat, the song's catchy hook is looped again and again so you can dance, should you want, until your feet drop off. It's so good, in fact, that the adjectives that best describe it sound like a dance version of the Seven Dwarfs: slinky, sexy, sparky, classy, funky, groovy and glittery.

> A dance version of the Seven Dwarfs: slinky, sexy, sparky, classy, funky, groovy and glittery.

The question is, of course, is it actually true that the music somehow sounds better if you are around? The answer, I guess, is that it all depends on who 'you' is. If we're talking about parents, for example, especially if yours are the sort who come in and turn the stereo down, then the music sounds quieter rather than better. If the 'you' in question is Timmy Mallett, then again, the answer is no – have some loon in silly glasses jumping around and shouting 'oh yeah!' is not likely to improve your musical experience. If we're talking someone attractive, which I think is what Thomas is Bangaltaring on about, then, well, how much attention are you paying to the music anyway?

Originally released on Bangaltar's own Roule label, 'Music Sounds Better With You' was picked up by Virgin and quickly rocketed up the charts. In fact, Virgin offered Bangaltar a reported three million dollars to record an entire album, but Bangaltar turned it down, preferring to get on with Daft Punk and leaving Stardust a one-song memory. Coupled with another Bangaltar collaboration, Bob Sinclair's 'Gym Tonic' (later finding its way to number 1 under the name 'Spacedust'), it remains the defining sound of a late-nineties summer.

Listen Here *Now That's What I Call Music Volume 41* (Virgin EMI, 1998). The solitary gem on a disc that includes Billie, Sash! and the Vengaboys.

Listen On *Discovery* – Daft Punk (Virgin, 2001). The day job.

Listen Further *Gym & Tonic* – Spacedust (East West, 1998). Don't drink and sit-up, you'll spill it.

No bracket required

Five hits with utterly unnecessary punctuation

'(Do) The Hucklebuck' – Coast to Coast

'(I Just) Died In Your Arms' – Cutting Crew

'Day Trip To Bangor (Didn't We Have A Lovely Time)' – Fiddler's Dram

'(Full Metal Jacket) I Wanna Be Your Drill Instructor' – Abigail Mead and Nigel Goulding

'Ain't Gonna Bump No More (With No Big Fat Woman)' – Joe Tex

12 Ooh Vicar – Saucy Hits

The rude, the crude and the lewd now, as we approach a selection of one hit wonders whose very naughtiness gave them enough notoriety to push them into the charts. Snogging, stripping, self-abuse, girlie magazines – they've all been the subject of hits over the years. There's a bit of being sexy (Jane Birkin talking French) and a bit of being sexist (the Monks and her legs) thrown in for good measure.

Of course, sex is everywhere when it comes to music. The saucier, the more suggestive the better when it comes to column inches and sales. What these songs do, however, is perhaps just cross over the line, go that little bit too far, push things a touch further than perhaps they should have. Like earlier gimmick songs, that's all very well and is great as far as getting attention goes. But the chances of being taken seriously in the long run? That's a lot trickier . . .

Je T'aime ... Moi Non Plus Jane Birkin and Serge Gainsbourg
No. 1 1969

'If you find a good woman and you have dinner, and you put a bit of Serge on, you're laughing.' David Holmes, sleeve notes to *Initials SG*

If a gherkin is what the Beatles would leave on the side of their plates, and a Jerkin is what Britney and Michael Jackson's music have in common (the producer Rodney), and a merkin is a nether-wig for the fairer sex (see Bush, the fake Nirvana), then a Birkin is a saucy-sounding duet between a beautiful young British actress and a forty-something French lounge lizard of the highest distinction.

More than anyone else in this book, Serge Gainsbourg is the one person to whom the phrase 'one hit wonder' feels unfairly applied. In any decent society, where talent and creativity were properly rewarded, Serge would be up there with the likes of Scott Walker, Burt Bacharach, Barry White and Leonard Cohen. He would be lauded as the man who inspired the music of Air and the attire of Jarvis Cocker, the man whose mixture of sixties pop, gallic funk, easy listening and lush orchestration was years ahead of its time; whose 1971 classic *Histoire de Melody Nelson* would be considered one of the great albums of the twentieth century.

Unfortunately for Serge, he was French. And that, as far as the British public were concerned, ruled him out of any possible musical credibility.

The first person to record 'Je T'aime' with Serge was another of his many lovers, Brigitte Bardot. But she refused to his request to release it, concerned at what people might think. So enter Jane Birkin. Famous for her part in Antonioni's brilliant but baffling *Blow-Up*, her part being wearing little more than a pair of lime-green stockings, she found herself starring opposite Serge in the French film *Slogan*. It didn't take long for Serge to get the urge. 'He always said he liked me because he was scared of breasts – although come to think of it, Bardot had the prettiest bosoms imaginable, so I'm not sure I should have believed him.'* Birkin was seduced, and before the year was out the new version of 'Je T'aime' was recorded.

Let us take a second to compare the performances of Brigitte and Jane. And sex icon that Brigitte is, it has to be said that Jane gives better aural sex. Where Brigitte's strategy is to give it some serious heavy breathing, Jane opts for the full range of groans and moans. The result is that she sounds up for it; Brigitte just sounds knackered. All of which is crucial for the song, because, *mmmm*, if the singer isn't, *ohh*, distracting you, you might start trying to fathom what the lyrics are all about. I love you ... me neither. What's that all about? I come and go between your kidneys? Let's move on.

'Je T'aime' was released in '69 – when else? – to exactly the response that Bardot had predicted. The

> 'Je T'aime' was released in '69 – when else?

---

* Interviewed in *The Insight*, April 2003.

sixties, it seemed, were not quite about free love after all. The Vatican condemned the song, the BBC banned it, and just as the song rose (surged?) to number 2, record label Fontana got all embarrassed and withdrew. Instead, they leased the song to another record company, Major Minor, and after a brief chartus interruptus, Serge commendably gathered a second head of steam, and Jane hit the top spot after all.

'Je T'aime' was the first time a foreign-language record had achieved that in the UK. And in two foreign languages for us Brits at that: French *and* hot loving. If you wondered what an English version of the song would sound like, listen no further than Frankie Howerd's version, released the following year. Woken up at 3.30 in the morning by a groaning June Whitfield (best not tell Terry, eh?), Frankie is not exactly overjoyed: 'Oh give over. Not again. Do you know what time it is? Speak English woman, what ever is the matter with you . . .'

Surge Forward, as *Private Eye* christened him, was not finished yet in shocking people. First, he turned his attention to the French, by rewriting 'La Marseillaise'. Then it was the turn of book buyers with his 1980 novel *Evguenie Sokolov*, a touching tale about a man who cannot stop farting. Next up was his 1985 duet with his fourteen-year-old daughter Charlotte, the ever so slightly dubious 'Lemon Incest'. But Serge saved his finest performance until last. Appearing on a French chat show with Whitney Houston in the late 1980s, a sizzled Serge leant across to the host and said, 'I want to fuck her.' The host tried to cover up by relaying to Whitney that Serge wanted to give her some flowers, but Serge was insistent. 'Don't translate for me. I said, I wanted to fuck her.' For that, Serge, I will always love you.

Serge sadly died in 1991, but his contribution to the world lives on. 'I was recently told by a taxi driver in London that he'd had three children to that record,' Jane said in an interview.* They may have had more hits, but really, could anyone say the same about Wet Wet Wet?

Listen Here *Initials SG* (Mercury, 2002). The Best of Serge. My French isn't fantastic, but even I can have a stab at what '69 Année Érotique' might be about.

Listen On *Histoire de Melody Nelson* (Mercury, 2001). Serge's finest album, in my opinion, now remastered.

Watch Further *Blow-Up* (DVD, 2004). Jane Birkin's in it. Beyond that, it all gets a bit confusing.

Nice Legs Shame About Her Face
The Monks
No. 19 1979

What's wrong with being sexy?
If recent years have seen songs and songwriters turning their attentions back(side)wards – 'Bootylicious', 'Booty Call', Kylie's most bootyful feature – in the late 1970s and early 1980s the thing to have was a pair of

* *The Scotsman*, April 1997.

legs. There was Rod Stewart having all the luck with his succession of 'leggy' blondes. There was Legs and Co., the *Top of the Pops* dance troupe who replaced Pan's People and went out with a squawk (see 'The Birdie Song'). There was the ZZ Top classic, 'Legs', all about a 'girl' who 'knows' how to 'use them'. And in spring 1979, just as Margaret Thatcher was taking control of the country, was this choice little ditty.

The Monks were two lapsed members of a strict Augustinian friary called St Michael's, near Hastings. Father Patrick and Brother George both confessed to having impure thoughts about a visiting nun, Sister Evangeline, and decided their future was outside the church. Actually, that's a lie. The Monks were in fact primarily John Ford and Richard 'Hud' Hudson, two former members of the Strawbs, the long-running folk-prog outfit who make slightly more sense after several pints of homemade cider. Together with Terry Cassidy and Clive Pearce, the Monks recorded a back-to-basics-style album, *Bad Habits*, from which this single came.

Apart from having a packet of pork scratchings and a dartboard stapled to the front, it is difficult to see how more pubby this pub rock record could be. Musically, 'Nice Legs' is second division Ian Dury, one part Squeeze to two parts Chas and Dave. Lyrically, it is Double Diamond on disc, employing a Hofmeister 'Follow the Bear' philosophy most recently brought back down to date by Finchy, the smooth-talking sales rep from *The Office*. The story goes like this: a monk agrees to go on a blind date to help a mate out, but the 'tasty bird' he was expecting turns out to be a right one. Great set of pins, admittedly, but not so hot in the head department. In verse two he takes her dancing as promised, but not 'getting far' (I wonder why?), he nips off to the bar, where everyone is in agreement: fantastic legs, plug mug. In verse three 'Nice Legs' starts getting choosy, asking to go bowling and then changing her mind after he's bought the tickets. Women! But despite three verses of dissing, in verse four our monk walks her home and is still expectant of his invitation indoors. Men who are boozy are not exactly choosy. Whereupon Nice Legs tells him to leg it and that he's not exactly an oil painting himself.

With its Ronseal cover of a pair of 'nice legs', the Monks raced to number n-n-nineteen in the charts. The follow-up, 'I Ain't Gettin' Any', didn't get any sales, except in Canada where inexplicably the band briefly became stadium-big. John and Hud rejoined the Strawbs, and the monks returned to a life-long vow of silence. Except in 2001, when the song was dusted down and performed in a place where outdated views were made to feel at home. That's right, John and Hud strummed the number at the Conservative Party Spring Conference, hell, even teaming up with rock hellraiser Michael Ancram for a couple of songs.

Nice.

Shame.

> Lyrically, it is Double Diamond on disc, employing a Hofmeister 'Follow the Bear' philosophy.

Listen Here *Bad Habits* (EMI, 1979). Further rib-ticklers include 'Johnny B Rotten'.

Listen On *Choice Selection of Strawbs* (A&M, 1992). Sixteen slabs of solid Strawb.

Listen Further 'Legs' – ZZ Top (Warner, 1985). The definitive song about the left one and the right one.

Centerfold
The J. Geils Band
No. 3 1982

Na na na na na na, na na na na na na na na na...

Picture the scene. It's 1981 and you're Peter Wolf (middle names 'and' and 'the'), lead singer of middling American rhythm and blues group the J. Geils Band. Perhaps you're on tour, all the groupies have gone home and you're feeling like a bit of a J. Arthur (see 'Turning Japanese' – the Vapors). You head for the newsagents to find yourself a 'girlie magazine', but as you flick through the pages of the *Playboys* and the *Razzles*, suddenly your, ahem, 'blood runs cold'. The centrefold star, the model with the staples in all the painful places, is looking a little familiar ...

In the early eighties, many years before the Internet and websites such as Friends Reunited, it was a lot more difficult to keep in contact with classmates from school. Maybe this was why Peter had lost touch with his 'homeroom angel', a beautiful, innocent slip of a girl, someone (you'll like this) it was impossible to 'stain'. But whereas once Peter's angel used to flash her 'baby blues' at him across the classroom, now she is flashing a whole lot more besides.

Pop songs have been written about all sorts of subjects – love, friendship, going out in North Wales (see 'Day Trip To Bangor' – Fiddler's Dram) – but 'Centrefold' is the only one with the courage to ask one of life's great questions: what do you do when your childhood sweetheart has become an international 'glamour' model? I can't offer any personal insight here – my girlfriends from school became, respectively, a bank clerk and a librarian – so should you ever find yourself in a 'centrefold situation', you could do worse than Peter's own four-point plan. First, deal with the hurt – come to terms with the feeling that your memories have 'just been sold'. This can be helped by point two, the reunion. Peter suggests catching up with your 'angel', see her when her 'clothes are on'. Third – and it's here where I differ slightly with his analysis – Peter wants his angel to take him for a drive, specifically to a motel, where they can hire a room and, ahem, take their clothes off 'in private'. Fourth, until this meeting can be arranged, Peter suggests easing the pain by buying the magazine (see 'All By Myself' – Eric Carmen).

> What do you do when your childhood sweetheart has become an international 'glamour' model?

In a slightly *Spinal Tap* career path, the J. Geils Band began life in the late sixties as the J. Geils Blues Band. Then Peter Wolf joined, and sixties blues became seventies rock. There followed a decade of moderate success, both on and off the record player. The band garnered a reputation as a great live band, while in 1975 Peter Wolf married the gorgeous Faye Dunaway. Then came the eighties. Faye moved in with fashion photographer Terry O'Neill and Peter moved in with his, well, I guess his collection of 'girlie magazines'.

'Centerfold' was the band's one and only international smash, helped in no small part by its 'na na na' chorus and also its ahead-of-its-time video – three minutes of cavorting schoolgirls when Britney was just a twinkle in Daddy Spears's eye. 'Centerfold' was followed by 'Freeze-Frame', which froze at number 27. Continuing the video analogy, the fast forward of the band's career quickly became rewind, stop and then eject, and the band split up a couple of years later.

J. Geils, if you're interested, was the band's guitarist. The J. stands for Jerome.

Listen Here *Life in the Fast Lane* – Various Artists (Telstar, 1987). There's also John Farnham, John Parr and Jon Bon Jovi.

Listen On *Full House Live* – J. Geils Band (WEA, 1999). Contains 'First I Look At The Purse', one of Nick Hornby's 31 songs.

Listen Further 'Centerfold' – Adam Austin (Media, 1999). Great song, crap version.

Kissing With Confidence Will Powers
No. 17 1983

With a little help, nobody does it better ...
Ah, kissing. Snogging. Spooning, as older readers of *Smash Hits* may remember. To tongue or not to tongue, that is the ingestion. A pastime fondly given much lip service in music: Prince's finest four minutes; the crazy, crazy knights of seventies glam metal; Deborah Harry's 'French Kissing In The USA'; Stephen 'Tin Tin' Duffy; kissing frogs (Peter Gabriel), brides (Elton), the dirt (INXS) and, um, the rain (Billie Myers). But despite all this, only one artist has ever turned his attention to what we really need to know: how to do it right.

I say 'his'. Will Powers, the singer of this bizarre song, is actually Lynn Goldsmith with the little help of a vocoder – a voice-altering box of special effects most famous for giving Cher a number 1 hit twenty years after her career had died. A hugely famous rock photographer, Lynn had snapped everyone from Springsteen to the Police when, in the early 1980s she decided to turn her attention to music. The resulting album, from which 'Kissing With Confidence' comes, boasts both a fantastically impressive range of contributors – Sting, Steve Winwood, Nile Rodgers, Todd Rundgren – and arguably one of the strangest concepts for a record ever committed to vinyl.

Dancing for Mental Health does exactly what it says on its rather odd tin. There's dance music, and then over the top (in every sense), there is Will Powers, a sort of Max Headroom meets Dale Carnegie character, offering his opinions on various psychological and emotional issues. 'The first optic-music artist,' is how Lynn describes the project, with the intention of fun first and information second. Anyway, the album and

> Arguably one of the strange concepts for a record ever committed to vinyl.

its accompanying videos did have the desired motivational effect: among those who used Will Powers were the US Department of Labor (to 'inspire' unemployed youths), the UK National Marriage Guidance Council and Harvard University. Two pieces even ended up in the New York Museum of Modern Art.

As for 'Kissing With Confidence' itself, it was helped by the contribution of an uncredited Carly Simon. Aside from her voice, Lynn felt she was appropriate for another reason: 'Carly's mouth is huge,' she explains, and she had to grow up with big lips when big lips weren't fashionable. While Carly sang the chorus Will chatted his way through some tonsil tennis advice: it doesn't matter how good-looking or great at dancing you are, if don't know how to kiss with confidence, you're not going to get past first base. There's a checklist (helpful) of questions to go through (example: is there any spinach in your teeth?). There's a chant to remember, though that's in Spanish (less helpful). There's some advice for anyone worried about getting pregnant from kissing (you can't). And if there's someone you know who burps or bites or drools, 'Will' suggests slipping them a copy of this record.

Lynn quickly discovered that the pop star world wasn't for her. Three days of being locked in a hotel room doing back-to-back interviews was not her thang. She quickly returned to her first love, the dark room. And as well as continuing with her photography career, she has recently returned more directly to the rock world, becoming good friends with World Party's Karl Wallinger and becoming his manager.

Listen Here *Dancing for Mental Health* (Island, 1983). Kissing and more sorted out, on one handy album.

Read On *Photodiary: A Musical Journey* (Rizzoli, 1995). Lynn doing her day job.

Listen Further 'Kiss' – Prince (Paisley Park, 1986). The finest four minutes about puckering up.

Male Stripper
Man 2 Man meet Man Parrish
No. 4 1987

They're not talking paint

In the mid-1980s, a full decade before *The Full Monty* was a twinkle behind someone's police hat, a body of pop stars got all excited about taking their clothes off. First of all there was Adam Ant, with his not exactly goody-two-shoes single 'Strip'. It's following 'ancient history' is the transparent argument of his lyrics. Not to be undone, Depeche Mode weighed in with their 'Stripped', in which Dave Gahan, rather unpleasantly in my opinion, wants to see you 'stripped to the bone'. Hmm. And then, in early 1987, came this Chippendale off the old block.

Man 2 Man were two men, who never went man 2 man themselves on account of being brothers. Paul and Miki Zone's route to stardom started in New

> Said stripper, the 'late night Adonis', modestly describes himself as 'built like a truck'.

York in the mid-1970s, as part of the New York Dolls-dominated glitter rock scene. Contemporaries of Blondie and the Ramones, their punk-pop four-piece the Fast got their big(ish) break when they were spotted by Ric Ocasek of the Cars.* A record deal and support slots in football stadiums followed. But when a second album, *Leather Boys from the Asphalt Jungle*, went as nowhere as the first, a change of direction was needed. So out went the drummer and bassist and in came synthesisers and drum machines. Out went punk-pop and in came Hi-NRG dance. Out went the Fast and in came Man 2 Man.

Enter Manny 'Man' Parrish, another New Yorker, though the sort to hang at Studio 54 rather than CBGBs. One of the pioneers of eighties electronic music, Man swapped critical success on tracks such as 'Hip Hop Bee Bop' and 'Boogie Down Bronx' for the commercial sort with Man 2 Man. Pitching their tent firmly in the centre of pop's camp site, 'Male Stripper' is the story of a 'male stripper' in a 'stripper bar'. Said stripper, the 'late night Adonis', modestly describes himself as 'built like a truck'.** He's more than happy to hump for a, well, you do the rhyme, but clearly his bar turns a blind eye to its no-touching policy. Backed by a pumping beat, a show-me-yours-I'll-show-you-mine chorus and 'Male Stripper' took (his clothes) off, all the way to number phwoar.

But just as soon as Miki and Paul were finally in the zone, Miki was tragically out of it. Many years of partying were finally catching up with him, and he died on New Year's Eve 1986, just as the song was taking off. Man 2 Man meet Man, now ostensibly the 2 Man Man meet Man, performed on *Top of the Pops* in February, achieving the rare feat of being a debut appearance and a swansong at the same time.

Interesting male stripper fact: Man Parrish went on to DJ at the delightfully named Sperm night in New York's delightfully named Cock bar. He also runs a number of adult websites.

Listen Here 'Male Stripper' – Man 2 Man (Hot Productions, 1995). Also includes the tender and poignant song, 'At The Gym'.

Listen On 'Hip Hop Bee Bop' – Man Parrish (Unidisc, 1994). Cutting cuts.

Listen Further 'You Can Leave Your Hat On' – Tom Jones (on *The Full Monty* soundtrack, RCA, 2001). More men. More clothes coming off.

I Touch Myself
Divinyls
No. 10 1991

It's not just the boys . . .

Before Kylie discovered that she had a bottom. Before Danni became pneumatically enhanced. Before (Good Golly) Miss Holly kiss-kissed her way to the upper reaches of *FHM*'s 100 Sexiest Women, there was another Australian who knew a thing or two about

---

* The Cars. Modest American new wavers, best known in Britain for their cigarette lighter anthem 'Drive', which, ever so slightly bizarrely, became part of the soundtrack to Live Aid in 1985.
** For a more detailed analysis of vehicular vocabulary, try *Ugly Women Look Like Buses, Gorgeous Men Like Trucks* by Professor Agatha Hoegaarden (P. Stake Press, 1994).

sex and sexuality. Her name was Christina Amphlett, nymphet lead singer of Aussie rockers Divinyls. And in 1991 they hit one hit wonderdom with a song about the 'wonder' of 'one' girl and her 'hit'.

Divinyls began in 1980 at (where else in Australia?) Sydney Opera House, where Christina was singing in a choir as part of a religious concert. Guitarist Mark McEntee was mesmerised as Christina's microphone lead got wrapped up in her stool, and she dragged her seat across the stage as though nothing was happening. Learning their craft in Sydney's salubrious King's Cross district, Divinyls developed their pop-rock sound and Christina her stage persona, all school uniforms and fishnet stockings. The band formed part of the so-called 'Australian Assault', the wave of emerging antipodean bands including Men at Work, Midnight Oil and INXS, but while the others found international success, Divinyls spent much of the 1980s boomeranging back to where they came from. Then in 1991 Christina and Mark teamed up with songwriters Billy Steinberg and Tom Kelly, the duo whose credits included Madonna's 'Like A Virgin'. The results, frankly, were never going to be polite.

Not, I should stress, that Christina 'touched' the subject for the very first time. In 1984 Prince introduced us to 'Darling Nikki', a girl who knew how to grind (coffee, I think), who when she was having a break from the beans, would perk herself up with the 'pages of a magazine'. Then, proving that girls sometimes just want to have fun, Cyndi Lauper recorded 'She Bop', a dirty little ditty about picking up some 'good vibration' and 'messing' with her 'danger zone'. And later on, Tori Amos would add 'Icicle' on her *Under the Pink* album: with her father running a religious

meeting downstairs, the group take from 'his body', while Tori 'takes' from hers upstairs.

Just in case anyone missed the point, the promotional pictures for 'I Touch Myself' featured Christina in nothing more than a fishnet dress and a couple of carefully placed hands. In an interview Christina explained, with wonderful rock perception: 'I was trying to be dressed and naked at the same time.' The video, meanwhile, featured a contortionist. But while the song enjoyed huge success around the world, this paean to female masturbation ended up rather more like the male version. Rather than enjoying hit after hit after hit, Divinyls had to make do with one solitary smash, and hard as they tried, could never quite hit the same peaks again. Wrangles with record companies delayed the follow-up album and while *Underworld* was a modest success in Australia in 1996, the moment, so like life, had passed. Christina has since turned her attention to acting.

Interviewed by the *Sydney Morning Herald* in 2003, Christina said the thing she loved most about the song was 'the feel'.

> Christina said the thing she loves most about the song was 'the feel'.

Listen Here *The Divinyls* (Virgin, 1991). Album also boasts 'Lay Your Body Down' and 'Love School'.

Listen On *Essential* (Chrysalis, 1991). Further touching songs.

Listen Further *Time after Time* – Cyndi Lauper (Columbia, 2001). Best-of that includes 'She Bop'.

Would You ...
Touch and Go
No. 7 1998

Umm ...

Do you come here often? How do you like your eggs done for breakfast? If I could rearrange the alphabet, I'd put U and I together. Is it hot in here or is it just you? What do you say we do some maths: add a bed, subtract our clothes and multiply. I think you've something in your eye: no, it's just a sparkle. Do you know why they call me Fred Flintstone? It's because I can make your Bedrock. Do you believe in love at first sight, or should I walk by again?

Ah, the perils of dating. Apparently, sometimes these lines don't work. And even more apparently, sometimes people don't like using them. Which is why, in 1998, the very nice Touch and Go came along and said it all for you, as main man David Lowe explains: 'If you fancy that guy or girl really badly, but you're a bit on the shy side, when the track comes on, hey presto, the question is already asked for you – you just have to look over and smile at your true love, and off you go.'* Certainly, it's hard to see how any sane person could resist the subtle argument of the lyrics. To paraphrase: one, I've been watching you; two, I think you're incredibly attractive; three, will you sleep with me? Well, if you put it like that, Mr Warthog, how can I say no?

Touch and Go is for all intents and purposes one

man, David Lowe, a technological mastermind from the not especially technological Malvern Hills. His first attempt at the charts was *Dreamcatcher*, a dreamy collection of Enigma and Deep Forest-style ethnic grooves. But when that didn't work out, he turned his attention to a simpler, stripped-down style, with simpler lyrics about, well, stripping down. Over a South American-style groove, the lyrics are spoken by a well-known but anonymous American actress. Actually, it's Jessica Lange. Actually, that's a lie. I've no idea who it is. David remains very secretive about the identity of his mysterious chanteuse.

'Would You ...' reached number 7 in 1998, and for a brief moment that trumpet solo sound was ubiquity itself. The song was hilariously parodied on Chris Moyles' Radio One show, with 'alternative' versions by Dale Winton ('Will You Go To Step Class With Me?') and Frank Bruno ('Will You Go Three Rounds With Me'). Its brassy, straight-talking – cheap? – style made a perfect complement for Asda, who used it for an advertising campaign in 2000. Meanwhile, Touch and Go's chart career was looking decidedly touch and go. The follow-up single, 'Straight To Number One', did anything but.

David returned to his day job, writing music for television, which, it has to be said, he is very good at: over 150 programmes under his belt, with everything from Jeremy Clarkson to Alan Titchmarsh to David Attenborough. But his biggest success is coming up

> To paraphrase: one, I've been watching you; two, I think you're incredibly attractive; three, will you sleep with me?

* Interviewed in *Sound on Sound*, January 1999.

with the current music for *BBC News,* if that's what you call the drum rolls and the Morse code tapping bursts that precede Huw Edwards saying 'Good evening'. The full version 'BBC News (Your Place Or Mine)' with backing vocals from John Humphrys and Jeremy Paxman has sadly never been released.

Listen Here *Now That's What I Call Music Volume 41* (Virgin EMI, 1998). Saucy side three of the double cassette also includes T-Spoon's 'Sex On The Beach'.

Listen On *I Find You Very Attractive* – Touch and Go (V2, 2000). A whole albummmm . . .

Watch Further The *BBC News.* Would you go to bed with Huw Edwards?

Their one hit was a cover version

'Wonderwall'
Mike Flowers Pops

'Whole Lotta Love'
Goldbug

'Smooth Criminal'
Alien Ant Farm

'Strawberry Fields Forever'
Candy Flip

'Funky Town'
Pseudo Echo

13 Eurostars
– Continental Hits

Europe. Great football players. Terrible musicians. How a continent of such great culture can produce such terrible music is a question that can never quite be addressed: the Eurovision Song Contest is an annual reminder that not only do we not sing from the same hymn sheet, we also do not dress from the same fashion sheet, dance from the same routine sheet or have the same taste from the same taste sheet. On one level, however cosy France and Germany get at our expense, we can always be ever so slightly smug at the fact that we've got the Beatles and the Stones and they've got Johnny Halliday and the Scorpions.

But let's not diss our European cousins too much. There are several perfectly decent musical strands around that we would be proud to call our own. France, for example, is fairly untouchable when it comes to slinky Gallic dance from the likes of Air and Daft Punk. Sweden, too, offers a whole host of very catchy pop from Abba through Roxette and perhaps one of the finest rock bands around in the Soundtrack of Our Lives. Italian house – Black Box and beyond – also enjoyed a respectable reign in the early 1990s. And Germany, as this book repeatedly demonstrates, serves to some extent as a retirement home for failed pop stars from elsewhere.

There are, however, pop moments that don't translate so well. Acts who come from different traditions that don't transfer so well into our charts. There may be a novelty factor here – the difference that feels first time round like endearing quirks. Long term, though, our tastes seem to diverge more and more. As close as we may move politically, culturally any union or harmony seems a long way off.

A Little Peace Nicole

No. 1 1982

Papa's girl

In April 1981, in a hard-fought contest in Dublin, Bucks Fizz squeaked past the German challenge of Lena Valaitis to claim the Eurovision Song Contest crown by a mere four points. That pulling-the-skirt-off gag, often imitated, never bettered, was the masterstroke. Which meant in 1982 that the host nation was the United Kingdom, Le Royaume Uni, with the microphone duties being given to the Katie Derham of her day, Jan Leeming. And where did the BBC choose to host the event, the glittering jewel of the European television crown? London? No, guess again. Birmingham? Further north. Manchester? A bit more across. Leeds? Up a touch. Newcastle? Lower. Scotch Corner? Ok, I'll tell you, you're not going to get it. The venue for the 1982 Eurovision Song Contest was Harrogate.

Quite.

The British attempt to keep hold of the trophy, and presumably allow Ashby de la Zouch its moment in the sun, fell to Bardo, a sort of Vauxhall Conference pop Torvill and Dean. He (Stephen Fisher) looked like a young Richard Madeley, she (Sally Ann Triplett) like Tiffany in a wig. Their song, 'One Step Further', seems in retrospect an admission of defeat from the word go. Another step, apparently, and they would have been 'there'. That might be true in the chart sense, where the song eventually stalled at number 2, but in Eurovision terms 'Six Steps Further' might have been more appropriate. Bardo finished in a sympathy-for-the-host position of seventh.

Instead, the night, and ultimately the number 1 spot, belonged to a seventeen-year-old German singer called Nicole. Until something miraculous happens, 1982 remains the only time that Germany has ever won the Eurovision Song Contest. Even Luxembourg, not so much a country as a postage stamp, managed it four times. 'Ein Bisschen Frieden' – I think that means 'A Little Fry-Up' – beat second-place Israel, no I'm never quite sure how they get to enter either, by a whopping 61 points. Nicole had long straight hair, a black dress with sparkly bits on and a twelve-string white guitar that looked far too big for her. And just to rub our noses in it, she sang the winning song again in *four different languages*. No one likes a smart arse.

> Nicole sang the winning song again in four different languages. No one likes a smart arse.

But as much as the song was a success, it was also a curse for German Eurovision. It was written by Ralph Siegel, a man who has since gone on to write the German entry many times – thirteen and counting. I guess his argument is 'I'm the only man to have written a winning song', rather than 'I'm the only man to have lost twelve times'. At least it makes it easier for the rest of us. Well, as long as we don't send along people who can't sing in tune like Gemini.

Nicole, meanwhile, has offered little peace to the German nation, remaining a popular and successful singer ever since. In 2001 she recorded a duet with fellow Eurovision winner Johnny Logan, the thanks-for-the-image single 'No One Makes Love Like You'.

Listen Here *The Story of Eurovision* – Various Artists (BS, 2002). Assorted winners and losers.

Listen On *Nur Das Beste* – Nicole (BMG Germany, 2000). If my German was better, I could make a cheap joke about some of the other titles.

Listen Further 'One Step Further' – Bardo (Epic, 1982). A plucky seventh place for the Brits. Something Gemini would have been proud of.

Live Is Life Opus
No. 6 1985

Less their magnum opus, more their Mini Milk

To Austria now, a country not noted for its musical success over the years. In the mid-1980s, however, it all briefly threatened to change. In 1986 Johann Holzel, better known as Falco, topped the charts all over the world with his brilliantly silly 'Rock Me Amadeus'. A sort of Teutonic Adam Ant, Falco somehow got away with singing in German (how often does that happen in Britain?), out of which the baffled listener picked out the occasional word – 'punk', 'excellent' and my particular favourite, 'po-po-leer'. But with his second top-ten hit, 'Vienna Calling', Falco – just – is ineligible for this book. Which

leaves us with this song by his fellow countrymen, Opus.

By 1985 Opus had already been going for twelve years. The less said about their early days the better. There were covers of Deep Purple songs. There was (dear God) a rock version of *Eine kleine Nachtmusik*. The strains of this classical influence were thankfully flushed out with their 1980 debut album, *Daydream*. By now the classic Opus line-up was complete: Kurt Rene Plisnier, Walter Bachkönig, Ewald Pfleger, Günther Grasmuck and Herwig Rüdisser. That may sound like the midfield line-up of a struggling Bundesliga side, and certainly with their requisite mullets and moustaches, they looked like one too.

Opus, though, were anything but struggling. In 1981 they played the Arena di Verona along with Christopher Cross and (is this allowed?) Lou Reed. In 1982 they released a concept album, called (are you ready for this?) *Opusition*. And after contributing to Falco's pre-'Amadeus' album *Junge Romer*, Opus turned their attention to their eleventh-anniversary concert at the Stadium of Oberwart. For which the band decided to write a new song, that all the fans could sing along to. Come on, all together now . . .

> Opus look like the midfield line-up of a struggling Bundesliga side, with their requisite mullets and moustaches.

Two competing interpretations have developed over the years with regard to the meaning of 'Live Is Life'. On one side is what is known as the Robbie Neville, C'est La Vie school of thought. This sees the song as a sort of Austrian 'Que Sera, Sera', a we're-all-in-this-together-vibe that translates the 'na na na na nas' along the lines of 'ho hum, mustn't grumble'. However, the competing argument, the Rock and Roll Star school, suggests that this interpretation is based on a mishearing of the lyrics: the song, it reminds listeners, is not called 'Life Is Life', but rather '*Live* Is Life'. This, coupled with the song's origins, not to mention the 'live' recording of 5,000 accompanying Austrians, positions the lyric as part of the music-about-music canon. Rock and roll, it suggests, is what life is all about. The Robbie Neville response to this line is that it renders the 'na na na na nas' completely meaningless. At which point, some thinkers have attempted to draw the two schools together by suggesting, 'isn't that like life?'

Whichever. All around the world, countries like Britain that had never even *heard* of Opus, were buying the record by the bucketload. And though off the radar here, they remain big in places like, erm, Bulgaria and Russia (in 1987, they sold out the Moscow Olympic Stadium three times). Sport remains a theme. In 1998 they recorded 'Viva Austria' to support the Austrian World Cup team. And in 2003 the DJ Otzi dance remix of 'Live Is Life' became an unofficial 'Swing Low' for the French rugby team. To whom, as world champions, we say (all together now) na na na na na ...

Listen Here   *The Greatest Hits of 1985* (Telstar, 1985). There's 'Clouds Across The Moon' by the Rah Band before it. There's 'Nineteen' by Paul Hardcastle after it.

Listen On   *Flying Higher: Greatest Hits* – Opus (Zomba Germany, 2003). A 'doppel' CD for those feeling brave.

Listen Further   *The Final Curtain: The Ultimate Best of Falco* (EMI Germany, 1999). Austria's other finest.

The Final Countdown
Europe
No. 1 1986

Diddle-lee dah! Diddle lee-di-dah!

Old songs never die. They just become mobile phone ring tones instead. You'd be amazed to find out how many songs you could type into Google and be offered the ring tone in return. Some old favourites, it has to be said, lend themselves more to being a cheesy mono-phonic annoying-people-on-the-train tune than others. And 'The Final Countdown', Europe's end-of-the-world-is-nigh riff, is right up there with the worst of them.

Europe began in Stockholm in 1979 – the band that is, not the continent – when they were known as Force. Led by lead singer Joey Tempest, the band got their big break in 1982 when they won a local music competition. Their prize, the recording of their first LP. Now called Europe, they called their debut album that too, added a keyboardist and followed it up with *Wings of*

The leather trousers! The poodle perm haircuts! The squiggly guitar solos!

Tomorrow. The band were slowly beginning to build a fan base in Scandinavia, before 'The Final Countdown' came along, and everything went global.

It would be easy to knock Europe, boasting as they did all the hallmarks of an eighties heavy metal band: the leather trousers! The poodle perm haircuts! The squiggly guitar solos! But really, they were no different or any worse in any of that from Bon Jovi or Van Halen or Whitesnake or any other band you care to think of. You wanted to be in a hard rock band in the eighties, you grew your hair long, dyed it blond and permed it – that's just how it was. You would, though, be on slightly safer ground with the music. There was always something slightly naff about Europe. Rather than, say, the fret pyrotechnics of fellow countryman Yngwie Malmsteen, there was instead a touch of cheesy synth to proceedings. Lyrically too, I'm sure a little was lost in translation. Whereas Nena's '99 Red Balloons' hit the button about hitting the button, Europe's story about leaving Earth behind and heading for Venus just seemed a touch post-post-apocalypse. Though whatever was wrong with planet Earth, at least they were heading in the right direction. Venus, as John Gray went on to tell us, is where women are from, so at least the Europe boys were following their rock and roll roots.

The single wasn't the final chart countdown the band were ever involved in, though it wasn't far off. A couple more albums, and the band split in the early 1990s. Joey Tempest went solo, with the band reforming for a millennium version of the song: 'The Final Countdown' 2000 hit number 36. But even this wasn't the final final countdown. A reunion proper was pencilled in for 2004.

Listen Here *Life in the Fast Lane* (Telstar, 1987). The final track on side one, of course.

Listen On *Europe 1982–2000* (Columbia, 2003). Includes the updated 'Final Countdown 2000'.

Listen Further *Marching Out* – Yngwie Rising Force Malmsteen (Polydor, 1982). More Swedish licking.

The Captain Of Her Heart Double
No. 8 1986

Less Double, more single

I hope that you're not thinking that just because Double – pronounced Doo-blay – come from Switzerland there is by definition some sort of link with those other Swiss musical giants, Yello. So the Swiss may not have had many hits over the years, but to assume that nation's musical output can be reduced to a mere handful of interconnected people would do a huge disservice to the no doubt thriving underground scene in Zurich and Geneva. It would also overlook the importance of the Montreux Festival, which in the 1980s was one of the high points of the musical calendar, most memorably for Frankie Goes to Hollywood doing a calculated 'Rage

> Toblerone Sade, with just a hint of A-Ha to proceedings.

Hard' by trashing the stage in front of the world's press. No, with Yello doing dance, Double – no, I don't know why you pronounce it Doo-blay either – doing their jazzy thing, and the Montreux Festival bringing in the rock, Switzerland in the 1980s was a rich and vibrantly diverse musical place. It is just one huge coincidence, then, that Felix Haug, one half of Double – or maybe it's more like double as in entendre – came to the band after playing with, er, Yello.

Vocalist Kurt Maloo, however, had nothing to do with the band without a 'w'. A former painter, he'd spent the seventies in experimental mode, first, with nine-piece band Troppo, and then with the equally curious release *Luna + 7 Notorious Maloo Home Works* – a record that was a 45rpm single on one side and a 33⅓ rpm album on the other. When Kurt and Felix met in 1981, they got themselves a bassist and called themselves Ping Pong. They even got Phil Manzanera from Roxy Music in on guitar for a bit. After modest success, including an appearance at the Montreux Festival – ok, so maybe the music scene isn't so big there *after* all – the band dropped the bass player and, let's be frank about this, really quite awful name, for one with a funny pronunciation. After a couple of well-received singles, they suddenly went global with this song.

'The Captain Of Her Heart' is a wonderfully mellow song, soothing in every sense from the smoothness of Kurt's voice to the sax fills and piano solos. It's Toblerone Sade, with just a hint of A-Ha to proceedings, partly through its melancholic pop feel, and partly through the not-quite-working-is-it metaphor at the centre of the song. How does one 'captain' someone's heart?

Do they have a navigational chart for that great pop staple, the sea of emotion? Certainly the lady in question is all adrift without her shipmate to guide her. She waits, he doesn't come back. She waits some more, he still doesn't come back. What can I say? Never trust a sailor.

There was an album, *Blue*, followed by another, *Dou3le* – God knows how you pronounce that – but despite featuring trumpet legend Herb Alpert and boasting an award-winning video, the single 'Devil's Ball' stalled at number 71. Double split up in 1987, but Kurt continues as a 'big in Switzerland' solo artist. The 1990 album *Single* (do you see what he did there?) was followed by 1995's *Soul and Echo*. He is currently working on a new album.

Listen Here   *The Hits Album 4* (RCA/Ariola, 1986). A mellow start to side four that also includes 'Radio Africa' by Latin Quarter.

Listen On   *Captain of her Heart* – Kurt Maloo (MMM, 1995). Four versions of the same song.

Listen Further   *The Best of Sade* (Epic, 2000). Similar groove. Fewer cuckoo clocks.

Call Me Spagna
No. 2 1987

Ring my bella

Do you remember that party trick in science lessons at school, the one with the Van der Graaf generator? Everyone would have to stand on a stool and slowly link hands until some poor sucker, normally the child the teacher really hated (I hope it wasn't you), got a whacking great electric shock? Do you remember as well that everyone's hair used to stand on end? Hilarious, wasn't it? In 1987 a singer from Italy made a name for herself with such a hairstyle – a 'fright wig' as *Smash Hits* would call it. Spagna somehow got to number 2 with a bleached pompon on her head and left a nation in shock.

Spagna (full name Spagna Bolognesa. That's a joke. It's Ivana Spagna.) was born in 1956 and started her recording career in the early 1980s with the dance duo Fun Fun. In 1986 she released her debut single, the I'll-leave-you-to-judge European disco smash 'Easy Lady'. Then came 'Call Me', not a cover of the Blondie classic but another slice of Italo-dance, in which Spagna repeatedly asks you to give her a ring. Actually, we can be more precise than 'repeatedly'. Spagna sings 'call me' a somewhat desperate-sounding twenty-eight times. Now I'm sorry that Spagna, as she puts it, is 'losing slumber' over the situation, but really, take the hint. The lad clearly woke up, saw your hairstyle, thought how much Hofmeister did *I* have last night and did a runner.

In one sense, however, Spagna wasn't alone: the mid-1980s saw pop stars everywhere not being able to get through on the telephone. Kirsty MacColl did her bit of telephonic telepathy on Billy Bragg's 'A New England': her phone not ringing meant she knew it 'wasn't you'. Then there was the ever so slightly stupid New Edition, who spent a whole song ringing 'Mr Telephone Man' to report a fault: the fault being that every time they ring their girlfriend's number, they always get a 'click'. The Rah Band, meanwhile, with their frankly barmy 'Clouds Across The Moon', described a desperate wife struggling to get through to her soldier husband fighting a war on the planet Mars. The only ones not to mope around were Curiosity Killed the Cat, who stuck the answer phone on, asked you to leave your name and number and headed out for the pub.

Meanwhile, back in Fright Wig Land, Spagna re-released 'Easy Lady' but it only got to number 62. And that was it for her British career, but on the Continent, particularly in Italy and Spain, she continues to be successful, both as a singer and a songwriter. In 1994 she enjoyed a huge hit with an Italian version of Elton's *Lion King* song, 'Circle Of Life'. In 1998 she sang the Italian World Cup song (they didn't win). Spagna has also worked with Whigfield (they share the same pop Svengali) and on her 2002 album *Woman* recorded 'Tears Of Love', a touching duet with Demis Roussos.

> Spagna sings 'call me' a somewhat desperate-sounding twenty-eight times.

Listen Here   *Dedicated to the Moon* (CBS, 1987). The debut album. Eighties Italo-pop to the max.

Listen On   'Easy Lady 2004' – Spagna vs Ice Cream (DST Germany, 2004). Is it just me, or is that not a fair fight?

Listen Further   *Mega Mixes* – Whigfield (Zyx, 1996). The nineties Spagna, except without the fright wig.

The Race Yello
No. 7 1988

Drive-time dance music

Hailing from Switzerland, a country so devoid of musical talent they even got Celine Dion to represent them in the Eurovision Song Contest, Yello are the exception. An eclectic, eccentric and sporadically excellent dance duo, whose long-running cult status finally spilt over into chart action in the late 1980s. On vocals, or 'concepts' as he prefers to call them, is Dieter Meier, a moustachioed aristocrat who looks like some sort of a cross between the Archduke Franz Ferdinand, Basil Fawlty and that bloke from Electric Six. His pre-rock and roll CV boasts such unlikely phrases as 'millionaire', 'professional gambler' and (I'm not making this up) 'member of the Swiss national golf team'. By contrast, his keyboardist and all-round music whiz can only boast a fantastic name: Boris Blank.

Formed in Zurich in 1979, the duo did their out-of-kilter synth pop thang on albums such as *Solid Pleasure* (1980) and *You Gotta Say Yes to Another Excess* (1983), but their ahead-of-their-timeness left them an acquired taste. Then in 1985 things started to turn with their song 'Oh Yeah', which found a home on *Ferris Bueller's Day Off*. It's the one that goes 'boom boom … chick chicka!' while headmaster Ed Rooney loses his marbles trying to prove Ferris is skipping school. With momentum gathering, the arrival of acid house and the increasing popularity of dance music shifted the musical landscape in Yello's favour. And with 'The Race' in 1988, they finally broke through.

While fellow European keyboard pioneers Kraftwerk also had an interest in cars and speed and races (think 'Autobahn', think 'Tour De France'), their clipped, minimalist tone couldn't have been more different from Yello's 'The Race', a more fast-paced, frenetic dash of a single, all mad brass bits and driving beat. Sorry. Interviewed in the *NME*, Dieter described the sound as playing the studio 'like the bongos of the twentieth century', whatever that means. The song was also helped by a fantastic video, Dieter driving round in one of those old-fashioned racing cars, while the world blurred past behind. Dieter had always been interested in the visual side of things, and this may have been one of the reasons why Yello are in this book. Film projects started to wrestle with the band for Dieter's creative attention, and the momentum, in this country at least, never returned.

Although the band failed to gain any more hits in

> A fast-paced, frenetic dash of a single, all mad brass bits and driving beat. Sorry.

the UK, they remained ubiquitous thanks to their continuous playing as background music on TV. Further albums *Baby* (1991) and *Zebra* (1994) did the business abroad, while *Hands on Yello* (1995) emphasised their influence on a whole generation of dance acts: Moby, the Orb and others remixing classic tracks.

Dieter, you'll be pleased to know, does not drive round those Swiss hairpins like the speed-merchant in the song: he's more like 'a fifty-year-old-chauffeur', he told the *NME*.

Listen Here *Essential Yello* (Universal, 2000). Does it also include 'Oh Yeah'? Oh yeah.

Listen On *The New Mix in One Go* (Mercury, 1986). All their pre-Race bits in all their glory.

Listen Further 'The Chain' – Fleetwood Mac (on *Rumours*, Rhino, 2004). The ultimate drive song for men of a certain age.

Boys (Summertime Love) Sabrina
No. 3 1988

One enormous hit. Or was it two?

A decade or so before any teenage witch came along, another Sabrina was casting her spell over young men of a certain age. Born in Genoa, 1968, Sabrina Salerno was apparently a shy, introverted child, but as her talents developed, she and they started to rise to prominence. First came the crown of Miss Liguria. Then came a job as a television presenter (media mogul and future prime minister Silvio Berlusconi predicted she would be a star). And then in 1987 came her pop career.

The level of subtlety that would drive Sabrina's career was indicated by her choice of debut single: 'Sexy Girl'. Some girls, as Morrissey once observed, are bigger than others, and Sabrina, it was hard not to miss, was bigger than most. Like a sultry Italian version of Pamela Anderson, Sabrina suffered from what I think was an elementary mistake in doing her washing at the wrong temperature. Certainly all her clothes were shrunk to the point that none of her tops would ever quite do up. In 1988 she released what would go on to be her one and only UK hit, though initially the single flopped. Well, if you will release a song about summertime love in February, what do you expect?

Rereleased in June, the single did the business. A trashy slice of Italian Europop, Sabrina sang her siren cry of boys, then boys, then boys again, announcing in perfect bad English that she was looking for 'the good time'. She was feeling 'right' for a bit of 'summertime love', and just in case anybody needed any further persuading, there was an accompanying video shot in a swimming pool, during which Sabrina had difficulty keeping her bikini top in place.

Unfortunately for Sabrina, the British took her at her word. Her singing career was very much a summertime love, and though Stock, Aitken and Waterman were hauled in for the follow-up, 'All Of Me', her moment had passed. On the Continent,

> Some girls, as Morrissey once observed, are bigger than others.

however, her career continued apace. There were cover versions of 'Lady Marmalade', Prince's 'Kiss' and, erm, 'My Sharona', a riotous performance in Moscow in 1989, in front of a crowd of 50,000 excitable, excited Russians. As well as TV work, Sabrina has turned her hand to acting (the film *Jolly Blue* came out in 1999) and her singing career continues. Still one to stir up controversy, she pipped Madonna and Britney to the post with a bit of female-on-female snogging in the video for her 1999 single 'I Love You'.

Unconfirmed tittle-tattle about a flirtation with the Italian prime minister aside, the story that won't go away for Sabrina is this: are her breasts real or not? Sabrina remains adamant that she is as nature intended, and has even gone to the lengths of being examined by a top plastic surgeon to prove it. But though she is perhaps the only person in the world to own a 'certificate of authentication', the rumours have never quite gone away.

Listen Here *Boys* (Elap Germany, 1999). Includes the wash-your-mind-out 'Like A Yo Yo'.

Listen On *As Heard on Radio Soulwax* – 2ManyDJs. One of the sadly unreleased sections, superbly spliced with Motley Crue's 'Girls Girls Girls'.

Listen Further *Hot Tracks – The Best of Samantha Fox* (BMG, 2000). Page Three. 'Touch Me'. Enough already.

Strike it unlucky

People whose hit single didn't make their fortune

St Winifred's School Choir
A 50 pence book token each

Toni Basil
$3,000 in royalties was all she saw

Toto Coelo
They didn't eat caviar

The Tweets
Should they have taken the session fee or the royalty?

The Singing Nun
She gave all her profits to the convent

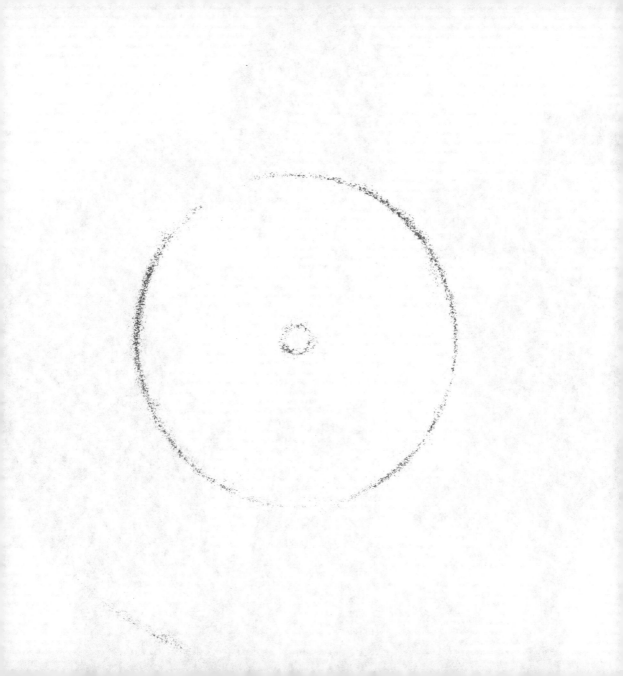

14 Funny Peculiar
– Bizarre Hits

I've come up with various theories and suggestions so far for why various types of songs become one-off hits. But there comes a point when no matter how hard you try and think things through, you finish reaching musical dead-end. I'm talking about songs whose overriding feature is that they are just a little bit *strange*.

There is a singing nun here. A man who sets fire to his head. An Italian American who told Vienna to 'Shaddap'. Women singing about eating cannibals, men telling ghost stories about dead marines, newspaper columns that ended up as number 1 hits. The question that each of them begs is 'why?' The simple answer is this: I'm not really sure.

Maybe we shouldn't look too hard for a reason. Maybe we should celebrate the fact that the chart is capable of throwing up oddities, the exceptions that prove that the chart can rule after all. After all, it's more interesting than a drip feed of endless anodyne boy bands.

Dominique
The Singing Nun
No. 7 1963

Twisted sister

In his poem 'Annus Mirabilis' Philip Larkin describes that glorious moment in 1963, specifically between the lifting of the ban on D. H. Lawrence's novel *Lady Chatterley's Lover* and the release of the Beatles' first album, when sex and the sixties began. Although society was changing, its permissiveness didn't stretch everywhere. Belgian nunneries, for example, didn't alter their age-old beliefs, even when they had a pop star in their midst.

Jeanine Deckers was born in Belgium in October 1933. In the 1950s, showing a keen pop eye for reinvention, she became Sister Luc-Gabrielle and became a Dominican nun at the Fichermont Convent. Popular with the other sisters for pulling out the guitar and playing one of her songs, she was persuaded by the other nuns to record an album, which she intended to give out as gifts. But then some smart cookie at the Philips Record Company saw the novelty potential in a singing nun. A deal was cut in which the profits would go to the convent, and the stage name Soeur Sourire or Sister Smile was adopted. 'Dominique', a happy and dare one say it, clappy celebration of her order's founder, St Dominic, rocketed up the charts. Top ten in the UK, it did even better in the US, hitting number 1 for four weeks and keeping 'Louie Louie' from number 1.

To begin with the Singing Nun decided to give up the singing and return to just being a nun. Back in America, Hollywood decided to follow the success of *The Sound of Music* with another nun movie – a musical of the Singing Nun's life, called, er, *The Singing Nun*, and starring the not especially nunlike Debbie Reynolds. In 1967 Jeanine changed her mind and left the convent to concentrate on her singing career. She changed her name *again*, this time to Luc Dominique, after Luc, the patron saint of artists. She released an album, perhaps appropriately titled *I Am Not a Star*.

The sixties, meanwhile, were finally catching up with our sister. First she ditched the habit for contemporary clothes. Then she recorded a song called 'Glory Be To God For The Golden Pill', which celebrated the arrival of oral contraceptives. Not that the Singing Nun would need them – her romantic involvement centred on a woman called Annie Pescher. The pair of them opened a centre for autistic children. Then it all started going tragically wrong. The Belgian government demanded tens of thousands of pounds in unpaid taxes from her music days – even though all the profits had gone to the convent. With the school facing closure, the Singing Nun and her lover took an overdose of sleeping pills and died together in a lettuce field in 1985.

Listen Here *Billboard Top Pop Hits: 1963* (Rhino, 1994). 'Blue Velvet', 'Wipe Out', 'Dominique': a vintage year for pop.

> A happy and dare one say it, clappy celebration of her order's founder, St Dominic.

Listen On   *The Singing Nun* – the Singing Nun
(Collector's Choice, 1999). She is a nun and she
sings.

Watch Further   *The Singing Nun* (VHS, 2002).
Debbie Does Dominique.

I'm The Urban Spaceman Bonzo Dog Doo-Dah Band

No.5 1968

The one with the fab producer

Boxing Day 1967 was the moment it all came together
for the Bonzo Dog Doo-Dah Band. To begin with, there
was the showing of the first-ever episode of *Do Not
Adjust Your Set*, the madcap TV show that boasted
both turns from the band and future *Monty Python*
types Eric Idle, Terry Jones and Michael Palin. And if
that wasn't enough, there was also the premiere of
the Beatles' *Magical Mystery Tour* – and who should
pop up halfway through, singing 'Death Cab For Cutie'
but, yes, the Bonzo Dog Doo-Dah Band all over again.

Originally called the Bonzo Dog Dada Band after
twenties cartoon character Bonzo Dog and anarchic
art movement Dadaism, the band apparently got
bored with explaining what Dada was, and switched
the word to Doo-Dah. Art school types to a tee, the
band's early music hinted of twenties nostalgia and
vaudeville, until saxophonist Bob Kerr left and took a
chunk of the group's stage routine with him. The
band became more rock but the bizarreness continued: how many other bands could boast not only a
cross-dressing tap dancer on drums (Legs Larry Smith)
but also a spoons player (Sam Spoons)? And we
haven't mentioned the fabulously named bass player,
Vernon Dudley Bohey-Nowell, surrealist singer Vivian
Stanshall, robot-obsessive Roger Ruskin Spear or duck-
on-his-head guitarist Neil Innes.

With both *Do Not Adjust Your Set* on the TV and a
suitably eccentric live show, the band's popularity
grew. And with a helping hand from producer Apollo
C. Vermouth, better known as Paul McCartney, that
elusive hit single finally arrived. One hesitates to pin
down precisely what this band were ever on about,
but with lines about having speed and being able
to fly, I'd wager that 'I'm The Urban Spaceman' might
having something to do with illegal substances.
Wacky enough to slip under the censor's radar,
the song eventually reached number 5.

The band released the brilliantly titled *The
Doughnut in Granny's Greenhouse*
but, with the British public inter-
preting eccentricity as novelty,
didn't have another hit. Splitting
up in 1970, the band briefly got
together for a contract-fulfilling LP,
Let's Make Up and Be Friendly
(1972), but otherwise pursued a
myriad of bizarre solo projects.
Roger let his robot frenzy go mad
with Roger Ruskin Spear's Giant Kinetic Wardrobe,
touring the country with his collection of homemade
wardrobes. Neil Innes rekindled the *Monty Python*
connection, appearing in both the *Holy Grail* film and

> One hesitates
> to pin down
> precisely what
> this band were
> ever on about.

Jabberwocky, as well as founding Beatles pastiche group the Rutles with Eric Idle. Singer Viv Stanshall, meanwhile, formed the Sean Head Showband, who released the single 'Labio Dental Fricative', was the narrator on Mike Oldfield's *Tubular Bells* and created the radio comedy character Sir Henry Rawlinson – later made into a film. He died in 1995.

Listen Here *The History of the Bonzos* (BGO, 1997). Two CDs of everything Bonzo.

Watch On *The Rutles – All You Need is Cash* (DVD, 2002). Macca produced Neil. Neil pastiches Macca.

Listen Further *Sir Henry at Rawlinson End* – Viv Stanshall (Virgin, 1995). Wonderful and weird in equal measure.

Fire Crazy World of Arthur Brown
No. 1 1968

It went out

Even in the 1960s some things were still far out. And at the outer edges of bizarreness was the pop star who set fire to his head. It sounds extreme and you'd be right. The only other pop star to try this trick was Michael Jackson while filming a drinks commercial in the early 1980s. And that was kind of an accident. Ow!

Born in Whitby during the Second World War, things started getting weird for Arthur Brown in Paris in the mid-1960s. Psychedelia was just starting to happen and in the midst of drugs, sex and general wildness, Arthur found himself playing gigs and Salvador Dalí coming to watch. And then came perhaps his defining moment. At a hotel in Montmartre, Arthur found a tin crown outside his door, complete with candles. The next time he played, he stuck it on his head, lit the candles and everyone went bonkers – in a 'How cool is that?' sort of a way, one presumes, rather than 'Oh my God! Your head is on fire!'

Back in England, Arthur met up with keyboardist Vincent Crane and formed the Crazy World of Arthur Brown. Drachen Theaker, who missed his audition for the Jimi Hendrix Experience by turning up too late, joined on drums. The band played Pink Floyd hangout the UFO Club, attracted the interest of Pete Townshend and got signed up by the Who's management. And before anyone knew what was happening, there was this strange bloke on *Top of the Pops* with a cape and a Bunsen burner on his head screaming about being the God of Hellfire. It's a touch unhinged, but 'Fire' is a great song, curiously both sixties and timeless, and it still gets a regular dusting down every time a lazy TV researcher needs a piece of music to illustrate a piece about flames.

> A touch unhinged, but 'Fire' is a great song, curiously both sixties and timeless.

Not that the band saw any of the money. In 1996 Arthur launched a lawsuit to try and finally get the missing royalties. Back in the 1960s the band split up under the pressure of success, and Arthur had to borrow money from his US tour promoter to buy a plane ticket back home. While his former band members went on to form Atomic Rooster, Arthur spent the early 1970s in experimental rock outfit Kingdom Come. In the late 1970s he moved to Austin, Texas, and with former Mothers of Invention drummer Jimmy Carl Black set up both an R&B band and a painting and decorating company (with their surnames Black and Brown, they chose the perhaps dubious title of the Gentlemen of Colour). After training as a counsellor in the 1980s, Arthur dusted down the old flame trilby and, with a new Crazy World line-up, got back on the road. One frightening episode at a gig in 1994 aside – on the bit in 'Fire' where he screams, Arthur passed out and suffered a brain haemorrhage – he continues to gig and set off sprinkler systems wherever he goes.

Listen Here *The Crazy World of Arthur Brown* (Polydor, 1991). A song called 'Spontaneous Apple Creation' could only have been written in the sixties.

Listen On *Tantric Lover* (Voiceprint, 2002). Can I resist a cheap joke about hot love? I do believe I can.

Listen Further 'Fire' – Jimi Hendrix (on *The Jimi Hendrix Experience*, MCA, 1997). More sixties pyrotechnics.

Kung Fu Fighting
Carl Douglas
No. 1 1974

Hoo. And if you will, haa

The mid-seventies now, and it wasn't only Don Revie's Leeds United who were handing out a good kicking. Kung Fu was cool, courtesy of Bruce Lee and films such as *Enter the Dragon* and David Carradine's TV show *Kung Fu* (in which the hero Kwai Chang Caine worked his way through the American Wild West with nothing but his feet). And catching the mood perfectly was this huge summer hit from Carl Douglas.

Originally from that hotbed of martial arts, Jamaica, Carl was a soul singer of moderate repute, singing with sixties bands such as Big Stampede and the Explosions. Some film work with Indian-born producer Biddu led to the producer calling Carl up again, to record a single, 'I Want To Give My Everything'. What Carl gave him was an idea for a B-side, 'Kung Fu Fighting'. Recorded, so legend has it, in ten minutes, the song was embellished with appropriate Oriental sound effects and Kung Fu shouts. Like a misjudged flying kick, it was all a touch over the top, but as a B-side its tongue-in-cheekness was fine.

> Like a misjudged flying kick, it was all a touch over the top.

'Kung Fu Fighting', however, was destined to become one of that long list of classic songs that a knowing record company switched from B-side to A list. 'Satisfaction' by the Stones and 'How Soon Is Now' by the Smiths are two other examples of a bright company seeing the hit potential the artist themselves couldn't. 'Kung Fu Fighting', complete with Carl suitably attired in black and orange 'angry' pyjamas, kicked the Osmonds off the top spot and saw off all-comers for three weeks. Attempts to capitalise on the Kung Fu theme with the follow-up single 'Dance The Kung Fu' stalled in the mid-thirties. Which was probably just as well: if people had danced the kung fu the dancefloors would have been carnage.

Carl did pop up again in the charts when he teamed up with Bus Stop (what kind of name is that?) for a nineties remix of his seventies smash. He now lives in Hamburg, Germany, where he runs a successful production company. As for that classic Oriental motif, it reappeared in the late seventies as the opening riff for another one hit wonder, the Vapors. But more about them later.

Listen Here *The Best of Carl Douglas* (Hot Productions, 1999). Track one, of course.

Listen On Follow-up single 'Dance The Kung Fu', also on the album.

Watch Further *Hong Kong Phooey* (Warner video, 2002). Penry, the mild-mannered janitor? Could be ...

Shaddap You Face
Joe Dolce Music Theatre
No. 1 1981

Midge Ure's favourite song

I don't know if anyone has ever done a survey of pub quiz pop questions, but if they did, then sneaking its sneaky way into the all-time top ten would be this: 'Which song kept "Vienna" by Ultravox off the number 1 spot in February 1981?' It is arguably not far from being the perfect pub quiz pop question. There's the classic tune for the music bore in the group to get all misty-eyed over; there's the roll-your-eyes moment when someone remembers the answer; and then there's the delicious sting in the tail, the words 'music' and 'theatre' in the name, with which the malicious quizmaster docks you that crucial half point for forgetting.

By the end of the 1970s Joe Dolce had swapped his home town of Painesville, Ohio, via California, for the Australian city of Melbourne. Here he was doing the rounds of the clubs with his stage act, the Joe Dolce Music Theatre, a pot pourri of folk, blues and country music, storytelling and characters. There was Joe Dolce, serious and sensitive artist, Big Joe Texas and an Italian by the name of Giuseppe, complete with pork pie hat and mandolin. It was in character as the latter that Joe tried out a song he'd written after remembering the banter at a big family meal back in America: all 'whatsa' this and 'shaddap' that. One night, playing in front of a particularly drunken crowd, Joe noticed that all the XXXXed Aussies were shouting 'Hey!' at the end of each line. He liked it, so he kept it in.

Enter the Australian Film Commission. Joe applied for a grant to record his stage show, and the commission, after some deliberation, gave him $2,000 to do a test segment – the segment, of course, being 'Shaddap You Face'. Joe recorded the song in two takes at a local studio for a knockdown $500 and then got to work on the video. It was when he was mixing the song that Joe got his crucial break. Mike Brady, the man responsible for 'Up There Cazaly', a hugely successful antipodean song about Aussie Rules Football, happened to be passing and spotted the song's potential. After failing to hawk the song around the major labels, Joe rang him up and got a deal. Mike Brady was right. A radio station was inundated with calls after the song was played on its breakfast show. Within a fortnight of being released in October 1980, the song was number 1.

First Australia, then the world. Elton John's Rocket Records heard the song and wanted to release it back in Blighty. When Joe said no, they decided to do their own version, with Joe replaced by Andrew Sachs, better known as Manuel from *Fawlty Towers*, and the song's Italianisms replaced with ever so predictable Spanish *que*s and what have you. But Joe was quicker out of the blocks. An injunction was issued against the rival version because permission hadn't been cleared to change the words. With a fortnight's head start, Joe's version was number 1 before Manuel's was even in the shops. (Note to what-if music philosophers: without the Andrew Sachs version, would Joe

Dolce's record have been released later, thus allowing Ultravox to get to number 1 after all?) It wasn't the only cover that Joe Dolce found himself up against. In Holland a singer called Dingetje recorded a whole album of versions in assorted dialects. In France his record company released both his single and a French rock and roll version by a singer called Sheila.

There were more singles – 'Christmas In Australia', 'You Toucha My Car I Breaka Your Face', 'Pizza Pizza' – but 'Shaddap' stubbornly remained Joe's solitary hit. He achieved the unique double of having the record company's highest-ever selling single and lowest-selling album. But I don't suppose Joe cares – in 2003 the song ratcheted up a record twenty-three years as most successful song in Australian music history. And with fifty alternate versions and counting (everyone from EMF to KRS-One, though Joe still puts Andrew Sachs's version as one of his favourites), those royalties and licensing deals are still coming in. Joe has had the chance to explore all his various musical ambitions, from folk to classical, and still plays and teaches in Australia.

So why was the song such a huge hit? Not even Joe is sure. 'No one really can answer that question with any authority. There is no formula for these type of original songs which fall outside of normal guidelines. It was the right time for this particular sentiment. Luckily it had a great melody as well – just the thought and idea without the tune wouldn't have stuck.' He's still very fond of it: 'I love it as much now as I did then. It is one of the handful of masterpieces in music I have made.'

> Put that in your pipe and smoke it, Midge.

And what does Joe think about Ultravox? 'I thought "Vienna" was a nice song – but pretty lightweight like so many of the pop songs that flit by – no one sings it or cares about it now. On the other hand, "Shaddap", which the Ultravox boys loved to put down, is still being covered to this day by other acts. That's the trouble with "flavour-of-the month" groups – they can't see the big picture – they can't see the forest for the trees. "Shaddap" was a true original. That's why it has endured.' Put that in your pipe and smoke it, Midge.

Listen Here *Chegger's Choice* (Global, 1999). Cheggers's first choice, more specifically.

Log On www.joedolce.net. Everything you could possibly want to know about Joe Dolce and a bit more besides.

Listen Further *The Collection* – Ultravox (Chrysalis, 1990). If you type 'Joe Dolce' into Amazon, it suggests you might also like this album.

I Eat Cannibals Part 1
Toto Coelo
No. 8 1982

Whatever did happen to Part 2?
In the early 1980s the charts were full of a different and – some would say – more dubious form of jungle music. Leaders of the Lion Pack were Tight Fit, who topped the chart with their 'wim-away' cover of 'The Lion Sleeps Tonight'. Then there was Baltimora – be ashamed of yourself, Irish singer Jimmy McShane – with his 1985 hit 'Tarzan Boy'. And clearing the path in 1982 was the all-girl group Toto Coelo, whose one and only hit was what can only be described as a somewhat random ditty about eating people.

Toto Coelo is in fact a Latin phrase that means 'utterly' or 'entirely'. Except in America, where it meant a phone call from Toto – the soft rockers who sang 'Rosanna', not Dorothy's dog – and a career-killing name change there to Total Coelo. The band consisted of Anita Mahadervan, Sheen Doran, Lindsey Danvers, Lacey Bond and Ros Holness. You may be thinking it and if you are then yes, you're right: Ros *is* the daughter of the legendary *Blockbusters* host. Dressed in what can only be described as a collection of neon bin-liners, the band's music is a sort of Bow Wow Wow without the wow – new wave crashing on to the quays of a particularly soggy synthesiser sound.

The band's solitary hit, the pub-quiz-point-docking-and-perhaps-over-optimistically-titled 'I Eat Cannibals Part 1', is either just a little odd or too rude for an early-eighties Britain to properly understand. Let's take the oddness angle first. Hall and Oates may have been mocked and laughed at for their drivelly disco sound, but maybe in Toto Coelo their prophecy about Maneaters comes frighteningly true. Watch out lads, they'd correctly warned: you'll get chewed up. Yum yum, respond Toto Coelo, licking their lips and taking the theory that we are what we eat to its logical con-

> Dressed in a collection of neon bin-liners the band's music is a sort of Bow Wow Wow without the wow.

clusion. They do, though, suggest a way to save your skin. The girls 'like the spice', so as long as you go for Brut instead, you might be ok.

If there is any innuendo in the song (lines about 'your love' being 'edible', giving the world 'a bone', requests to 'eat me' and so on), it is down to my addled brain having listened to too many AC/DC records. When I talked to lead singer Anita, she hadn't a clue what I was on about, so I dropped the subject before I got all embarrassed. As far as she was concerned, the song was 'pure nonsense' and 'just a bit mad' and in keeping with the band's tongue-in-cheek set list. Other Toto Coelo songs included 'Calorie Counting', 'Japanesi Panasonic', 'Mucho Macho' and 'Milk From The Coconut'. Mind you, 'Milk From The Coconut' was banned for being too suggestive so maybe I am right after all.

Anita (who was a vegetarian at the time of the single) looks back on the band fondly, if not the bank balances. The Svengali behind the band was the same as that behind Toni Basil, and the group made just as little money. Supporting Rose Royce at the Hammersmith Odeon was one highlight; *Top of the Pops* was another, particularly as Anita had once been a member of Legs and Co. But the band came to a halt before an album was even released. Anita briefly joined hard rock band the Cherry Bombz, before moving into acting, presenting and then qualifying as a counsellor. Lindsey took to the stage, appearing in West End musicals such as *Cats*; and Lacey was most recently spotted in the Orlando Bloom film *The Calcium Kid*.

Listen Here   *The Best One Hit Wonders in the World . . . Ever!* (Virgin, 2003). Nestled nicely halfway down the second CD.

Listen On   *I Eat Cannibals* – Toto Coelo (Razor and Tie, 1996). There's even part two.

Listen Further   *Past to Present – Toto* (Sony, 2000). Soft rock yes, Coelo no.

Spirit In The Sky
Doctor and the Medics
No. 1 1986

Two one hit wonders for the price of one

If there was ever a prize awarded for the most one-hit one hit wonder, it would fall to 'Spirit In The Sky', a song that has been the solitary hit for not one, but two acts over the years. Originally written and recorded by Norman Greenbaum, the first version of 'Spirit In The Sky' hit number 1 in 1970 and succeeded where Greenbaum's other singles failed. Mind you, if you release a song called 'The Eggplant That Ate Chicago' it is fair to say that *Top of the Pops* isn't necessarily in the bag. The inspiration for the song, apparently, came from Norman watching country singer and sometime Dolly Parton partner Peter Wagoner on his TV show. Wagoner was singing a religious song and God, Greenbaum realised in a moment of divine inspiration, was the key.

Fast forward to the eighties and a band set up in

order to win a five-pound bet. Clive Jackson may have failed to get into medical school, but that didn't stop him risking the wrath of the British Medical Association by calling himself the 'Doctor' and running a nightclub called the 'Clinic'. If you want to add a joke about pills at this point, please feel free to do so. The healthcare theme continued with his band, the Medics: Steve McGuire on guitar, Richard Searle on bass, the Anadin 'brothers' Wendi and Colette on backing vocals and Vom on drums. Probably best not to, actually – it deadens the sound.

At both the Clinic and new club Alice in Wonderland, the Doctor tried – with minimal success – to kickstart some sort of psychedelic revival. Out on the road, meanwhile, the band were getting noticed for their live show and rave-esque gigs – Chislehurst Caves and Clacton Butlins were just two of the surprise venues the Medics would coach their fans to. A record deal followed, and after a couple of indie hits – 'Happy But Twisted', 'Miracle Of The Age' – the band crossed over into the charts proper. 'Spirit In The Sky' mark 2 is, to be honest, not vastly different from the first, a little more oomph on the guitars aside, but if it ain't broke, there's no need to give Bob the Builder a call. Add in a new generation of listeners who had no idea who Norman Greenbaum was, a church-hall video with swirly bits of card hanging from the ceiling, and number 1 was theirs. A mention should be made of the Doctor's stage get-up at this point. Sort of Pete Burns meets Adam Ant: there was a long swishy cape, eyebrows that made Denis Healey's look reserved and a sticky-up triangle of hair that Cameron Diaz was to mimic in *There's Something About Mary*. Let's not go into how he got *his* to sit upright.

'Spirit In The Sky', according to which article you read, was number 1 in 18 countries and sold 2.3 million copies, or was it number 1 in 32 countries and sold over a million? It did the biz, put it that way. For a couple of years, all the trappings of fame were theirs, trappings being touring the song to death and appearing on charity records (Ferry Aid's 'Let It Be' – a fund to pay the former Roxy Music frontman to end his solo career). But with follow-up singles 'Burn' and 'Waterloo' failing to tempt the charts, the band split up. Vom joined a band called the Armageddon Dildos; Richard joined actually-quite-good jazz-funksters Corduroy; Wendi started a family with the Doctor; Colette got work as a body double for Gwyneth Paltrow; Steve went on to work in production, most notably for Badly Drawn Boy; and the Doctor set up a snail farm in Wales. Yeah, like you do.

In the mid-1990s the Doctor got himself a new bunch of Medics and went back on the road, doing by all accounts a nice line in eighties revival tours and the like. In 2003 'Spirit In The Sky', even if it was for charity, was somewhat mangled by Gareth Gates. Indeed, he arguably did to the song what Jordan had done to him. Wouldn't it be neat if his career went the same way as Norman Greenbaum's and Doctor and the Medics'? Meanwhile, expect the next cover of the song to hit number 1 some time in 2019 . . .

> The Doctor had a sticky up triangle of hair that Cameron Diaz was to mimic in *There's Something About Mary.*

Listen Here *Now That's What I Call Music Volume Seven* (EMI, 1986). Who wouldn't want to be sandwiched between Amazulu and Bananarama?

Listen On *Laughing at the Pieces* – Doctor and the Medics (IRS, 1986). A whole album of musical medicine.

Listen Further *The Best of Norman Greenbaum* (Repertoire, 2002). The original spirit.

Camouflage
Stan Ridgway
No. 4 1986

Now you see him, now you don't

Storytelling is one of the neglected arts of modern pop music, and one of its best practitioners is Californian-born Stanard Ridgway. A little bit Johnny Cash, a touch Tom Waits, perhaps a hint Raymond Chandler, his music adds a cinematic twist to traditional American folk and country. A class maverick in other words, and quite frankly the last person you would expect to find nestling in the top five of the singles charts.

From 1979 to 1983 Stan was lead singer with art rock outfit Wall of Voodoo. Respected without being huge, their biggest success was grazing the US top forty with single 'Mexican Radio'. Musical differences later, Stan found himself going solo and finally released his first album, *The Big Heat*, in 1986. Described by Greil Marcus as 'the most compelling portrait of American social life to appear on a rock and roll LP since Bruce Springsteen's *Nebraska*', the album was universally praised with one exception. The 'sole clinker', said *Rolling Stone*. 'Is it camp? Is it serious?' asked *Spin* magazine. 'Climbing this week to number 4 . . .' said Bruno Brookes.

'Camouflage' draws its inspiration partly from Phantom 309, a truck-driving ghost story by country ledge Red Sovine, and also the experiences of Stan's cousin Peter, who fought in Vietnam. In the song, the narrator is on a patrol in Vietnam in 1965, and with the enemy moving in, things are not looking good. Then along comes a 'big marine' by the name of Camouflage to save the day. They fight side by side, Camouflage swats away a bullet with the narrator's name on it, and then just as soon as he arrived, he is gone. When the narrator returns to his base, he discovers the ghostly truth: the soldier called Camouflage had died the night before, but his final wish was to save a young marine . . .

Perhaps 'Camouflage' served as an eerie counterpoint to *Platoon* and *Rambo* and all the other war films around at the time. Or maybe it was the Americana 'Ernie'. Whichever, with its ghost-story verses and shades of *Rawhide* chorus, 'Camouflage' sounded like nothing else around and sneaked its way to number 4 with nobody sure quite how it had got there. There weren't further hits, but a successful solo career still rumbles quietly along, together with an additional career in film scores – *Rumblefish* and *Pump up the Volume* included.

> Perhaps 'Camouflage' served as an eerie counterpoint to all the war films around at the time.

Listen Here *Now That's What I Call Music Volume Seven* (EMI, 1986). There's Pete Wylie before him. And there's Max Headroom afterwards.

Listen On *The Big Heat* (EMD/IRS, 1993). More Stan than you can shake a stick at.

Listen Further *In Country: Folk Songs of Americans in the Vietnam War* (Flying Fish, 1992). As it was to the strum of a guitar.

Everybody's Free
(To Wear Sunscreen)
Baz Luhrmann
No. 1 1999

The one about the columnist, the novelist and the film director

May 1997. Mary Schmich, journalist for the *Chicago Tribune* newspaper, is walking along the shores of Lake Michigan, thinking about what she is going to write for her column, when she has an idea. It's graduation time, so why doesn't she write a pseudo-graduation speech, full of advice people would really find useful? And then she sees a young woman sunbathing and the following thought pops into her head: I hope she's wearing sunscreen.

Soon after her column appears, something strange starts to happen on the Internet. People start emailing each other the article, passing its pearls of wisdom to everyone they know. But as the column whips its way across the world, there's one small but noticeable change. No one is quite sure how it started, but Mary's name is nowhere to be seen. Instead, authorship is credited to cult American novelist Kurt Vonnegut, the article now a speech he gave to students at MIT. A hoax, a mistake, who knows? But that's where the story might have ended, had the email not turned up in Baz Luhrmann's inbox.

> Have *you* done your scary thing for the day yet?

The acclaimed Australian film director of *Strictly Ballroom* and *Romeo and Juliet* (as well as the love-it-or-loathe-it musical *Moulin Rouge*), Baz Luhrmann was between film projects and filling the time by putting together an album. When he saw the words, he quickly got the actor Lee Perry to read them to music – Rozalla's 1991 top-ten hit 'Everybody's Free (To Feel Good)'. And though the song was only meant to be an album track, the record company changed their mind after it was picked up by radio. Capital Radio's Steve Penk got so many calls about the song that he gave out EMI's phone number on air to get rid of them. An oddball number 1 smash was inevitable.

It's probably a little churlish to pick at the lyrics to the song as they were only ever intended to be a newspaper column and not for posterity, but hey. What the heck. Five years on, the advice for the class of '99, like the beauty Mary told you to enjoy, has started to fade a little. Keeping love letters? That'll win over your new girlfriend. Throwing away your bank statements? Not if you fill out your own tax return. Not feeling guilty about not knowing what to do? If you still don't know, I say *feel* guilty – five years is too long to be loafing around. Some of the comments still make sense – the wearing sunscreen bit I can't argue with – but I reckon that the further away we get, the more dated most of the suggestions will become. It's that nineties mix of New Age philosophy meets Feel the Fear and Do It Anyway meets Hallmark cards. And although lots of people bought it, I wonder how many people still follow its advice? I mean, have *you* done your scary thing for the day yet?

Listen Here   'Everybody's Free (To Wear Sunscreen)' (EMI, 1999). The single with a lovely orange cover.

Listen On   'Everybody's Free' – Rozalla (Pulse, 1991). The original music.

Read Further   *Slaughterhouse-Five* – Kurt Vonnegut (Bantam, 1991). Some words he did write.

Helping hands

Famous people who did their bit to make the song a hit

Paul McCartney

Producer on the Bonzo Dog Doo-Dah Band's 'I'm The Urban Spaceman'

Pete Townshend

Who guitarist does production duties on Thunderclap Newman's 'Something In The Air'

Carly Simon

Vocals on Will Powers's 'Kissing With Confidence'

William Orbit

Manned the decks for Harry Enfield's Loadsamoney single

Nik Kershaw

Penned Chesney's one and only classic

15 The One and Onlies
– Eighties Greaties and Nineties, … aah Fineties Hits

A selection of classic pop songs now from the decade that taste forgot (copyright whichever decade you want to write about). Actually, no one's really put the boot into the nineties yet, have they? The seventies got the abuse for years but at some point stopped being naff and started being a retro treasure chest to explore. The eighties are starting to go the same way. But the nineties? Were they less the nineties and more the nonentities, too derivative of other stuff (Britpop and the sixties and so forth) to escape pop-culture censure? Or will we hit a point in about five years' time when we groan at the crassness of lad culture, see Oasis as some sort of end-of-the-century Slade and think as badly of Tony Blair as we now do about Margaret Thatcher? Only time will tell.

There were plenty of songs I could have included here. 'Mary's Prayer' by Danny Wilson. '(Feels Like) Heaven' by Fiction Factory. Alphaville, Dream Academy, Jennifer Paige, Olive. The ones who made the cut, though, were the ones I felt I couldn't leave out. Have they dated? Possibly. Do they still capture a moment? In their various ways, I think they do.

(I Just) Died In Your Arms Cutting Crew

No. 4 1986

They weren't a crew. And let's be honest, they weren't really that cutting

This song has one of those eighties starts that your brain needs to hear about point five of a second of before the recognition factor kicks in. Here it's that pseudo-church-organ keyboard sound, ba-ba-ba-ba-ba-ba-ba-ba, followed by what sounds like it should be a cello underneath, but I suspect may be a synth noise instead. Classy, you think. Different. Wrong. Because pretty quickly '(I Just) Died In Your Arms' – don't get me started on the brackets – straightens out into fairly standard eighties rock. A little bit Foreigner, a touch sophisticated Big Country and for my money, a soupçon Mr Mister. It's what is known in the soft rock terminology as a plodder: not slow enough to get the cigarette lighter out, but not fast enough for a head-nod either. Instead, the correct response of the listener is to sway wistfully or, if you can manage it, poignantly, from side to side.

Three-quarters British, one-quarter Canadian, Cutting Crew were front man Nick Van Eede, squalling guitarist Kevin MacMichael, bassist Colin Farley and drummer Martin 'Frosty' Beedle. That's his nickname rather than my comment by the way. I've never met the guy, and I'm sure he's very nice. It all started in the early eighties when Nick's then band the Drivers were supported on a Canadian tour by Kevin's band, Fast Forward. There is a (I suspect apocryphal) story about how Fast Forward were involved in a car crash and Kevin was the only member unhurt. Whatever the truth, Kevin followed Nick back to England, and Cutting Crew were formed. Success was pretty much instant. The first single from their first album *Broadcast* '(I just hate it when people use brackets) Died In Your Arms', hit number 4 in the UK and number 1 in the US.

Of course, Cutting Crew didn't literally die in your arms. It's one of those rock metaphor things, singer Nick thoughtfully coming to terms with the fall-out of infidelity and trying to not be put off by Kevin MacMichael's guitar not exactly gently weeping in the background. The band toured the US supporting the likes of Huey Lewis and the News and Starship (if anyone has a bootleg tape . . .), but follow-up single 'I've Been in Love' failed to dent the top twenty no matter how many times it was released (three). Two more albums followed – *The Scattering* (1989) and *Compus Mentus* (1993) – but when their record company was taken over by EMI, they were dropped like a hot brick. Nick auditioned for the vacant vocalist slot in Genesis (eventually taken by Ray from Stiltskin) and has continued writing. A new album, under the name *Grinning Souls*, is due for release this year. Kevin, meanwhile, went on to join Robert Plant's band and fretted all over the 1993 album *Fate of Nations*. Sadly, he died of lung cancer in late 2002.

> A little bit Foreigner, a touch sophisticated Big Country, an for my money, a soupçon Mr Mister.

Listen Here *The Best One Hit Wonders in the World . . . Ever!* (Virgin, 2003). Track 4, got to number 4.

Listen On *The Best of the Cutting Crew* (Disky, 1995). Not one but two versions of '(I Just)' included.

Listen Further *Fate of Nations* – Robert Plant (Fontana, 1993). What Kevin did next.

Calling All The Heroes
It Bites
No. 6 1986

Once bitten. Twice shy

Bonnie Tyler was holding out for one. The Stranglers said no more of them. David Bowie said we could be them, but only for about twenty-four hours or so. And It Bites, the band with arguably one of the worst names ever to grace the *Guinness Book of British Hit Singles* – it's just *rubbish*, isn't it? – they were calling out for them in 1986.

The Bites hail from Cumbria, where singer Francis Dunnery originally played in a punk band called Waving at Trains. The original line-up had a good time doing the Cumbrian club circuit, until drunken behaviour and turning up late saw them banned – though, frankly, what do they expect from a rock band? Reconvening in London, the band squatted in Peckham (that's as in living arrangements rather than crouching on the floor), before getting that all-important deal. First single, top ten, it must all have seemed a bit of a doddle.

Lyrically, 'Calling All The Heroes' is all a bit cowboys and Indians. With the men off doing whatever men do, the downtown fortress was left unguarded, and a stack of bandits moved in, attacked the women and stole all the gold. The men came back, saw what happened, tracked the bandits down and, as far as I can gather, knocked the crap out of them. Whether this constitutes heroism or simply making up for an earlier dereliction of duty, I'll leave up to you. Musically, the song was sort of Marillion meets Nik Kershaw, with arguably an element of Level 42 musicianship in there for good measure. There's a great moment two-thirds of the way in where the song stops, there's enough silence for John Cage to consider suing, and then the chorus kicks in again. It's a fantastic piece of tension and anticipation, unfortunately spoilt by many a DJ filling the gap with the sound of a custard pie splat.

'Calling All The Heroes' was both It Bites' blessing and curse. In essence, the band wanted to be a proper rock band: a little bit Genesis, a touch, yes, Yes. In reality, their debut single was bought by thirteen-year-old *Smash Hits* readers. Can *you* spot the discrepancy? When the band went rock – and the It Bites logo soon morphed into something suspiciously Yes-like – the thirteen-year-old girls weren't interested. The proper rock fans, meanwhile, were ever so slightly sceptical of

> It Bites wanted to be a proper rock band: their debut single was bought by thirteen-year-old *Smash Hits* readers.

the band's pop success. However fickle fate is, credibility is even more so. The debut album, the brilliantly named *Big Lad in the Windmill* (it just makes me laugh I'm not sure why) only reached number 35, and after two further studio albums, the band split and Francis went solo. The nineties were punctuated by various albums and collaborations (he contributes to both Lauren Hill's *The Miseducation of Lauren Hill* and Ian Brown's *Music of the Spheres*). He also developed his skills as a psychological astrologer. Having been dormant for many years, a mooted reunion and It Bites tour were pencilled for 2004 at the time of writing.

Listen Here *Calling All The Heroes* (EMI, 2003). Calling all the best songs.

Listen On *Big Lad in the Windmill* (Virgin, 2002). A touch of the Bobby Robsons in the title here?

Listen Further *Music of the Spheres* – Ian Brown (Polydor, 2002). A little bit of bite to the former Stone Roses frontman.

Cuddly Toy Roachford
No. 4 1989

In terms of hits, it's all a little bear

Early April 1994. In the same week as Kurt Cobain committed suicide, Oasis released their first single, 'Supersonic'. It was the end of grunge, the birth of Britpop, a shift of rock's tectonic plates. And as the musical baton was passed to a new generation, so an elder statesman, a 'ledge', was there to witness the transition. As Bob Dylan had met Woody Guthrie, as the Sex Pistols met David Bowie,* so on 7 April Oasis returned to the Forte Crest Hotel in Glasgow, following a triumphant live performance on Radio One. There, in the bar, Liam, Guigsy and Bonehead were suitably starstruck by the star in their midst. 'Roachford!' Liam yelped, mobbing him. '"Cuddly Toy", man! Tune of the eighties!'**

Guitar rock stroke pop stroke soul stroke funk is one of music's most maligned subgenres. Prince is definitely its undisputed star. In the mid-eighties everything he touched would turn to purple – 'Let's Go Crazy', 'When Doves Cry', 'Kiss'. Michael Jackson, wigging out with Eddie Van Halen ('Beat It') and Slash ('Black or White') was up there for a while too. Continue down the corridor and you'll get to the

* I say met. In July 1973 David Bowie was playing the Hammersmith Odeon. The night before, Paul Cook and friend broke in and stole his PA (Jon Savage, *England's Dreaming*, page 75).
** John Harris, *The Last Party*, page 146. Liam and Noel would go on to wind up the evening by winding each other up in the notorious 'Wibbling Rivalry' interview.

office of one Leonard Kravitz. Further down again, neither fish nor fowl, you'll find Terence 'Trout' D'Arby.* And if you travel further still, round the corner, down another flight of stairs, second door on the end, there, *there*, you'll find one Andrew Roachford.

In the summer of 1988 Roachford released his debut single, 'Cuddly Toy'. Nothing happened. So in January the following year he released it again. This time it shot to number 4. A fat slice of funk-rock, 'Cuddly Toy' kicks off with a guitar riff the approximate size of Belgium. It has a classic 'come and get me' rock lyric, the story of a maligned man who everyone thinks has a laydee in every town (subtext: good in bed), but is in fact home alone and single (subtext: sensitive and misunderstood). It has a great bit near the end where Roach asks his 'girl' to 'feel for me', first one time, then three times and so on, each 'time' backed up by a funk 'stab' from the band.**

Roach, of course, has but one 'joy' back home. His cuddly toy. And then being the eighties, there is only one possible candidate for such an honour. Orange, feline, it was, *naturellement*, a Garfield ('the coolest mascot in the world' according to his debut album sleeve). In an interview with *DJ* magazine in 2002, Roach reveals: 'I've still got it on top of my wardrobe and he still has that stoned smile on his face. I've always thought that if you look at Garfield, you can tell he's definitely a stoner.' His words, not mine, Jim.

Personally, I don't think for a second that there was any subliminal drugs reference going on here.†
Instead, I just think the song's one hit wonderness springs purely from its unfortunate choice of lyrics. I mean, 'Cuddly Toy'. It's so English, so *Generation Game*, so naff, it had to end up upending the nation's perception of young Roach. And indeed, unfortunately for Roachford, his first hit single was also his last. Lacking any further feline foam inspiration, none of his subsequent singles hit similar heights. After a second, unsuccessful album – the disappointing *Get Ready!* – Roachford changed direction. Albums such as *Permanent Shade of Blue* were subtler, slinkier, and if he didn't trouble the charts again, his R&B-flavoured soul has kept him ticking over nicely ever since.††

> A fat slice of funk-rock, 'Cuddly Toy' kicks off with a guitar riff the approximate size of Belgium.

Listen Here *Roachford* (Sony, 1992). The debut album. File under cuddly.

Listen On *Permanent Shade of Blue* (Sony, 1994). Roach grows up.

Read Further *Garfield: Survival of the Fattest* (Ballantine, 2004). The fortieth Garfield book apparently. Who, apart from possibly Roachford, is still buying them?

---

* As *Smash Hits* used to call him. They also had a long-running joke about Roland Orzabal and a kangeroo, but that's another story.
** If you go and see him live, as I did at Nottingham's Rock City in 1989, this goes up to five, seven, nine times, until the band can count no more. I was young.

† Though there is, if you're feeling brave, a seven-minute 'X Rated Acid Toy Mix' available.
†† When I saw him down the bill in the dance tent at V99, it was still 'Cuddly Toy' that was the highlight of the set. And yes, the three times, five times, seven times shtick was still going strong.

The One And Only
Chesney Hawkes
No. 1 1991

Need I say any more?

1991 offered up some of the best albums of the nineties – *Blue Lines*, *Nevermind*, *Screamadelica*, *Achtung Baby* – and some of its worst singles. For sixteen long summer weeks Bryan Adams's *Robin Hood* theme 'Everything I Do' ruled the roost. And then there was a nineteen-year-old Home Counties boy with the beach-blond flick, the singular mole and the leather jacket and jeans: the one and only Chesney Hawkes.

'The One And Only' was taken from the film *Buddy's Song*, which Ches 'starred' in with the Who's Roger Daltrey. Rog played Ches's dad, which was sort of ironic, because Ches's real dad was a real 'rock' star – 'Chip' Lee Hawkes of sixties band the Tremeloes. The Tremeloes auditioned for Decca Records the same day as the Beatles. Decca in their wisdom turned down the Fab Four and signed the Tremeloes. With such family pedigree, how could Chesney fail?

'The One and Only' sounds contemporary for about four and a half seconds, as an electric guitar does a passable impression of a Formula 1 car going through the gears. Then in comes Ches. It's a strange mix – a naive fifties feel (*Time Out* described him as a 'secular Cliff Richard') backed by a full range of eighties furniture: Diet Coke guitar riffs, Korgonzola synth blasts, booming snares and that all-important chorus-up-a-

key at the end. It was written by Nik Kershaw, who hadn't had a top-ten hit since 'Don Quixote' in 1985, and it showed. Nik Kershaw used to wear a green snood, but that's another story.

It's hard to know which went worse – Ches's musical or acting career. *Buddy's Song* didn't exactly set the box office charts ablaze, but it did a darn sight better than Ches's only other outing on the big screen, *Prince Valiant* (1997), in which Ches played a stable boy. The follow-up to 'The One And Only', 'I'm A Man Not A Boy', was kept off the top spot by the aforementioned Bryan Adams. Well, ok, Bryan Adams and twenty-five others. But 27 was as high as Ches was ever going to get again. The next single 'peaked' at 57, the next one at 63, the 2001 comeback single 'Stay Away Baby Jane' burst into the top 75 at a spectacular 74.

Bad news ladies, Ches did the decent thing and got married in 1997 to a model, Kristina. They had their one and only child, Casey, in 2001. It is too early to say whether he will follow in the family tradition, but here's hoping.

> It was written by Nik Kershaw who hadn't had a top-ten hit since 'Don Quixote' in 1985, and it showed.

Listen Here *The Best One Hit Wonders in the World . . . Ever!* (Virgin, 2003). It wouldn't be the best without him.

Watch On *Buddy's Song* (VHS, 1990). The film the song came from.

Listen Further *The Essential Nik Kershaw* (Spectrum, 2000). Are there *really* seventeen essential Nik Kershaw songs?

Sleeping Satellite
Tasmin Archer
No. 1 1992

What the dickens . . .

For some curious reason, there has always been a discrepancy in pop talent between the two sides of the Pennines. While cities such as Liverpool and Manchester have offered up everyone from Oasis to the Beatles, the Smiths to the Stone Roses, a *Now That's What I Call Yorkshire Hits* would offer a more prosaic selection from the likes of Embrace, Joe Cocker, Shed Seven and Tasmin Archer. Yes, that is Tasmin rather than Tamsin, Bradford born and bred, who in 1992 hit number 1 with her debut single, 'Sleeping Satellite'.

Although it felt like Tasmin had appeared from nowhere, she had in fact been trying to crack the pop thing for many years before. Even the song 'Sleeping Satellite' was four years old by the time it got into the charts. Having left school at sixteen, Tasmin had done the obligatory roll call of dead-end jobs (including cleaning toilets) before she hooked up with musicians John Beck and John Hughes. Originally calling themselves the Archers, it took a while for anyone to notice any of their songs, but once they did, they couldn't have asked for any more backing. With the person who signed them at EMI having been promoted to head of A&R, the full armoury of a major record label, with tens of thousands of pounds of radio advertising, was put behind Tasmin's debut single.

Of course, if a single is shit, it doesn't matter how much support a record gets. 'Sleeping Satellite' was anything but and quickly knocked the Shamen's 'Ebeneezer Goode' from the top spot. Even now, the song feels something of anomaly, shiny adult pop with a message, sort of Seal meets Sting. In essence, Tasmin's argument is the same as one Prince raised in 'Sign O' The Times' – why are we sending people to the moon when there's all this crap to sort out down here – though Tasmin is more concerned about the planet than Prince's cousin doing horse. What she lacks in funk she makes up in philosophy – are we a species up to carrying the 'concept' of controlling Mother Nature, she asks at one point. When was the last time Kylie asked us to think about that?

> What she lacks in funk she makes up in philosophy.

There was a Dickens vibe to Tasmin. The title of her debut album *Great Expectations* came from her love of the character Pip. Her trademark dress sense, all waistcoats and long sleeved white shirts, was a sort of Artful Dodger, urban urchin look. But from such lofty beginnings, Tasmin's success began to slide. She won the 1993 Brit award for Best Newcomer, but her follow-up single, the child-abuse-themed 'In Your Care', barely scraped the twenty. The pressure and the promotional schedule also took their toll. A collection of Elvis Costello recordings, *Shipbuilding*, filled the gap between albums. By the time *Bloom* eventually appeared in 1996, both the record company and the general public had lost interest, and in 1997 she was dropped. She has taken time out since then, but has recently returned to writing and recording.

Listen Here *Great Expectations* (EMI, 2000). Great expectations indeed.

Listen On *Bloom* (EMI, 1996). Her career didn't.

Watch Further *Man Alive* – Harry Hill (VHS, 1997). Is it just me or is Tasmin Archer Badger the pick of the Badger Parade?

Would I Lie To You?
Charles and Eddie
No. 1 1992

Their debut album was called
***Duophonic.* Their chart career was**
more mono

History repeats itself, Karl Marx once said, first as tragedy, then as farce. Pop history repeats itself too, but in a different sort of way. The first time it is as tragedy, the second as some sort of PR exercise. In the early 1960s Keith Richards and Mick Jagger bumped into each other on a station platform, striking up a conversation over the records Keith was carrying under his arm. Nearly thirty years later singer Charles Pettigrew bumped into singer Eddie Chacon on the New York subway. Eddie was carrying a copy of *Troubled Man* by soul legend Marvin Gaye. Charlie struck up a conversation. A pop duo was born.

I don't want to cast aspersions over the story of how Charles and Eddie got together, but put it this way: if you were a publicist, struggling to sell a Hall and Oates for the nineties to the music press, coming up with some sort of story would give your press release a much-needed hook. And the story's veracity matters because Hall and Oates's – sorry, Charles and Eddie's – debut chart-topper was all about honesty. Would I lie to you? they ask, all sweetness and light. It's a different tack from the one Annie Lennox took with the Eurythmics' song of the same name. There Annie sounds like she'd rip your head off with her bare hands if you so much as raised the possibility. Charles and Eddie, by contrast, go for the I'm-innocent-really angle, the musical equivalent of arms open, palms out, butter-wouldn't-melt smile.

> If the chance meeting was made up, they really pushed it.

I'll give Charles and Eddie their due. If the chance meeting was made up, they really pushed it. The follow-up single, 'NYC (Can You Believe This City)' saw the boys at it again – a song with a lyric about bumping into future musical partners on the subway. Obviously some people thought they were protesting too much, as the single only reached number 33. Subsequent singles and a second album – 1995's *Chocolate Milk* – failed to rekindle the duo's original success, and the pair split to work on solo projects. Eddie wrote songs for bands such as Eternal, while Charles's singing included a stint with Talking Heads offshoot the Tom Tom Club. Tragically, he died from cancer in 2001.

Listen Here *The Best One Hit Wonders in the World . . . Ever!* (Virgin, 2003). It's the truth.

Listen On *Duophonic* (Capitol, 1992). Hear how the boys met in NYC.

Listen Further *Ultimate* – Darryl Hall and John Oates (BMG, 2004). Thirty-seven slices of the original pop-soul duo.

Your Woman
White Town
No. 1 1997

A do-it-yourself number 1

In 1988 Jimmy Cauty and Bill Drummond, better known as the KLF, released a rather wonderful book called *The Manual*. Its subtitle – *How to Have a Number One the Easy Way* – explained its purpose. Drummond and Cauty had got to number 1 as the Timelords with 'Doctorin' The Tardis', and they reckoned that anyone could follow their plan of campaign and also hit the top spot. If you didn't, they'd refund your purchase. A brilliant book it may be, but in 1989 a band called Edelweiss followed the KLF's rules and only reached number 5 with the (admittedly dreadful) 'Bring Me Edelweiss'. And then, eight years later, a man called Jyoti Mishra made even the KLF's plan seem profligate, with a number 1 single he recorded in his bedroom.

Born in India in 1966, Jyoti Mishra moved to Britain when he was young and ended up in Derby. He played in various bands in the eighties under names such as Daryl and the Chaperones and Whizz For Atoms. After seeing the Pixies in 1989, he formed a more indie-sounding White Town who at their third gig found themselves supporting Primal Scream. As the other members dropped off one by one, White Town became a one-man band, and Jyoti moved away from guitars towards a more keyboard sound. The early nineties were punctuated by a succession of small label singles and a 1994 album, *Socialism, Sexism and Sexuality*.

Jyoti was a big fan of Dennis Potter's *Pennies from Heaven*, on the soundtrack of which was a 1932 song by Lew Stone called 'My Woman'. It was this that inspired his number 1 single. He sampled trumpeter Nat Gonella for the song's opening riff, and put the song together himself using a second-hand sequencer, a sampler, a couple of Casio keyboards and an electric guitar. At this point in *The Manual*, the KLF tell you to get yourself a plugger who can push the single to the radio stations. Jyoti went one better. He cut out the middle man and sent it to Radio One himself. Mark Radcliffe heard it, liked it and played it. The song was picked up and the number 1 slot followed soon after.

> Being a bloke, the chances of Jyoti being anyone's woman are always going to be remote.

The thing about 'Your Woman', I think, was that the song sounded fresh. The thirties trumpet riff helped it stand out, the lo-fi simplicity of the production allowed the melody to breathe, and the whole thing grooved along in an oddly eighties way. Added to which was a nice bit of gender confusion in the lyrics – the last thing I would want to do would be to cast aspersions on Jyoti's sexuality, but being a bloke, the chances of him being anyone's woman are always going to be remote. And finally, Jyoti's original weakness – the fact that he was an anonymous bloke in his bedroom – flipped over into being his biggest asset. Publicitywise, it was a gift.

An album, *Women in Technology*, followed, as did a single, 'Undressed', which peaked at number 57. Meanwhile, 'Your Woman' hit number 1 in another seven countries, and Jyoti used the proceeds to build himself a proper studio. In 2002 he released a new album, *Peek and Poke*, which was critically acclaimed if not commercially successful.

Listen Here *The Best One Hit Wonders in the World . . . Ever!* (Virgin, 2003). Between the Mock Turtles and Belouis Some.

Listen On *Peek and Poke* (Bzangy Groink, 2002). Worth buying for the name of the record label alone.

Listen Further *The Best of Lew Stone* (Clave, 2000). Includes 'My Woman'.

Bubbling Under

Five one hit wonders that almost made the worst top ten

Owen Paul
'My Favourite Waste Of Time'
(No. 3, 1986)

Commentators
'N-N-Nineteen Not Out'
(No. 13, 1985)

Brighouse and Rastrick Brass Band
'The Floral Dance'
(No. 2, 1977)

Aneka
'Japanese Boy'
(No. 1, 1981)

Fred Wedlock
'Oldest Swinger In Town'
(No. 6, 1981)

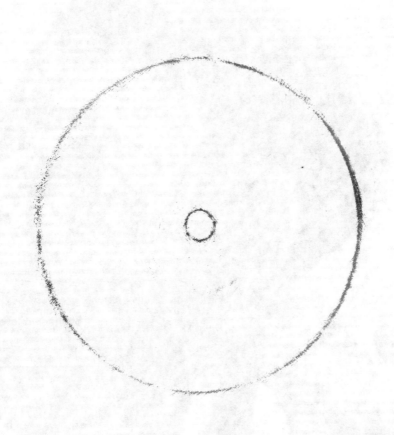

16 Rock Bottom
– Just Awful Hits

Ok. So I said this book was a celebration of one hit wonders. An attempt not to put the boot in, but to understand. Dear reader, I have lapsed. I've been nice about 'Mr Blobby' and 'The Birdie Song' and the Joe Dolce Music Theatre, but there comes a time when even I have to draw a line, and this is that point.

It has been quite disturbing to note just how much my musical taste has wobbled by writing this book. Actually, it's more than wobbled, it's gone off the scale. I have developed a taste for early-eighties American rock, all those mullet bands with names of cities like Chicago and Boston. I have rediscovered a long-dormant love for Tears for Fears. I have even – nervous readers may want to look away now – bought myself a second Roachford album. And listened to it.

To start with, I tried to balance it all out with repeated playing of *Kid A*. But in the end what saved me (and probably my relationship) was the discovery of one hit wonders that even I in my most generous moments still could not stand. They are, in my personal opinion, songs that are beyond redemption, hits beyond my meagre comprehension.

I should probably issue a health warning before we continue. These songs are very contagious, and no one is immune. Their insidious tunes may well infest your brain for many hours, if not days to come. You are reading on at your own risk, and I cannot be held responsible for what follows. If you are feeling sensitive, you would be well advised to skip to the next chapter now . . .

Grandad Clive Dunn
No. 1 1970

OAPless

If you were making a television show in the sixties or seventies, and you wanted someone to play the bumbling but basically lovable old codger character, the first phone call you would make would be to Clive Dunn's agent to see if he was available. Best known for his role as Corporal Jones in *Dad's Army*, Dunn played similar characters in *My Old Man*, *Bootsie and Snudge* and the one I can't quite forget, *Grandad*, a children's show by *Rentaghost* writer Bob Block, in which Dunn plays Charlie Quick (as the actress said to the dealer), the doddery caretaker of Parkview Rehearsal Hall. To find the blame for that show, we have to look back to this number 1 record. And to find the blame for that record, we have to look back to, well, Ronnie Corbett.

If Ronnie Corbett hadn't been on *This is Your Life* none of this might ever have happened. For it was at the after-show meal that Clive Dunn found himself sat next to Herbie Flowers, sometime bassist and songwriter. The two cooked up the idea to record a single, and Flowers got his friend Kenny Pickett, singer with sixties rockers the Creation, to write the words. If you ever thought the lyrics were somewhat chocolate-boxy, you'd be right. Part of the inspiration for the words came from the pictures on a tin of Quality Street that Kenny had on the table.

In order to explore the true awfulness of this single,
let us linger for a second on the musical calibre of the people who wrote it. You may not have heard of Herbie Flowers, but you will have heard his playing. His finest moment came with his bass part to Lou Reed's 'Walk On The Wild Side'. He also played with T Rex and David Bowie. Kenny Pickett's the Creation, meanwhile, are one of those influential sixties groups whose attitude and music get Britpop types all starry-eyed. Indeed, they were loved so much by Alan McGee that he named his record label after them. If this was a school report, Flowers and Pickett would get an E when they are clearly capable of an A. 'Very, very disappointing,' the teacher would write with a sigh.

> If this was a school report, Flowers and Pickett would get an E when they are clearly capable of an A.

There was one last shot at keeping 'Grandad' out of the charts. The electrical unions went on strike (supposedly over something else, but maybe they'd heard the record . . .) and the record company couldn't press any more copies. But it didn't do any good – Ed Stewart's *Junior Choice* was deluged with requests and 'Grandad' eventually went to number 1 anyway. Flowers and Pickett went back to proper music (T Rex and roadieing for Led Zep respectively), and Clive continued his funny old bloke act. He retired to Portugal in the 1980s, no doubt a very rich man.

Listen Here *Chegger's Choice* (Global, 1999). Next to 'There's No One Quite Like Grandma'. Where else?

Watch On *The Very Best of Dad's Army* (DVD, 2001). Dunny being funny.

Matchstalk Men And Matchstalk Cats And Dogs
Brian and Michael
No. 1 1978

Clogging up the charts

The seeds of this song go back to T. Walls and Sons, a factory in Oldham, where Brian Burke and Michael Coleman used to work. Writing songs together in their lunch hour, the pair formed a folk music-cum-comedy duo under perhaps the not fantastic title of Burke and Jerk. But one song in their repertoire did not quite fit in: a warm paean to local painter L. S. Lowry. Lowry was famous for his paintings of northern working life, particularly the 'matchstalk' figures that adorned them. Looked down upon by critics but loved by many, he had died in 1976, and the duo had the idea of writing a song about him. And when they tried it out, the positive response they had to it led to the idea of recording it as a single.

Scraping £1,000 together, Brian and Michael went to Pluto Studios in Stockport to record the song. The owner of Strawberry Studios (the posh one downstairs) suggested they use St Winifred's School Choir

as this was where his children went. From such simple beginnings ... The wonderfully named Tintwhistle Brass Band was also added as this was the village where producer Kevin Parrot lived. The money ran out before the B-side could be recorded, but fortunately another studio-friend stepped in to help out. Having finished the recording, the Burke and Jerk name was dropped in favour of Brian and Michael, and the song was released in November 1977.

A lot happened in the six months between the song being released and April the following year, when it finally hit number 1. First, for reasons that aren't quite clear, Brian and Michael became Kevin and Michael, after one half of the duo left, originally because his wife was ill, but the temporary split soon became permanent, and Kevin – who had played with Michael back in the 1960s – became 'Brian' full time. At the same time, the chart compilers were highly suspicious of the song because the sales of the record were predominantly from the north. But despite these setbacks, there was no stopping the song, and it knocked 'Wuthering Heights' by Kate Bush off the top to become their first and only number 1.

'Matchstalk ...' is a funny mix of a song. The lyrics aren't actually bad at all, and indeed, the song went on to win a coveted Ivor Novello award. And if it had just been sung acoustically, maybe it would have become a much-loved modern folksong, a northern 'Streets Of London', if you will. But as it is, the kitchen-sink production of brass band and school choir ladles

> The kitchen sink production of brass band and school choir ladles the sentimentality on with a trowel.

the sentimentality on with a trowel and hams up the song's northern roots, and I think this is why the song is less fondly remembered in some quarters.

'Brian' and Michael recorded two albums without much further success, before going on to pursue other interests. In 1986 they wrote and produced another one hit wonder, Claire and Friends' 'It's 'Orrible Being In Love When You're 8½'. Michael went on to write a musical about Lowry, and 'Brian' ended up in advertising. Brian, meanwhile, started an ice-cream business, before going full circle and ending up back in factory work.

Listen Here 'Matchstalk Men And Matchstalk Cats And Dogs' (PYE, 1979). The single.

Listen On 'It's 'Orrible Being In Love When You're 8½' – Claire and Friends (BBC, 1986). Claire had a friend called Brian and another one called Michael.

Read Further Michael Howard – *L. S. Lowry: A Visionary Artist* (Lowry Press, 2000). The man the song was all about.

Day Trip To Bangor (Didn't We Have A Lovely Time)
Fiddler's Dram
No. 3 1979

Dramalamdingdong!

Before we get started on the song, we'd better get the issue of the title out of the way. They're not the first band to do this, and I don't suppose they'll be the last and maybe I'm making an example of them, but just listen to this. Day Trip To Bangor open brackets Didn't We Have A Lovely Time close brackets. Why? What possible reason is there for this song to have a subtitle? Either it's part of the title or it's not. It's not even as if it tells us anything useful. If a song is the theme for something or other – for example, 'Three Lions (The Official Song of The England Football Team)' – it almost makes sense. But otherwise, people just go bracket crazy. Take Coast to Coast. One terrible hit, emphasised by its appallingly punctuated title: '(Do) The Hucklebuck'. Either the song's called 'The Hucklebuck' or it's called 'Do The Hucklebuck'. Just make a decision and move on. It's as Phil Collins almost once said: when it comes to music there's No Brackets Required.

> What possible reason is there for this song having a subtitle? Either it's part of the title or it's not.

Folk music gets a bad name in this country, which is a great shame because if you look in the right direction, there's actually lots of good stuff around. Kathryn Williams is rather fine, and there's a young singer from Yorkshire called Kate Rusby who has got one of the most gorgeous voices going. And don't get me started on Nick Drake. The problem that folk has, though, is that on the rare occasions it pops up in the charts, it is with a risible little ditty such as this, which reinforces all the stereotypes the population at large has about folk types. We're only five lines into the song, for example, when the first bottle of cider is opened.

'Day Trip To Bangor (Which Almost Sounds Like A Welsh Porn Film When You Think About It)' reinforces the feeling that folk is stuck in some sort of time warp (which it's not: check out Eliza Carthy). While pop music was jetting off to Barbados (Typically Tropical) and Sunny España (Sylvia), the folkies were trundling along to North Wales for the delights of a cup of tea, the Ferris wheel, a pedal boat, the sound of a brass band and eels – all in, don't you know, for less than a quid. Talk about letting your hair down. And how do Fiddler's Dram describe their day out? Lovely. Not 'lovely' as you or I would say it, but 'lovely' translated into irritating Ye Olde Englyshe folkspeak, where somehow it has acquired an extra syllable. Luvverly. Or maybe not.

Fiddler's Dram, who dissolved quite quickly after this single, are actually all very talented folk musicians, which makes this irritating single so much worse. Frankly, they should have known better. Lead singer Cathy Lesurf went on to sing with the Albion Band and Fairport Convention. Alan Prosser and Ian Telfer remain the backbone of long-running folk group the Oyster Band. Chris Taylor has gone full circle, teaching music in Canterbury, where the band originally came together. And Ian Kearey (bass) is an editor and writer. I wonder what his house style on brackets is?

Listen Here   'Day Trip To Bangor' (Dingles, 1979)
A single ticket, rather than a return.

Listen On   *Pearls from the Oysters* – Oysterband (Recall, 1998). Where Alan and Ian went next.

Listen Further   *Little Lights* – Kate Rusby (Pure, 2001). Folk at its most fantastic.

Mickey Toni Basil
No. 2 1982

Pom tiddly pom

'Mickey' is one of those songs that is so seared in the public consciousness that all you need to hear of it to get that groan of recognition is a split second of those drums at the beginning. You know the ones, the almost tribal beat that launched a thousand cheerleading routines, Butterkist Butterkist ra ra ra. Indeed, teen-favourite flick *Bring It On*, the 2000 cheerleading 'classic' starring Kirsten Dunst, would have felt bereft without its presence. Though why they got B*Witched to rerecord the song is anyone's guess.

Antonia Basilotta, it might not surprise you to

learn, had once been a cheerleader. Indeed, she set up a cheerleading squad at school before there were even any teams to cheer for. But between leaving Las Vegas High and making 'Mickey', she enjoyed a life well beyond the pompons. There was an acting career at the cutting edge of sixties counterculture: dancing with Davy Jones in the Monkees' psychedelic career suicide film, *Head*; frolicking with Peter Fonda in *Easy Rider*. In the seventies Toni built up a reputation as a much-in-demand choreographer, both for films (*American Graffiti*) and for music (*Diamond Dogs*-era David Bowie).

But it was another seventies phenomenon that was to propel Toni to pop stardom. Mike Chapman and Nicky Chinn were the songwriting team *du jour* of glam rock, penning hits for Sweet, Mud and many more. If they had platform shoes, they probably wrote for them. Another of their successful acts were the not especially racy Racey (biggest hit 'Some Girls', which got to number 2 in 1979), and someone had the bright idea of Toni rerecording their song 'Kitty', except with 'Kitty' taken out and 'Mickey' put in its place. Toni had the idea of adding in the cheerleading stuff, and *voilà*! A hit was made. Using all her choreographing skills, Toni got herself some actual cheerleaders (from LA's Carson High School) and made what was one of the most iconic videos of the early 1980s.

Mickey reached number 2 in the UK and went one better in the US when it was released a month later. But the follow-up, the fatefully titled 'Nobody', stalled at number 52. And not only that, but due to contracts

> Antonia Basilotta, it might not surprise you to learn, had once been a cheerleader.

and other people writing the song and what have you, Toni's reward for her stardom was equally minimal: $3,000 in royalties is all she has ever received. Still, it's not all bad, and pop was only ever one of Toni's many talents. A still from the video ended up in the Museum of Modern Art; her choreographing goes from strength to strength (*That Thing You Do*, *My Best Friend's Wedding* and more); and she still does the odd bit of singing, one of the wild ones in the Latin group Cecilia Noel and the Wild Clams.

Listen Here *The Best One Hit Wonders in the World . . . Ever!* (Virgin, 2003). They've taken the Mickey and put it halfway down side two.

Watch On *Easy Rider* (DVD, 2000). Toni Basil and Peter Fonda. Who'd have thought it?

Listen Further *Some Girls* – Racey (Disky, 2002). Contains 'Kitty', from which the Mickey was taken.

Down Under
Men at Work
No. 1 1983

Strewth

Australia, I think it is fair to say, has offered the UK charts more than its fair share of one hit wonders over the years. And that's before we get on to all those formers actors from *Neighbours* trying their luck. Think Mental As Anything. Think Midnight Oil. Think – was there ever a more appropriately named band? – Flash and the Pan. But none was more successful, or more one-off, than this 1983 chart topper: an unofficial national anthem for XXXXers everywhere.

Men at Work started out as acoustic duo Colin Hay (vocals) and Ron Strykert (guitar), before becoming a band with the addition of John Rees (bass), Jerry Spesier (drums) and Greg Ham (a little bit of everything). Getting their name from (where else) a road sign, Men at Work soon developed a healthy following on the Melbourne pub scene, even releasing a self-financed single, 'Keypunch Operator'. It was on the B-side of this that 'Down Under' made its first outing. A proper record deal followed, and their first release, 'Who Can It Be Now?' went to number 1 in Australia. If the band thought that was good, the follow-up did even better. It went to number 1 *everywhere*.

'Down Under' starts with some empty bottles. I would guess beer, but I'd hate to be accused of stereo-typing. Anyway, Ron Strykert was messing around at home, filling the bottles up with water and trying to play himself a tune. That messing around became the beginning of the song. Then in comes Colin with his celebratory tune and definition of what being an Australian is all about. The verse about the bloke walking into a bakery in Brussels, trying to converse in French and discovering the man was Australian apparently happened to a friend of his.

There are three reasons in particular why this song deserves to be in this section. First, it should probably be charged for rhymes against humanity. The characteristics of an Australian are limited to those that rhyme with 'under'. So they 'plunder'. And sometimes they 'chunder'. And just occasionally, there's a little bit of 'thunder' for good measure. Second, there is the 'Vegemite sandwich', which, as a lifelong Marmite loather, I feel should clearly not be countenanced on the grounds of decency. But perhaps most damning of all, there is the disturbing discovery that lead singer Colin Hay *is not even Australian*, but was in fact born in Scotland where he lived for what should have been fourteen formative years. I rest my case.

With a suitably wacky video, 'Down Under' wowed a fledgling MTV and briefly the band were huge. As well as reaching number 1 in the UK, in the United States they won a Grammy for Best New Artist, and the accompanying album, *Business as Usual*, stayed at number 1 for fifteen weeks there. In Britain, though, success was slightly shorter lived, and the follow-up, 'Overkill', hit the buffers at

> Lead singer Colin Hay *is not even Australian*, but was in fact born in Scotland.

number 21. It was perhaps an appropriate choice of single, because although Australia was ready for the band's second album *Cargo* ('Down Under' had been a number 1 there over a year earlier), the belated success in the UK meant that the second album was released three months after the first. That, clearly, was too much Men at Work for anyone.

Men at Work released one further album, *Two Hearts*, before the band started shedding members and Colin Hay became a solo artist. In the late 1990s, for reasons that are best described as unfathomable, the band were rediscovered in South America and reformed for two hugely successful tours. There was a further outing for the song in 2000, when Colin performed it at the closing ceremony of the Sydney Olympics. As well as a recent tour with that most hallowed of one-hit call-ups – yup, the Ringo Starr All Starr Band – Colin has recently recorded *Man at Work*, an acoustic collection of band favourites.

Listen Here   *Super Hits* (Sony, 2003). All the hit and nine more.

Listen On   *Man at Work* – Colin Hay (Compass, 2003). Includes 'Down Under' in different versions.

Listen Further   'And The Band Played Waltzing Matilda' – the Pogues (on *Rum Sodomy and the Lash*, Warner, 1994). Irish rather than Scottish, but poignant and affecting.

Solid Ashford and Simpson
No.3 1985

Still not not not not not not not not

I have a soft spot for soul music. My favourite soul song of all time is 'Memphis Soul Stew' by King Curtis, a funky little number in which said King runs through the recipe of his superior soul music. He starts with a half a pound of bass, then adds in a pound of fatback drums, a tablespoon of 'bawling Memphis guitar', a pinch of organ, and half a pint of horn. I mention this because sometimes, you see, soul music can be extremely tasty. At others, however, it can be overdone, overcooked, unpalatable and to continue the King Curtis analogy, well, stewed.

Nicholas Ashford and Valerie Simpson first met in the early 1960s at White Rock Baptist Church in New York, where they were both members of the choir. They started writing songs together and after their 'Let's Go Get Stoned' was a hit for Ray Charles, they got jobs at Motown as writers and producers. Marvin Gaye, Diana Ross, the Miracles, all benefited from the Ashford and Simpson experience, though perhaps their best song was saved for Chaka Khan, 'I'm Every Woman'. At the same time, Val and

> The song's low point is the bit where they tell us that the 'thrill' (i.e. the shagging) is still 'hot'.

Nick started having ideas about performing themselves. Valerie went first, but when her solo career didn't take off, it was duo time. They started having hits in the US – 1977's 'So, So Satisfied' a hint at what was to come – until finally, in 1985, they scored this international 'success'.

Reasons why 'Solid' is execrable no. 1. It is smug. This song is the musical equivalent of those newly married couples, who spend the whole time inviting you to their house, where they can show off the furniture and regale you with tales of how wonderful they and their family are. Ashford and Simpson, who'd been married for about ten years or so by this point, want to tell the world how they are so much still together. And that's great guys. Good for you. The problem is that they're so damned *pleased* about it, it's almost as if they're taunting the singletons of the world. 'Hey lonesome! Look what we've got! Bet you wish you were like us, huh? Rock solid, yeah!'

This smugness then combines with reasons why 'Solid' is execrable no. 2. The words. It seems almost unfathomable that Ashford and Simpson are actually respected and successful songwriters when you listen to 'Solid', because the lyrics appear to have come straight out of The Big Book of Rock Clichés. How many can *you* spot? My tally is seven – solid as a rock, sky turning grey, batting an eye, down the line, gone with the wind, knock on wood and against all odds. And it would be more if they didn't keep on repeating that interminable chorus.

Finally, we move on to reasons why 'Solid' is execrable no. 3. The vocals. First, there's those dreadful throat-clearing 'woah woah woahs' between each verse. Then there's the way that the word 'solid' is not pronounced 'solid' with its first syllable 'Sol' as in beer,

but somehow has an 'ow!' injected into proceedings. Sow-lid! And then there is perhaps the song's low point, the bit where they tell us that the 'thrill' (i.e., the shagging) is still 'hot'. Hot hot hot hot hot hot hot hot. If that wasn't nauseous enough, again the pronunciation comes into play. 'Hot' becomes a laughing-at-the-rest-of-the-world 'ha!' Ha ha ha ha ha ha ha ha. My hackles are rising, just thinking about it.

Ashford and Simpson are still going, and in 1999 celebrated their twenty-fifth wedding anniversary, still, alas, very much solid as a rock. They now own a restaurant in New York, the suitably saccharine Sugar Bar. In 1992 they sang at Bill Clinton's presidential inauguration, which considering everything that was to happen with Monica Lewinsky proves that maybe the Americans do have a sense of irony after all.

Listen Here   *The Hits Album 2* (WEA, 1985). Odd track-listing positions 'Solid' after Phil Collins's less solid 'Easy Lover'.

Listen On   *The Very Best of Ashford and Simpson* (Rhino, 2002). Fifteen 'classic' cuts.

Listen Further   *I'm Every Woman: The Best of Chaka Khan* (ESP, 1999). They can write songs, after all.

My Toot Toot
Denise Lasalle
No. 6 1985

Whatever you do, don't mess with hers

There is a lesson to be learned with this particular one hit wonder and it is this: if you are a reasonably successful and talented blues singer and your record company rings you up and asks you to record a version of a novelty song that's doing the rounds, the answer is no.

Zydeco is a type of music that, until its brief spurt of popularity in the mid-1980s, had not travelled much beyond its home state of Louisiana. It's a sort of accordion-led dance music, mixing rhythm and blues with a touch of Cajun and a helping of traditional French music. In 1984 a zydeco artist called Rockin' Sidney Simian wrote and recorded a throwaway little number called 'My Toot Toot'. And despite being buried deep on the second side of his new album, the local radio stations started going crazy for it and it was released as a single.

As the song spread out from being a regional hit to national success, so did that predictable novelty record pattern of bigger record companies getting in on the act. Fats Domino did a version, as did Jean Knight, and when Malaco Records had their offer for

> Denise has got one and she doesn't want you to 'mess' with it.

the record turned down, they turned to one of their other singers, Denise Lasalle, to cover it instead. Denise, the self-styled 'Queen of Soul Blues', hails from the Big Momma Don't Go Messing With Her School of Soul Singers and had been having R&B hits since the early 1970s, songs with titles such as 'Trapped By A Thing Called Love' and 'I'm So Hot'.

And when 'My Toot Toot' came out, hot Denise suddenly was. Ignorant of the song's Louisiana origins, unaware of Denise's music credentials, as far as the British public was concerned, here was an unknown singer with a funny song about a Toot Toot. So what the hell *is* a Toot Toot anyway? The lyrics, unfortunately, aren't that helpful. We know that Denise has got one, she doesn't want you to 'mess' with it, and if you so much as try to touch hers, she's going to 'break your face'. Nice. There is one further clue. We know that the potential Toot Toot toucher has 'another woman'. So maybe what Denise is referring to is what Ricky Martin would call his bon-bon. But before we dust down all those cheap 'rock bottom' jokes, the truth is that 'toot' is actually an old Creole term of affection, from the French *tout*, thus meaning something like 'my everything'. Which I think refers to a loved one, unless Denise is particularly proud of her posterior.

Rockin' Sidney got a Grammy award for the song, while Denise got the international hit. She's still very much doing her thing. Sure there may have been the odd boat trip in the Caribbean (the 'Ultimate Blues Cruise', which is a concept we don't really have time to go into here), but in 2002 she released *I'm Still the Queen*, and it would take a braver man than me to argue otherwise. The album contains such no-prisoner soul-fests as the gloriously titled 'You Should Have Kept It In The Bedroom'.

Listen Here *The Hits Album 3* (WEA, 1985). Funny how the *Hits* series folded while the *Now* series goes strong.

Listen On *Right Place, Right Time* (Malaco, 1995). Denise gets saucy on 'Bump And Grind'. You have been warned.

Listen Further 'My Toot Toot' – Rockin' Sidney (Maison de Soul, 1987). The original tooter.

Achy Breaky Heart
Billy Ray Cyrus
No. 3 1992

His big breaky was short-livedy. Thank goodnessy

Remember Chris Waddle from Spurs midfield duo Glenn and Chris, with their 1986 hit 'Diamond Lights'? Imagine, if you will, that following said single, instead of returning to his mazy-dribbling career on the football pitch, Chris decided to give up sport altogether. Instead, Chris packed his bags and headed off for the US of A, where he was to spend the next six years eating a succession of large hamburgers and working out. Imagine, too, that rather than having his hair cut, Chris let his trademark mullet grow, mutate into some form of world-beating giant rat's tail. Dress him in a red lumberjack shirt, add a guitar and hip shake and *voilà!* You've got yourself your very own Billy Ray Cyrus.

I'm not a big fan of country music at the best of times, and 1992 was not the best of times for country music. It's got a bit more mainstream since then (Shania 'Man!' Twain and the Dixie Chicks) and also a bit more credible (assorted Americana acts, Calexico and the like), but back in the early 1990s in the UK at least it was all a bit Stetson this and Dolly Parton that. Billy Ray, born in Kentucky in the early 1960s, was the bright new hope, ready to give Garth Brooks a run for his money. His musical career had begun in a band called Sly Dog, but hit problems when the Ohio bar they were the house band for was mysteriously burnt to the ground, with all their equipment inside. Strange that. It didn't stop Billy though, who eventually scored a record deal and released his debut album *Some Gave All* in 1992.

The mullet and the country music are general rather than specific reasons for loathing 'Achy Breaky Heart'. A more specific factor is the words. I mean, achy breaky heart? Purlease. There's a time and a place for coochie-coo lover's language, and it's not on a single. Billy Ray, it transpires, is happy for you to do anything just as long as you don't break his achy breaky boombox. Here are some alternatives he suggests in the verses: burning his clothes, telling your friend what a klutz he is, getting your dog to bite his leg, allowing your brother Cliff to punch him, or explaining to your mother that Billy Ray has moved to

> I'm not aware of exploding hearts being a common cause of death, even among mullet-wearing cowboys.

Arkansas. Or if you're feeling a little weirder, try one of these for size: tell Billy's lips to have a word with his fingertips, a word about how they won't be touching anything any more; or mention to Billy Ray's eyes to keep a look out for his mind, as it might be about to walk out at any moment. Or maybe, given all of the above, it's already buggered off.

I'm not saying that Billy Ray has a touch of the dramatics, but here's the threat he's laying down to his cowgirl. If you leave, and break his heart, the achy breaky one, it is likely to 'blow up' and in the process kill Billy Ray. Now. I'm not a world expert on human biology, but I'm not aware of exploding hearts being a common cause of death, even among mullet-wearing cowboys. As last throws of the dice go, it is a pretty paltry one, and if Billy Ray's cowgirl has had any form of schooling, she won't be staying after all, but trying not to laugh as she closes the door behind her.

Fortunately for Billy Ray, there are plenty more cowgirls in the ranch. He turned into one of those unfathomable heart-throbs, even when the words 'line' and 'dancing' were added to the equation. His second album, the depressingly titled *It Won't Be The Last*, unfortunately did not turn out to be his last. There have been another six long-players, plenty of success in Nashville if not beyond, most recently the God-friendly *The Other Side* (2003).

Listen Here *Achy Breaky Heart* (Spectrum, 2001). Billy's best bits. And 'Achy Breaky Heart'.

Listen On *The Other Side* (World, 2003). Billy does God.

Listen Further *The Most Awesome Line Dancing*

Album Volume 1 (Music for Pleasure, 1997). Awesome? Awful.

Breakfast At Tiffany's
Deep Blue Something
No. 1 1996

Lunch was another matter

In the 1980s British music was plagued by winsome, wistful, jangly bands who eschewed any sort of rock edge in favour of showing how sensitive they were. Artists like Scritti Politti. Danny Wilson. China Crisis. Hue & Cry. To borrow a band name from the era, they were wet wet wet. Fortunately, they were easily identified with their flowery shirts and preponderance of waistcoats, and thus easily avoided. In the 1990s the disease spread across the Atlantic, despite the heroic attempt of grunge to kill it off. Once again, thankfully, such bands could be spotted and avoided, this time by helpfully sporting ridiculous names such as Hootie and the Blowfish.

Deep Blue Something, however, briefly slipped through the net. At the (soft) centre of the band are brothers Todd and Toby Pipes, who strum and share vocal duties. In 1992 they formed a university band with drummer John Kirtland and guitarist Clay Bergus, later replaced by Kirk Tatom, and went under the Bowie-inspired moniker Leper Messiah. I told you these bands were easy to spot. Changing their name to Deep Blue Something, the band recorded an album in 1993, *11th Song*, on a small local label. Nestling in at track ten was a certain 'Breakfast At Tiffany's', though with production values at a minimum, the record wasn't deemed good enough for radio and sales were minimal. In 1995 the band started work on a second album, *Home*, and this time the first single, a rerecorded 'Breakfast At Tiffany's', was picked up. A major label stepped in, and an international hit was theirs.

'Breakfast At Tiffany's' tells the story of a relationship nearing its end. From the lyrics, it's sounding like she is dumping him: they've got nothing in common, she says. Scrabbling around to prove her wrong, the best our singer can come up with is the observation that they both like the film *Breakfast at Tiffany's*. The insinuation is that, hey, I'm a romantic kind of guy, my liking of funny, quirky black-and-white films shows that I'm not some shallow Hal but a Man With Feelings. We're two romantic peas in a pod, so maybe we should stay together after all. Thank you Audrey, you might just have saved my relationship!

Now, I don't know who Mr Pipes was going out with, but if you listen carefully, you'll discover that in fact she's rather smart. Carefully, cuttingly, she rips his Audrey Hepburn trick apart. *Breakfast at Tiffany's*? she muses. Yes, yes, I 'think' I remember that film, she responds indifferently. But here's the killer. Her recollection is that both her and Pipey 'kinda liked it'. Not loved it. Not even liked it. But kind of liked it. If that isn't a response laced with sassy feminine sarcasm, I don't know what is. And what is Pipey's response to this sassy piece of feminine sarcasm? Like a true bloke, he completely misses the point. See? he responds triumphantly. We have got something in common after all.

I don't know whether Deep Blue Something intended this reading of the song when they wrote it. My guess is that rather than writing a multi-layered song about the subtleties of male–female relations, they probably only included words like 'think' and 'kinda' in order to make the lines scan better. This is also only another guess, but I reckon that the nod to *Breakfast at Tiffany's* is one of those lazy romantic references shoehorned in to give a song some semblance of credibility. A credibility, it has to be said, that is needed to cover the fact that the music is almost offensively inoffensive and that the chorus is repeated six, yes that's six times.

But spare a tear, if you will, for the deep blue boys. They may not have been deep, but they were quickly blue. As 'Breakfast At Tiffany's' rocketed up the charts around the world, their original record company rereleased the band's first album with the original version of the song on it. The band slapped a lawsuit down, and the record company responded with a counter-suit, stopping the band from recording or releasing anything else. If that wasn't bad enough, guitarist Kirk was replaced by original member Clay, and guess what? Another lawsuit ensued. And just when things couldn't get any worse, their current record company was merged with another, and the new conglomerate wasn't that interested in scheduling the new Deep Blue Something album. Back to court the band went again, in order to get themselves out of their contract. By the time all

Breakfast at Tiffany's is one of those lazy romantic references shoehorned in to give a song some sense of credibility.

this was sorted out, and the new album, *Deep Blue Something*, was released, it was 2001, and the momentum had gone.

Wouldn't it be nice if somewhere in Midwest America, there is a couple on the verge of splitting up, and as a last throw of the commonality dice, the boyfriend says, What about 'Breakfast At Tiffany's'? And the girlfriend goes, God yes! *I* remember that song. She smiles and says, you know, if I remember rightly, we both kinda hated it. And the boyfriend nods yes, and they laugh together for the first time in weeks. What were they called? the girlfriend asks. No idea, the boyfriend grins, their relationship suddenly salvageable after all.

Listen Here *The Best One Hit Wonders in the World . . . Ever!* (Virgin, 2003). Unnecessarily prominent at track three.

Listen On *Home* (MCA, 1996). The album sleeve is not deep blue. It's yellow.

Watch Further *Breakfast at Tiffany's* (DVD, 2000). Audrey Hepburn at her very best.

Wassuup Da Muttz
No. 11 December 2000

Buddy awful
Philadelphia, the mid-1970s. As well as being the home of soft cheese and soul music of the same distinction (see 'Move Closer' – Phyllis Nelson), Philadelphia was where four friends – Paul Williams, Fred Thomas, Charles Stone III and Scott Brooks – lived and greeted each other with their tongues out like this. Whassup?! Wassuuup. *Wassuuuuuuup.* Waaaaaaaaaaaaaaasup. Ah, how quickly the eighties must have come round. All of which would be fine, except fifteen years later, Charles decided to make a short film of the grating greeting – a short film that found its way into the hands of Budweiser and their advertising team. Charles and his Philadelphia mates were famous. Sitting at home. Watching the game. Having a beer. Making a fortune. True.

The first wave of the Wassup attacks happened before the adverts were even out in the UK. Email inboxes everywhere became clogged up with video messages from wacky friends in the States. Then came the adverts themselves: on the telly, at the cinema, retold down the pub. There was the sitting at home ad. The guy delivering pizza ad. The Japanese chef 'wasabi' ('Wassssabi!') ad. The posh English 'What is up' ads. Then back clogged the email inboxes as the spoof adverts arrived, spliced together by people with too much time on their hands: the hilarious *Star Wars* one; the side-splitting *Scooby Doo* version; the Mahir 'I Kiss You' take. Bill Gates, *The Matrix*, *The Sixth Sense*, the Teletubbies: you name it, they've got their own Wassuup special somewhere on the Internet.

And then. Then. Then came this execrable cash-in single by two British producers who thought they

'Wassuup' is a couple of people shoutin' 'Wassup?' set to the music of MC Hammer's 'Can't Touch This'.

could make a quick buck or two. Alex Rizzo and Elliot Ireland are two perfectly respectable dance fellows, with an eclectic track record that includes remixing Eminem, Kirsty MacColl, Alison Limerick, Osibisa and Incognito. They also go under the names of Shaft and Skeewiff and Ikon. But in 2000 the name was Da Muttz, and the public bought it.

'Wassuup' isn't just a couple of people shouting 'Wassup?' set to music. Oh no no no. 'Wassuup' is a couple of people shouting 'Wassup?' set to the music of MC Hammer's 'Can't Touch This', all topped off with a lumping beat and a handful of sirens (the taste police?) thrown in for good measure. It doesn't take much imagination to picture the scene in Toff's Nightclub, the cheesy DJ turning down the sound and the drunken throwing their hands in the air and shouting 'Wassssuuuuuuuup!!' About as much imagination as it took to put this single together.

Listen Here 'Wassuup' (WEA, 2000). The single.

Listen On '(Mucho Mambo) Sway' – Shaft (Wonderboy, 1999). Alex and Elliot in a different guise.

Listen Further *The Hits* – MC Hammer (EMI Gold, 2000). U Can't Touch This without someone going 'Wassuuuuuuuup!' over the top.

Bubbling Under

Five one hit wonders that almost made the best top ten

Soho
'Hippy Chick'
(No. 8, 1991)

Alannah Myles
'Black Velvet'
(No. 2, 1990)

Fiction Factory
'(Feels Like) Heaven'
(No. 6, 1984)

Dream Academy
'Life In A Northern Town'
(No. 15, 1985)

It's Immaterial
'Driving Away From Home (Jim's Tune)'
(No. 18, 1986)

17 Singled Out – Great Hits

The thing about a thunderstorm is that afterwards the sun comes out. And after the downpour of dreadful one hit wonders, it is only fair to bring your ears some rays of golden joy – and leave the Rays of Billy Cyrus behind us. You're slightly at the mercy of my own personal taste, which you may well be having doubts about by now, but here, I hope, you'll think I'm spot on.

A quick word about the selection of Nena. '99 Red Balloons' may be a slightly controversial choice for some, and I would admit it is a slightly sentimental choice on my part, but I would be doing a disservice to my eleven-year-old self if it was left out. Also, its inclusion echoes what this book is partly about: it's not about being cool but being honest about what we really like. And I still like that song, so in it goes.

The surprising thing about all the artists in this chapter is that they only ever had one hit. If they can produce three and a half minutes of such brilliance, how come they never achieved it again? As Strawberry Switchblade so poignantly put it, all they left us with are our 'thoughts of yesterday'. But what thoughts.

Something In The Air
Thunderclap Newman
No. 1 1969

A lightning career

The late 1960s were a time of great opportunity and possibility: Altamont, the Beatles splitting up, My Lai, the Irish troubles, the election of Richard Nixon, Harold Wilson and the devaluation of the pound, the Six Day War, Rolf Harris and his two little boys ... ah, happy days. But as bad things will, the seventies were coming, waiting round the corner with a large mallet to finish off the remains of sixties idealism, all of which makes this particular song all the more poignant.

Thunderclap Newman were an odd mix of a band, brought together by Pete Townshend of the Who. The main man and singer was John 'Speedy' Keen, a long-time Who acolyte, who had written 'Armenia City In The Sky', the opening song on the Who's *The Who Sell Out* album. Added to the mix was pianist Andy 'Thunderclap' Newman and sixteen-year-old guitar wunderkind Jimmy McCulloch. With Pete Townshend producing, their debut single hit number 1 in Bryan Adams's mystical summer of '69, nestled between the Beatles' 'Ballad Of John And Yoko' and the Rolling Stones' 'Honky Tonk Woman'.

Everything about 'Something In The Air' is optimistic, right down to the chord sequence that shifts up and up and never comes down. It lacks the edge of cynicism that John Lennon gives to its nearest equivalent, the Beatles' 'Revolution'. And the Beatles' credo is more of a political one. Thunderclap Newman's feels more permissive, more personal. The lyrics about getting it together work on both a relationship and a revolutionary level. It works both ways, which is one of the reasons it is so good. There's a poignancy there too, a sense of pathos, but I'm not sure whether that was there originally or if it's just me listening with hindsight. I'll leave that up to you.

What I can't not offer an opinion on, though, is Andy 'Thunderclap' Newman's contribution a couple of minutes in. The song's all spaced out and chilled and loved up and groovy and then suddenly the guitars all stop and there's this rinky-dink piano solo that wouldn't be out of place in the back room of an East End – or should that be Hackney? – pub. What's that all about? Where has the revolution gone? Who invited Chas and Dave along? It's quirky and quite odd, and the words 'first', 'against' and 'the wall' spring to mind.

What happened to Thunderclap Newman, more than anything, was that the seventies arrived. An exorbitant delay in the follow-up single didn't help. 'Accidents', which reached number 46, didn't come out until almost a year later; the band split up soon after, leaving behind one album, *Hollywood Dream*. Newman and Keen went on to release solo albums before turning their hands to production; McCulloch, meanwhile, joined Wings and sadly died in 1979. Nothing, though, can

> Suddenly the guitars all stop and there's this rinky-dink piano solo that wouldn't be out of place in an East End pub.

take away the magic of 'Something In The Air', a little bit of the sixties, captured for ever.

Listen Here *Hollywood Dream* (Polydor, 2000). The first, and last, Thunderclap Newman album.

Listen On Follow-up single 'Accidents', also on the same album.

Listen Further *The Who Sell Out* – the Who (Polydor, 2000). Kicks off with Keen's 'Armenia City In The Sky'.

My Sharona
The Knack
No. 6 1979

For four minutes, they had it

What Badfinger were to the start of the seventies, the Knack were to its conclusion. There were two double-edged words, power pop, which are both music to my ears and the kiss of death to many a band's commercial success; and one band, the Beatles, whose legacy hung heavy in the air. With Badfinger, the comparison sort of made sense. Picked up by Paul McCartney and sounding just a touch like the Beatles in places, you could see where the accusations came from. With the Knack, it's not so much a musical thing; if there's a soupçon of the sixties in the mix, it's of the Kinks or Who variety. Instead, it was more things like *Rolling Stone* calling them 'the new fab four' and the jacket

sleeve to their debut album, *Get the Knack*, sharing the black-and-white photo feel of *With the Beatles*.

Certainly, for a few months in 1979, everyone got very excited about the Knack. With disco at its peak, the band had thirteen record companies falling over themselves to try and sign this great-sounding rock band. Hailing from Los Angeles, the band consisted of Doug Fieger (vocals/guitar), Berton Averre (lead guitar), Prescott Niles (bass) and Bruce Gary (drums). Enter Capitol Records, triumphant at their signature, and producer Mike Chapman, fresh from working with Blondie. The resulting album, *Get the Knack*, was one of the fastest-selling debut albums of all time in the US, and this single number 1 for six weeks.

The Sharona in question is Sharona Alperin, a Beverly Hills real estate agent, and Doug Fieger's one-time fiancée. The result is everything that is great about guitar pop. First, there's the thumping great tom-tom drumbeat. Then in comes the bass, sitting on that octave jump in superb staccato style. And topping the riff off is the guitar, crisply crunching along in unison over the top. The lyrics have a requisite dollop of sex to them, all dirty minds and things running down thighs, with the chorus adding in a 'My Generation'-style stutter 'M-m-m-my Sharona'. And talking of the words, has there ever been a more thrilling line written than 'My my my I Yi Woo'?

> Has there ever been a more thrilling line written than 'My my my I Yi Woo'?

The problem with instant success is that people, especially rock fans, get very suspicious of it. Releasing a second album eight months after the first probably didn't help. Neither did a band policy not to give any interviews. But even so, the resulting press backlash and briefly fashionable 'Knuke The Knack' T-shirts all seem a little harsh. Following a third album, *Round Trip*, the band split up in 1981. Since then, the group's lives have been punctuated by solo projects and getting back together again: first in 1986–7, then in 1991, and most recently in 1997. 'My Sharona', meanwhile, got a new lease of life from being used in the film *Reality Bites* and crept back into the charts. More recently, its gorgeous riff was lifted hook, line and sinker for the Girls Aloud single 'No Good Advice'. Or maybe that's just me.

Listen Here *Get the Knack* (Capitol, 2002). The debut album, now stuffed with bonus tracks.

Listen On *... But the Little Girls Understand* (Razor and Tie, 1993). The little girls didn't, and neither did anyone else.

Listen Further 'No Good Advice' – Girls Aloud (Polydor, 2003). Just my opinion. What do I know?

Video Killed The Radio Star Buggles
No. 1 1979

Oh-a oh-a!
Buggles was the brainchild of two seventies session musicians, Trevor Horn and Geoff Dowse, who first met as members of disco star Tina Charles's backing band. Trevor was also trying to make it as a producer, but after a succession of bad punk bands who went nowhere, decided he'd be better off making his own music. The band name was apparently chosen to be as repulsive as possible, though if so it doesn't quite work. In fact, it's kind of cute.

The inspiration for 'Video Killed The Radio Star' came from a short story by science fiction writer J. G. Ballard, of whom Trevor was a fan. 'The Sound Sweep' tells the story of a futuristic city where audible noise is considered pollution and music has been replaced by ultrasonic sound. For those who were worried about their house containing remnants of sound, a sound-sweep was hired, who would use his 'sonovac' to suck it all away. In the Buggles song the concern is more contemporary but ostensibly the same: the medium of video is taking over at the expense of music. It's a story of technology over talent, style over substance, and one that was to prove prophetic. Two years later, when a new channel, Music Television, or MTV for short, began, Buggles was the first song the station played.

> Trevor Horn sounded like he was singing and holding his nose at the same time.

With its insistent piano chords, backing singers going 'oh-a oh-a!' and Trevor Horn sounding like he was singing and holding his nose at the same time, 'Video Killed The Radio Star' hit number 1 in sixteen countries. What happened next can only be described as curious. Trevor and Geoff joined prog-rock band Yes. Replacing leaving members Jon Anderson and Rick Wakeman, the new line-up toured to mixed reactions. Trevor's strained vocal cords left him unable to sing, and bottles were thrown at the stage. Pretty soon, the pair left as quickly as they had arrived: Geoff went on to join rock supergroup Asia, while Trevor turned his hand to production.

It has to be said, what a phenomenal production career Trevor has had. ABC's definitive eighties album *The Lexicon of Love*? That was him. Frankie Goes to Hollywood's iconic eighties singles 'Relax' and 'Two Tribes'? That was him too. Propaganda, if you remember them, Seal, the Art of Noise, Dollar, even Russian lesbian schoolgirl duo Tatu have enjoyed his touch. Ooer. All of which goes to show that for all the power of MTV, the demise of the radio is ever so slightly exaggerated. As long as there are people like Trevor Horn writing and producing quality pop music, there'll be a couple of years in the old wireless yet.

Listen Here   *The Age of Plastic* (Island, 1999). There's a Miss Robot, an Astro Boy and Johnny on the Monorail in Buggles' vision.

Listen On   *Adventures in Modern Recording* (Imports, 1998). Geoff having gone to Asia, Buggles begins to turn slowly Trevor.

Listen Further   *The Lexicon of Love* – ABC (Mercury, 1996). One of the great pop albums of the eighties, thanks in no small part to Trevor's production.

Ring My Bell
Anita Ward
No. 1 1979

My ding-a-ling

Now this in my mind is a thing of beauty: disco as light and delicate as it is possible to be. So much so, in fact, that the whole thing floats from the speakers for its three and a half minutes. There's chirruping guitar and a right funky bass in the background, there's someone tinkling on the top end of a xylophone, but best of all there's repeated use of one of those classic disco noises (*pow!*), the sort that sounds like someone firing an effeminate sci-fi stun gun.

And over the top, but not so at all, sings Anita and her bell stars. Anita sings high, helium-high at times, and slightly spookily for my money: think the Bee Gees meet Eartha Kitt, with a touch of Sandra Dickinson thrown in for good measure. The lyrics, in a nutshell, are thus: she wants you to ring her bell, and, well, that's pretty much it. Quite what her bell is and how one rings it are never made clear, but the way Anita sings the song, there's little hint of any insinuation or innuendo. Her keenness for bell-ringing is reinforced by the backing singers, who gamely work their way through phrases such as 'ring it!', 'ding dong ding' and 'ring a ling a ling'.

> Quite what her bell is, and how one rings it, is never made clear.

Born in Memphis, Tennessee, in 1957, Anita got into singing through the gospel route and ended up as a member of the Rust College A Cappella Choir. She hadn't really thought about singing as a career – she had a degree in psychology and a job as a teacher – but her unique voice was spotted and she was put in touch with dance producer Frederick Knight. After they recorded an album together, mainly of ballads and mid-tempo songs, Frederick decided that the record was one dance song short. He then pulled out a song he'd written for Stacy Lattisaw, his eleven-year-old prodigy who'd go on to have a huge hit with 'Jump To The Beat'. 'Ring My Bell' was originally about teenagers yakking on the phone, but with a few lyrical tweaks, the song was Anita's. The rest, as they say . . . With nothing similar on the album, Anita's star, like so many disco acts, faded as quickly as it had appeared.

Listen Here *Ring My Bell* (Charly, 2001). Ringing it in single and extended versions.

Listen On 'Ring My Bell: Greatest Hits Remixed' (Hypnotic, 1999). Five remixes of Anita's top tune.

Listen Further 'Jump To The Beat' – Stacy Lattisaw (Atlantic, 1980). The child prodigy who should have sung the song.

Pop Muzik M
No. 2 1979

New York. London. Paris. And, so I've heard, Munich

The alphabet of pop is to say the least, a mixed bag: there's A (dodgy rock), Mel B. (zig a zig nah), Mr C (he's, er, goodish), D:Ream (D:Ire), Sheila E. (funky drummer), Adam F. (friend of Redman), Mel G. (see Mel B.), H (lead twonk from Steps), iPod (the one with all the hits), Jay Kay (two for the price of one), LL Cool J (soppy rapper), *NSYNC (Justin didn't, the others did), Roy Orbison (the Big O), P. Diddy (it stands for Puff), Q-Tips (like PG, but funkier), R KID (rib-tickling Oasis catalogue numbers), S Express (superfly guys), Mousse T (they're horny, etc.), UB40 (red red whine), VW (the logos the Beasties wore around their necks), XTC (1,2,3,4,5), Bill Wyman (il est un rock star) and, of course, ZZ Top. But as much as some of these have their moments, none quite matches up to the sheer joy of the solitary hit of letter number thirteen.

M is in fact a bloke called Robin Scott, who hails from that most rock and roll of places, Croydon. In the late 1960s he went to Croydon Art College, where he met, befriended and briefly lived with the future driving force of punk, Malcolm McLaren and Vivienne Westwood. But turning down the opportunity to get

> Pop Muzik celebrates pop at its most ephemeral and effervescent – fun, fleeting and fizzy.

involved in the Chelsea clothes shop they were setting up, Robin turned his hand to music instead. In
1969 he released his first album, the singer-song-
writer-styled *Woman from the Warm Grass*. More
strumming and various bands punctuated most of
the seventies. He managed R&B band Roogalator and
released Adam and the Ants' debut album on his Do-It
record label. It wasn't until the end of the decade and
he was living in Paris that Robin acquired his new
moniker, taken from the fluorescent 'M' that denotes
a Métro station. It was here that 'Pop Muzik' was
recorded.

A mixture of DIY-disco, bendy guitar lines, female
'do wops' and scattergun spoken lyrics, 'Pop Muzik' is
both a summary and celebration of twenty-five years
of bubblegum and boogie. There are nods, if you listen
closely to the words, to the Beatles and the Stones,
also rock and roll, soul and nursery rhymes. But what
'Pop Muzik' is really about, for me at least, is celebrating pop at its most ephemeral and effervescent – fun,
fleeting and fizzy. Phrases like 'shoobie doobie' belong
to the international language of music, which M
speaks very well, almost more fluently than his
English.

A huge hit across the globe, M never captured the
same heights again. There were further minor hits –
'Moonlight And Muzak', 'That's The Way The Money
Goes' – and a smattering of albums, with a proto-
Level 42 in support. When the record company
decided not to release the third album, *Famous Last
Words*, that was pretty much it. Robin moved into production and DJing and now lives in Portugal. In the
late 1990s 'Pop Muzik' got a new lease of life and a
hefty wedge of remixes, when it was used by U2 as
the opening song on their PopMart tour.

Listen Here   *Pop Muzik* (Collectables, 1998). M is
for magnificent.

Listen On   *Woman from the Warm Grass* – Robin
Scott (Demon, 2001). M is for Mmmm.

Listen Further   'Last Night On Earth' – U2
(Island, 1997). Bono and the boys offer up a 'pop
mart' version. M is for middling.

Echo Beach Martha and the Muffins
No. 10 1980

Faraway in time

I don't know about you, but I just go goosepimply
when I hear the opening guitar riff to this song. I've
played it again just now, and nearly twenty-five years
on that shiver down the spine is still there. It's a little
bit pop Stranglers, perhaps just a touch Toyah, but
mainly just great: new wavey, spacey and romantic at
the same time. Pop music, in many senses, doesn't get
much better than this.

Martha and the Muffins started out in Toronto,
Canada, in the late 1970s. With punk happening and
their art-school backgrounds, they had the perfect
new wave combination. Various names were discussed (among those rejected were the Confused
Tourists and the Gel Heads) before Martha and the
Muffins was chosen. It was meant to be a reaction
against the knee-jerk violent punk names and was

only ever meant to be temporary. As these things happen, though, it quickly became permanent.

The band's route to the charts was fantastically simple. They sent a tape to the music critic of a New York magazine. He liked it, played it to a guy from Virgin Records and a deal was signed. If only everything else was that simple. 'Echo Beach' quickly became an international hit. It was a song written about a summer job that songwriter Mark Gane had spent in a wallpaper factory, dreaming about being somewhere else. Like any great song, 'Echo Beach' taps into some sort of universal sentiment: the feeling of being a romantic trapped in some dead-end situation. We all have our own Echo Beach we think about escaping to. Back in the song, meanwhile, 'Echo Beach' doesn't refer to a particular place, though apparently Sunnyside Beach on the shore of Lake Ontario plays a part.

For a second, everything in Muffin world was great. They had their hit single, they had their support slot on Roxy Music's arena tour. But success came too soon, too quickly, and by the end of the year tensions and musical differences led to the six-piece being slimmed down to a four-piece. Ironically, this was where the band felt they made their best music. With the help of upcoming producer Daniel Lanois (later to become U2's knob-twiddler of choice), they recorded *This is the Ice Age*, a more experimental and free-form sound. Another Lanois album, *Danseparc*, followed in 1983.

In 1984 the band slimmed down again, to a two-piece of Mark Gane and singer Martha Johnson. More crucially, and you can see why they did it, but perhaps not a great idea in retrospect, they decided to get rid of the band name. Bored of being Muffins, Mark and Martha became M+M instead. It wasn't until the early 1990s that they changed back again. Since then, there has been a succession of film and television work, Martha has recorded music for children (her 1995 album *Songs from the Tree House* won the Canadian equivalent of a Brit award), and perhaps most importantly, Mark and Martha have had a daughter. Aw. A new compilation of their best work, *Then Again*, has left the door open for some new material at some stage.

> 'Echo Beach' taps into the feeling of being a romantic trapped in some dead-end situation.

Listen Here *The Sound of the Suburbs* – Various Artists (Sony, 1997). They weren't from the suburbs, but let's not get picky here.

Listen On *Then Again* (Imports, 2001). The best bits of Martha. The best bits of the Muffins.

Listen Further *Acadie* – Daniel Lanois (Warner, 1989). Muffin producer in atmospheric and quite good album shocker.

Turning Japanese
The Vapors
No. 3 1980

The one that isn't about wanking

The Vapors are perhaps the best thing ever to come out of Guildford, with the obvious exception of a train leaving the dreary commuter drop-off for the bright lights of London. Consisting of lead singer and songwriter Dave Fenton, guitarist Ed Bazalgette, bassist Steve Smith and drummer Howard Smith, the band got their big break playing a gig at Scratches, a pub just outside Godalming. In the audience – I say in, he probably *was* the audience – was Bruce Foxton, bass player of the Jam. So excited was he by what he saw, he offered to manage them, along with John Weller, the Jam's manager, or Paul's dad as he is more commonly known. A support slot swiftly followed (on the Jam's Setting Sons tour), as did a record contract with UA (head of press, Bruce's girlfriend) and a debut LP produced by John Vic Coppersmith, producer for the Woking trio.

Before the band knew what was happening, they were basking in the glory of a top-three hit with their second single. 'Turning Japanese' is just fantastic: crisp, clipped, punchy, punky, everything a three-and-a-half-minute pop song should be. Described by Dave Fenton as 'just a love song', it came to him in one of those middle-of-the-night moments. The Japanese riff and lyrical theme fitted in with one of pop's then pre-occupations: Alphaville's 'Big In Japan' and Aneka's 'Japanese Boy' were two other contemporary Far East hits. In retrospect, however, the song's lyrics have taken on a second meaning. When the band went to the US to promote the song, turning Japanese was taken to be English slang for masturbation. Bored as bands get on promotional tours, they thought the suggestion funny and went along with it. The claim subsequently stuck.

But like the song's apocryphal subject matter, 'Turning Japanese' was a heady and vibrant couple of minutes, followed by an overwhelming sense of anticlimax and disappointment. The song became a worldwide smash, its peak of number 3 in Britain eclipsed by reaching number 1 for several weeks in Australia. But the speedy success in Britain coupled with following the song's success around the world meant that the Vapors had no fan base to build on back home. At the same time, all the good luck that had propelled them to stardom suddenly turned bad. First, their record company was bought out by an indifferent EMI. Then, when their follow-up single, 'News At Ten' was released, a Musician's Union strike kept *Top of the Pops* off the air. And third, Paul's dad decided the Jam required all of his attention and resigned as their manager. In August 1981, as quickly as the band had got together, they split up.

Dave set up a new band, the Vapor Corporation, which suited him better: it was more rocky and he wasn't the frontman any longer. He eventually

> A heady and vibrant couple of minutes, followed by an overwhelming sense of anticlimax and disappointment.

returned to the legal career he'd left to start the band in the first place. A couple of years ago the band were offered a deal to re-form and got as far as a smattering of rehearsals, before day jobs and children made it too impractical. The songs still sounded as good as ever, though, apparently.

Listen Here   *The Sound of the Suburbs* – Various Artists (Sony, 1997). They were from the suburbs, so that's ok.

Listen On   *The Best of the Vapors* (EMI, 2003). 'News At Ten' is corking too. As is 'Jimmy Jones'.

Listen Further   'Big In Japan' – Alphaville (WEA, 1984). More Far East Fascination. Same number of hits.

99 Red Balloons
Nena
No. 1 1984

They were red, and there were ninety-nine of them

Before I start writing about Nena, I should probably fess up to a slight vested interest here. When '99 Red Balloons' came out, I was eleven years old and fancied Nena something rotten. Shaved armpits or no shaved armpits (let's get that boring tabloid moan out of the way right now), there was something about the dress sense (that classic eighties combination of black

baggy T-shirt over a fluorescent pink top, matching pink headband and huge hooped earrings), rock-chick looks (the missing link between Chrissie Hynde and Susanna Hoffs?), and that old favourite, speaking English with a foreign accent, that well and truly did it for me. But enough about the bass player, let's move on to the singer.

> The song ignores one of the golden rules about songwriting and doesn't actually have a chorus.

A former vocalist with a group called the Stripes (it was the eighties, so they were probably bright green rather than white), Gabriele 'Nena' Kerner formed the band Nena along with Carlo Karges (guitar), Uwe Fahrenkrog-Petersen (keyboards), Jürgen Dehmel (bass) and Rolf Brendel (drums) in the early 1980s. They hit number 1 in Germany with their first single, 'Nur Geträumt', and then came its even bigger follow-up, '99 Luftballons'. One quick (and slightly approximate) translation later, and the band had an international hit on their hands.

Now. It has to be said that one of the problems with much of the music recorded in the eighties was the addition of the keyboardist to the classic rock line-up of bass, guitar and drums. Every time you got something approximating a half-decent song, up popped some poodle-permed pianist to add his synthy soup into the mix. It was a bit like Manchester United buying Juan Sebastian Veron: he may be a great player and can do some fancy showing-off stuff, but at the same time he was utterly expendable and had a tendency to get in everyone else's way. Occasionally though, in the same way that Veron has the odd fantastic game, the pop-rock line-up can knock out a killer song. And '99 Red Balloons' is one example. All the key signatures of the dreaded line-up are there – a touch of slap bass, chugging punk guitar, cheesy Korg chords – but for once they work brilliantly.

So much so that no one ever notices two of the most interesting facts about '99 Red Balloons'. First, the song ignores one of the golden rules about songwriting and *doesn't actually have a chorus*. There's just a lot of verses, each ending with a line about red balloons, occasionally interspersed with a funk-style drop down. And second, Nena's got a great distinctive voice and everything, but if you listen to the lyrics carefully, her and her blessed balloons *have just triggered World War Three*. One minute she's letting them go at dawn in some cutesy and symbolic fashion, the next minute the fighter planes are being scrambled, people are doing their Captain Kirk impressions and it's all, as Nena would put it, 'super scurry'. Forget the supposed point of the song being all about Cold War paranoia. The true message is this – if you live near a war zone, for God's sake keep hold of your balloons, or we're all buggered.

Thankfully, World War Three didn't happen. But neither did Nena's follow-up single – 'Just A Dream' – leaving her career in this country floating away like a balloon in the sky. In Germany, though, Nena remained huge, and though Nena (the band) split up in 1987, Nena (the person) didn't. That would have been horrible. Four children and a hugely successful solo career later, Nena celebrated twenty years in the music business in 2002 with the slightly confusingly titled *Nena feat. Nena*, an album updating many of her classic hits. The re-reworked '99 Luftballons' is, in my opinion, nothing to write home about. It's a bit

like when Eric Clapton revisited 'Layla' on that unplugged album of his: it's all very nice and pleasant, but it's not a patch on the original. And there's new material too. In 2003 Nena teamed up with, of all people, Kim Wilde, and had a huge hit on the Continent with their duet 'Anyplace, Anywhere, Anytime'. If you want to add a lecherous joke at this point, please feel free to do so.

Listen Here *The Best One Hit Wonders in the World . . . Ever!* (Virgin EMI, 2003). Track one, side one, what more can I say?

Listen On *20 Jahre Nena: Nena feat. Nena* (WSM Germany, 2002). Remixed version of You Know What, not much cop in my opinion.

Listen Further *Tausend Sterne* – Nena (Zwekwerk, 2002). One of a number of Nena albums for children.

Since Yesterday
Strawberry Switchblade
No. 5 1985

Razor sharp and fruity
It was as if two members of the Bangles had got drunk and dressed up for a laugh. Or Boy George had two naughty little sisters. Alisha's Attic a pair of ever

so slightly bonkers aunts. A couple of bridesmaids on acid. What you get if you cross a goth with a Dalmatian. Mari Wilson on a bad hair day. The Dance of the Sugar Plum Fairy meets *The Rocky Horror Picture Show*. A strawberry, if you will, crossed with a switchblade.

The White Stripes may have their red-and-white outfits, Slipknot may have their masks, Bros their Grolsch bottle tops attached to their shoes, but has any pop act had such a fabulous image as Strawberry Switchblade? Kitsch in the mid-eighties which, let's face it, took some doing, the duo Jill Bryson and Rose McDowell were, in every sense of the word, dotty. Polka dotty, to be precise, with an entire haberdashery of ribbons pouring down from their back-combed hair, the polka dots matching those on their polka-dot party dresses. The video for 'Since Yesterday', directed by Cure favourite Tim Pope, saw them dancing round in a studio full of – how did you guess? – lots and lots and lots more dots.

Rose and Jill originally became friends in Glasgow at the height of punk in the late seventies. Rose, for a while, was in a band called the Poems who, so the story goes, financed their singles by shoplifting. It was James Kirk, guitarist with then rising stars Orange Juice, who suggested that they form a band, and even came up with the name from a song he was writing. Originally four, but ultimately two, Rose and Jill toured the country with Orange Juice, and for a while were also signed to their label, the fledgling indie label Postcard Records.

Help from famous friends continued. The girls caught the eye of Bill Drummond, then manager of Echo and the Bunnymen, who would go on to success with Jimmy Cauty as, among others, the KLF and the Timelords. Drummond persuaded Ian McCulloch to release the band's first single on his 92 Happy Customers label. 'Trees And Flowers', a song about Jill's agoraphobia, featured contributions from two members of Madness and Aztec Camera's Roddy Frame on guitar.

Released in November 1984, 'Since Yesterday' meandered its way up the charts, reaching number 5 in February the following year. It's pop at its most gloriously bubblegum – light, fluffy and fun, but at the same time underpinned by the 'looking back' of the lyrics, a can't-quite-put-your-finger-on-it melancholy, a bitterness to its sweetness, almost as if the duo knew what was coming next.

Because pretty soon, all Strawberry Switchblade did have left were their thoughts of yesterday. Subsequent singles failed to sell, not even the last-throw-of-the-dice cover of Dolly Parton's 'Jolene'. Under pressure from their record company and with the original sense of fun no longer there, the band split up. Jill, with all that innate fashion sense, found work as a buyer for a clothes designer. In 1990 she got married to a man named Frog. Rose, meanwhile, continued singing, first as a backing vocalist for bands such as Bronski Beat and Primal Scream, then for herself as Candy Cane, Spell, Sorrow and now she performs under her own name.

> Has any pop act had such a fabulous image as Strawberry Switchblade?

Listen Here   *The Hits Album 2* (WEA, 1985). Closes side one, following Dead or Alive, Howard Jones, King and Nik Kershaw.

Listen On *Strawberry Switchblade* (WEA, 1997). Japanese release of 1985 album, including nine extra songs.

Drink Further At Ghoul School, 'Hollywood's Only Dark Underground Alternative', you can order yourself a Strawberry Switchblade, 'a strawberry vodka cocktail, sweet and cute but deceptively deadly'.

Crash The Primitives
No. 5 1988

Way, indeed, too fast

Girl-fronted guitar bands were all the rage in the late 1980s. There were successful and fabulous acts such as the Bangles (Susanna Hoffs – sigh), who took their hooks and looks from the Go-Gos and the like. Then there were successful but iffy acts – step forward Transvision Vamp, I'm talking about you. And back in indieland, there was a predilection for adding a touch of Blondie to proceedings. There were the fairly dreary Darling Buds. For the gothically minded there was All About Eve with Julianne Regan up front. For the more booky, there was the Sundays. And for those who liked great pop tunes, there were the Primitives.

The Primitives formed in Coventry in 1985. The line-up fluctuated somewhat (this perhaps was one of their problems) but constants were lead singer Tracy Tracy (not I suspect her real name), who ticked the indie boxes of petite, blonde and pretty, and guitarist and songwriter Paul Court. These were accompanied by bassist Steve Dullaghan (later replaced by Paul Sampson) and drummer Pete Tweedie (later replaced by Tig Williams). Older readers may at this point remember an amusing story about a cat, which is probably best not to repeat here. With a bit of Blondie, a touch of the Ramones and a great big bag of melodic hooks, the Primitives started out sounding a little, well, primitive. They rattled through their early gigs at a pace of knots, shooting up the indie charts at the same speed with singles such as 'Thru The Flowers' and 'Really Stupid'. Then came the major label deal, the glossy recording and the gorgeous first hit single.

> Tracy's vocals have that just-right texture of tunefulness, suavity and boredom.

'Crash' is pretty much as close to indie guitar pop perfection as it is possible to be: it is both compact and crunching, fast and fun, bubblegum and brilliant. Like any great song, there's a freshness there that just doesn't seem to date. Tracy's vocals have that just-right texture of tunefulness, suavity and boredom. Basically, the gist of the song is this: everything is going too fast too quickly – if someone doesn't put their foot on the brake, it's all going to end in tears. I take it as referring to the heady days of a new rela-tionship, that exhilarating, out-of-control sensation of not being able to stop things. But that's just me; maybe the band were big fans of Nigel Mansell or something.

An album, *Lovely*, appeared, and it is: twelve tight gorgeous pop songs. But the initial burst of fame proved short-lived; as in the song itself, everything happened too fast. There were line-up changes, there were follow-up singles that didn't scale the same heights, and for the second album *Pure* there was an unfortunate image change: bored of dying her hair blonde, Tracy returned as a redhead. The album got mixed reviews and even more mixed sales and the band split up in 1991. Tracy did a fashion course, went back to her native Australia for a bit and was last heard tinkering on various dance projects.

Listen Here *The Best of the Primitives* (Camden, 1996). It's got 'Crash' on it, but, oddly, not 'Really Stupid'.

Listen On *Pop Said . . .* – the Darling Buds (Columbia, 1989). Like the Primitives, but not as good.

Listen Further *Baby I Don't Care* – Transvision Vamp (Spectrum, 2002). Like the Primitives, but nowhere near as good.

A Final Thought from Joe Dolce

I can't finish this book without mentioning another theory about one hit wonders that Joe Dolce suggested to me: they don't exist. 'There is no such thing as a "one hit wonder" in the real world,' he argues. 'It is a marketing term invented by disc jockeys and industry people. Kids never use the term. They like a song or they don't. They don't pigeonhole things in that way. "One hit wonder" is also a term tied into the competitiveness of the chart world. In real music, it's not about being number 1 or number 2 – it's about being unique.'

Whatever your thoughts about Joe Dolce, no one can argue with his uniqueness. And his theory about one hit wonders? Although I think he protests a little too much, his thoughts are worth bearing in mind. For as important as chart placements are to anally retentive people such as myself, they are not the only way to judge a music act. And though a band like, say, Martha and the Muffins had only one bona fide hit, it doesn't mean that they didn't produce other equally wonderful tunes – tunes that perhaps the band are ultimately more proud of.

I end with this thought, because over the course of writing this book, I have grown strangely fond of its inhabitants. These are people who had fame cruelly snatched away just as soon as we gave it to them, who have then had to suffer living down the moment down for the rest of their careers. And for that, we, the music-buying public, should take some of the blame. It's not their fault they ended up with only one hit; that responsibility lies with us. And so for all the derision and the jokes that one hit wonders have had to suffer over the years (and, in places, over the last 200 hundred pages or so), I'd like to utter one short, poignant, five-letter word: sorry. Chesney, if you're reading this, I think the nation owes you a pint and I'd be more than happy to buy it for you. I just hope yours isn't bitter.

Acknowledgements
and References

One Thanks Wonders

Huge thanks to the many people who have given their time, talents, and on some occasions both, towards the writing of this book. In particular, I would like to thank Noel Edmonds, Joe Dolce, Lynn Goldsmith, Tara Daynes, Adrian Bennett, Simone Hyams, Anita Nurse, Dave Fenton, Phill Jupitus, Andrew Collins, Ellie Smith, Merlin Cox, Jim Stoddart, Richard Marston, David Mackintosh, Joe Sutton, Barbara Daniel, Sophie Lazar and Time Warner Books for the flexibility and understanding.

Three people deserve special thanks: Martin Toseland, for coming up with the idea in the first place, and for being as nice an editor as a writer could wish for; Simon Trewin for the advice, agenting and numerous conversations about bad music; and Joanna, my wife, for putting up with me in 'writer mode', being woken up by members of the Tweets and suffering all of the above music for the past year or so.

One Lit Wonders

As well as the numerous piles of old magazines thumbed for information, some still with us (*Q*, *Smash Hits*, *NME*), others sadly no more (*Melody Maker*, *Select*, *Number One*), the following books proved useful and are worthy of further investigation:

Altered State, Matthew Collin (Serpent's Tail, 1997)
British Hit Singles, David Roberts, ed. (Guinness World Records, 15th Edition, 2002)
England's Dreaming, Jon Savage (Faber and Faber, 1991)
99 Red Balloons ... and 100 Other All-Time Great One Hit Wonders, Brent Mann (Citadel, 2003)
One Hit Wonders, Chris Welch and Duncan Soar (New Holland, 2003)

Rock Bottom, Pamela Des Barres (Little Brown, 1996)

Rock: The Rough Guide, Jonathan Buckley and Mark Ellingham, eds. (Rough Guides, 1996)

The Best of Smash Hits, various (EMAP, 1985)

The Encyclopedia of Classic 80s Pop, Daniel Blythe (Allison and Busby, 2002)

The Encyclopedia of Cult Children's TV, Richard Lewis (Allison and Busby, 2001)

The Last Party, John Harris (Fourth Estate, 2003)

The Manual, Jimmy Cauty and Bill Drummond (KLF Publications, 1988)

The Nation's Favourite, Simon Garfield (Faber and Faber, 1998)

Top Ten: The Irreverent Guide To Music, Alex Ogg (Channel 4 Books, 2001)

Whatever Happened To ... ?, Bill Harry (Blandford, 1999)

One Click Wonders

Out of the many websites visited in researching this book, the following may tickle your musical taste buds further:

www.disco-disco.com

www.patrickmacnee.com

www.noeledmonds.tv

www.ratfans.com

www.cultofflateric.cjb.net

www.davethompson.org.uk

www.geocities.com/pieroumiliani

www.spectropop.com

www.crashtestdummies.com

www.sabrinasalerno.com

www.harrynilsson.com

www.cubans.freeserve.co.uk

www.joedolce.net

www.parengstrom.com/vapors.htm

www.raywilson.co.uk

www.commercialbreaksandbeats.co.uk

www.manparrish.com

www.sylvia-vrethammar.de

www.loubega.de

www.geocities.com/moron200/gainsbourg

www.babylonzoo.net

www.bbc.co.uk/totp2/trivia/legs_and_co

www.stanridgway.com

www.thepodule.com

www.lynngoldsmith.com

www.ericcarmen.com

www.minnieriperton.com
www.timmymallett.co.uk
www.doctorandthemedics.com
www.whitetown.co.uk
www.divinyls.com
www.itbites.com
www.kennyloggins.com
www.knack.com
www.marthaandthemuffins.com
www.berlinpage.com
www.thetoydolls.com

www.ivanaspagna.it
www.colinhay.com
www.godofhellfire.co.uk
www.bazmark.com
www.nana-mouskouri.net
www.tasminarcher.com
www.opus.at
www.garyjules.com
www.nena.de
www.chesneyhawkes.com

Index of Songs

Index